SOCIO-LEGAL TRAJECTORIES ACROSS EUROPE: COMPARATIVE PERSPECTIVES

What are the different institutional, intellectual and biographical trajectories in socio-legal studies, and how can they be compared? This book brings together scholars from across Europe to reflect on the socio-political, legal and academic contexts in which they became the academics they are today. The chapters in this book link individual scholars to the historical and contemporary factors that have shaped or influenced their work and careers – a novel approach that combines scholarly self-reflection with a historical perspective on the development of socio-legal studies between law and the social sciences. The editors provide a heuristic framework for comparing and making sense of these different, dual trajectories, and show how professional scholarly biographies can be both contextualised and analysed with a view to shedding light on broader academic fields, both nationally and internationally.

Oñati International Series in Law and Society

A SERIES PUBLISHED FOR THE OÑATI INSTITUTE
FOR THE SOCIOLOGY OF LAW

Recent titles in this series

The Legacies of Institutionalisation: Disability, Law and Policy in the
'Deinstitutionalised' Community
Edited by Claire Spivakovsky, Linda Steele and Penelope Weller

Gender and Careers in the Legal Academy
Edited by Ulrike Schultz, Gisela Shaw, Margaret Thornton
and Rosemary Auchmuty

Contesting Austerity: A Socio-Legal Inquiry
Edited by Anuscheh Farahat and Xabier Arzoz

The Right to the Continuous Improvement of Living Conditions:
Responding to Complex Global Challenges
Edited by Jessie Hohmann and Beth Goldblatt

Supporting Legal Capacity in Socio-Legal Context
Edited by Mary Donnelly, Rosie Harding and Ezgi Tascioglu

What Is a Family Justice System For?
Edited by Mavis Maclean, Rachel Treloar and Bregje Dijksterhuis

Combining the Legal and the Social in Sociology of Law:
An Homage to Reza Banakar
Edited by Håkan Hydén, Roger Cotterrell, David Nelken and Ulrike Schultz

Criminal Justice and The Ideal Defendant in the Making of Remorse
and Responsibility
Edited by Stewart Field and Cyrus Tata

Socio-Legal Trajectories Across Europe: Comparative Perspectives
Edited by Christian Boulanger, Naomi Creutzfeldt and Jennifer Hendry

For the complete list of titles in this series
see www.bloomsbury.com/uk/series/oñati-international-series-in-law-and-society/

Socio-Legal Trajectories Across Europe

Comparative Perspectives

Edited by
Christian Boulanger
Naomi Creutzfeldt
and
Jennifer Hendry

Oñati International Series in Law and Society

A SERIES PUBLISHED FOR THE OÑATI INSTITUTE FOR THE SOCIOLOGY OF LAW

•HART•
OXFORD • LONDON • NEW YORK • NEW DELHI • SYDNEY

HART PUBLISHING

Bloomsbury Publishing Plc

Kemp House, Chawley Park, Cumnor Hill, Oxford, OX2 9PH, UK

1385 Broadway, New York, NY 10018, USA

Bloomsbury Publishing Ireland Limited, 29 Earlsfort Terrace, Dublin 2, D02 AY28, Ireland

HART PUBLISHING, the Hart/Stag logo, BLOOMSBURY and the Diana logo are trademarks of Bloomsbury Publishing Plc

First published in Great Britain 2025

A catalogue record for this book is available from the British Library.

A catalogue record for this book is available from the Library of Congress.

ISBN: HB: 978-1-50998-262-2
ePDF: 978-1-50998-264-6
ePub: 978-1-50998-263-9

Typeset by Compuscript Ltd, Shannon

For product safety related questions contact productsafety@bloomsbury.com

To find out more about our authors and books visit www.hartpublishing.co.uk. Here you will find extracts, author information, details of forthcoming events and the option to sign up for our newsletters.

Acknowledgements

WE ARE GRATEFUL to the Max Planck Institute for Legal History and Legal Theory, Frankfurt, without whose backing this book and the wider 'Socio-Legal Trajectories' project would not have been possible. We are particularly indebted to Institute Directors Marietta Auer and Stefan Vogenauer for their support of this project, both financial and intellectual.

This collection is the result of an excellent workshop that took place at the International Institute for the Sociology of Law (IISL) in Oñati in April 2023. We thank the Institute for hosting this event and providing a beautiful environment in which to consider socio-legal trajectories across Europe and beyond. Particular thanks are due to Ulrike Schultz, whose extensive international scholarly network was integral in facilitating connections necessary for both the Oñati workshop and the resultant edited volume.

We had the good fortune to present aspects of this collection in several different forums, notably the Socio-Legal Studies Association Annual Conference 2024 in Portsmouth, the *German Law Journal*'s Transatlantic Seminar Series 2024 in Bristol, and the Sociology of Law Department at Lund University. We are appreciative of the scholars who took the time to reflect on ideas raised and to provide feedback. Our thanks also to the series editors of the Oñati International Series in Law & Society, the anonymous reviewers, and our editors at Hart Bloomsbury: Kate Whetter, Sinead Moloney and Sasha Jawed.

Finally, our grateful thanks – as editors – are due to the contributors, whose wholehearted engagement with a truly dastardly brief comprising auto-ethnographic self-reflection, socio-legal history and academic legal-cultural positionality generated uniquely personal chapters. We appreciate them sharing their own socio-legal trajectories with us, and hope that this collection inspires in you reflection on your own.

JH, NC, CB
Lund, December 2024

Contents

Acknowledgements .... *v*
List of Contributors .... *ix*

1. *Zooming In, Zooming Out: Socio-Legal Trajectories between Country Studies and Scholarly Self-Reflection* *1*
   Christian Boulanger, Naomi Creutzfeldt and Jennifer Hendry

2. *The Comeback of Law: Theoretical Foundations and Research Traditions of Socio-Legal Studies in Poland after 1989* *19*
   Marta Bucholc

3. *Socio-Legal Studies in Contemporary Hungarian Legal Scholarship: Successes and Challenges* *39*
   Balázs Fekete

4. *Sociology of Law in the Western Balkans: Instrumentality, Liminality and Beyond* *61*
   Samir Forić

5. *Outline of a Danish Socio-Legal Trajectory Interconnected with Sociology of Law in Norway and Sweden* *87*
   Ole Hammerslev

6. *At the Crossroads of Sociology and Law: An Essay in Socio-Analysis* *105*
   Liora Israël

7. *Interdisciplinary Labour Law Studies: From Critical Legal Studies to the Sociology of Law and Back Again* *119*
   Eva Kocher

8. *On the Matter of the Law and Socio-Legal Identifications* *135*
   Revital Madar

9. *A Eurolatin Career in Comparative Public Law: From Analytic Legal Theory to Sociology of Law* *151*
   Francisca Pou Giménez

10. *Socio-Legal Studies in the United Kingdom: A Personal Reflection* *173*
    Sally Wheeler

Index *187*

List of Contributors

Christian Boulanger is a Senior Research Fellow at the Max Planck Institute for Legal History and Legal Theory (Frankfurt/Main). He has a PhD in political science from the Free University of Berlin. His research interests include the sociology of law, digital humanities and comparative judicial studies. Previously, he has held positions at Humbodt Universität zu Berlin and the Wissenschaftskolleg zu Berlin (Institute of Advanced Studies). He is part of the editorial board of the *German Journal of Law and Society* (*Zeitschrift für Rechtssoziologie*).

Marta Bucholc is Professor of Sociology at the Faculty of Sociology, University of Warsaw, and Associate Researcher at the Centre de recherche en science politique, Université Saint-Louis Bruxelles. From 2015 through 2020 she was Research Professor at Käte Hamburger Centre for Advanced Studies 'Law as Culture', University of Bonn. She was visiting scholar at the universities of Jena, Cambridge, Graz and Saint-Louis Bruxelles, as well as Bronisław Geremek Fellow of the Institute of Human Sciences in Vienna. Her research focus is sociology of law and historical sociology. In 2022, she started a five-year ERC Consolidator project 'Using Human Rights to Change Abortion Law: Involvement Patterns and Argumentative Architectures in the Global Figuration of Human Rights (Abortion Figurations)'.

Naomi Creutzfeldt is Professor of Law and Society at the University of Kent and Affiliated Scholar at the Max Planck Institute for Legal History and Legal Theory (Frankfurt/Main). She teaches public law and socio-legal theory and methods. Her interests in administrative and civil justice systems and alternative dispute resolution (ADR) (as pathways of informal dispute resolution) have a broader scope, addressing questions of access to justice, vulnerability, digitalisation, AI and consumer protection.

Balázs Fekete is Professor and Department Head at the Eötvös Loránd University, Faculty of Law, Department of Legal and Social Theory and Senior Research Fellow at the Centre for Social Sciences, Institute for Legal Studies, both in Budapest. His main research areas include rights consciousness, legal alienation and comparative legal studies methodology. His most recent book is *Paradigms in Modern European Comparative Law: A History* (Oxford, Hart Publishing, 2021).

Samir Forić is Assistant Professor at the University of Sarajevo, Faculty of Political Science, Department of Sociology. He holds a PhD in Sociology, MA in Sociology, BA in Law and BA in Political Science. His current research interests include legal professions, histories of sociology of law and deviance and social control. He is the author of socio-legal concepts in the first glossary of essential constitutional concepts in Bosnia and Herzegovina, *Citizens, Constitution, Europe* (Sarajevo, 2023). He holds the role of research associate at the Centre for Legal Education and Social Theory at the Faculty of Law and Administration, University of Wroclaw, and is an Editor-in-Chief of the *Sarajevo Social Science Review*.

Ole Hammerslev is Professor at the Sociology of Law Department, Lund University. He has previously held positions at the Department of Law, University of Southern Denmark, and the Department of Criminology and Sociology of Law, University of Oslo. Hammerslev's research spans legal professions, legal aid and welfare state law, with a particular focus on marginalised groups. His work also explores dispute transformation, state transformation and socio-legal theory and methodology.

Jennifer (Jen) Hendry is a Professor at The Chinese University of Hong Kong (CUHK) Faculty of Law, and a Visiting Professor at the University of Leeds School of Law. She is presently also an Affiliated Scholar at the Max Planck Institute for Legal History and Legal Theory, Frankfurt (MPILHLT) and an Academic Associate at 23ES Barristers' Chambers (Crime). Jen is former Vice-Chair of the UK Socio-Legal Studies Association (SLSA, 2017–19) and current Co-Editor-in-Chief of the *German Law Journal* (Cambridge University Press). Her research expertise lies in comparative law, socio-legal studies, jurisprudence and criminal law and justice: within these broad fields she researches on legal pluralism, legal culture, Indigenous justice and civil/criminal hybrid proceduralism. Jen's current project on 'Problematising Preventive Justice: Exposing the Injustices of Civil/Criminal Procedural Hybrid Orders' is funded by the Arts & Humanities Research Council (AHRC).

Liora Israël is a sociologist of law and justice. She is Professor at EHESS (School of Advanced Studies in Social Sciences), Paris. Her dissertation focused on judicial resistance during the Second World War, using notably the cause lawyering framework of analysis. She has mostly worked since on the political mobilisation of law in various contexts. Her most recent book, published in 2020, is entitled *A la gauche du droit. Mobilisations politiques du droit en France (1968–1981)*. She is currently working on lawyers at the Conseil d'Etat and Cour de Cassation in France from a socio-historical perspective.

Eva Kocher is Professor for European and German labour law and the Head of the Center for Interdisciplinary Labour Law Research (C*LLaS) at the Law Faculty of European University Viadrina Frankfurt (Oder), Germany. She is the chair of the 'Vereinigung für Recht und Gesellschaft' (German Law & Society Association). Among her most recent publications are the books *Digital Work*

Platforms. At the Interface of Labour Law (Oxford, Hart Publishing, 2022) and the collection of articles *Das Andere des Arbeitsrecht. Perspektiven feministischen Rechtsdenkens* (BadenBaden, Nomos, 2024).

Revital Madar is an interdisciplinary scholar specialising in state criminality and legitimate violence in liberal democracies. Her research explores the intersections of law, culture and power, with a focus on how legal systems shape and regulate identities as legitimate targets. Drawing on critical theory, political philosophy and feminist thought, she has published on topics such as the regulation of bodies, sovereignty and conflict-related sexual violence. Her work has appeared in journals like *Identities* and *Conflict and Society*. Madar is currently a Marie Skłodowska-Curie Research Fellow at the Robert Schuman Centre for Advanced Studies at the European University Institute.

Francisca Pou Giménez is Senior Researcher at the Institute for Legal Research of the National Autonomous University of Mexico (UNAM) and a Senior Member of the Mexican National System of Researchers. She holds a law degree from Pompeu Fabra University in Spain and Master's and Doctorate Degrees from the Yale Law School. Her work focuses on judicial review, judicial design and performance; Latin American constitutionalism; gender and constitutionalism; constitutional change; and fundamental rights. In the area of rights, she addresses both comparative normative discussions and rights protection mechanisms. Her most recent co-edited book in English is *Women, Gender and Constitutionalism in Latin America* (Abingdon, Routledge, 2024). She is a member of several international academic networks, such as the International Society of Public Law and the American Society of Comparative Law.

Sally Wheeler is a socio-legal scholar working in the areas of corporate behaviour and contractual relationships. She is currently Vice-Chancellor of Birkbeck, University of London and previously worked at the Australian National University and Queen's University Belfast.

1

Zooming In, Zooming Out: Socio-Legal Trajectories between Country Studies and Scholarly Self-Reflection

CHRISTIAN BOULANGER, NAOMI CREUTZFELDT AND JENNIFER HENDRY

I. THE AIM OF THE BOOK

THIS BOOK IS the result of a workshop we organised in April 2023 in Oñati (Gipuzkoa), Spain at the International Institute for the Sociology of Law (IISL). We invited scholars from across Europe and encouraged them to investigate, self-reflectively, what they were doing as socio-legal scholars, what motivated the questions they were asking and the methods and theories they were using. Furthermore, and as if that wasn't enough of a challenge, we also asked for this reflection to occur against the backdrop of the legal and academic context in which they worked, inclusive of considering its distinct historical trajectory. In short, we were looking for contributions that overtly connected the individual scholar with their own intellectual, institutional and political context, which is to say, to those things that have influenced them, and to which they have responded or reacted. Our contributors were invited to ponder questions like: What is the relationship between a socio-legal scholar's academic biography and the intellectual and institutional context(s) in which they have been socialised? How do their personal and disciplinary trajectories align, intersect or collide? What were the main influences on their work? These are the questions explored in this volume, articulated by and through the voices of socio-legal scholars telling their own stories.

In this introductory chapter, we take the opportunity to share insights that arose from discussions at our Oñati workshop. First, we provide a theoretical underpinning for those questions to contributors, as listed above. We then outline the theme of the book, noting its deliberate situation at the intersection of biographical and socio-historical narratives. We bring together this book's unique stories through a heuristic framework; for pragmatic reasons, this framework takes primarily a European comparative perspective.[1]

II. COMBINING MICRO- AND MACRO-PERSPECTIVES ON SOCIO-LEGAL STUDIES

We are interested in comparing what we refer to as different 'socio-legal trajectories' across Europe. Before we explain what we mean here by the term 'trajectories', the more substantial conceptual challenge is to clarify what we mean to encompass through our intentional reliance on the term 'socio-legal'. As Liora Israël notes in her chapter, '"Socio-legal studies" do not translate easily into French', for example. In relation to traditional boundaries in the national academic world, the sociology of law has been the closest field of research to such an interdisciplinary approach.[2] Israël continues to observe that these two labels in fact emphasise different things, for example: 'the sociology "of" law indicates a direction, from sociology to law, the latter being the subject of inquiry of the former'.[3] Socio-legal studies, by contrast, is less disciplinarily specific and so more inclusive. In a similar vein, Marta Bucholc insists 'on distinguishing the sociology of law (in Polish: socjologia prawa) from socio-legal studies …, despite the fact that in daily academic circulation the two expressions tend to be almost synonymous'. Bucholc understands socio-legal studies to be those 'studies of law having an empirical component demonstrably anchored in the theories and methodologies of social sciences, as opposed to purely speculative philosophical reflection or to legal dogmatics'.[4] This operative distinction also exists in the UK,[5] although the comparatively minor role played by sociology of law research and scholarship contributes to its subsumption under the 'big' umbrella of socio-legal studies.[6] It is in Bucholc's broadly inclusive sense that we employ the term, although not with the aim of achieving conceptual or definitional clarity. Rather, we hope to contribute to a more nuanced and differentiated use of 'socio-legal studies', ideally one that is less obviously Anglo-centric in origin.[7]

[1] For a more systematic inquiry into a sociology of law in Europe, see Volkmar Gessner and David Nelken, 'Introduction: Studying European Ways of Law' in Volkmar Gessner and David Nelken (eds), *European Ways of Law. Towards a European Sociology of Law* (Oxford, Oñati International Series in Law and Society, Hart Publishing, 2007).

[2] Israël, p. 117.

[3] Israël, ibid.

[4] Bucholc, p. 20.

[5] Roger BM Cotterrell, 'Law and Sociology: Notes on the Constitution and Confrontations of Disciplines' (1986) 13 *Journal of Law and Society* 9.

[6] J Hendry, 'One Umbrella or Two? Comparative (Socio-)Legal Studies in light of Globalisation' (2021) 16(2) *Journal of Comparative Law* 552–68, 534–35.

[7] A more practical reason for continued reliance on 'socio-legal studies' is that this edited collection arose in conjunction with a research project that compares socio-legal studies in the UK with *Rechtssoziologie* (sociology of law) in Germany, and terminological continuity was preferable. See www.lhlt.mpg.de/2512903.

As for 'trajectories', this term denotes two aspects – macro and micro – of the same idea, that is, a pathway or progressive direction. On one hand, we look at the distinctive ways in which 'socio-legal studies' has developed in different jurisdictional academic contexts. On the other hand, we allow the individual biographical narratives of the authors to feature in the story. This juxtaposition of the societal and the individual facilitates a unique perspective – unique insofar as no previous systematic attempt has been made to unite analysis of the histories of socio-legal studies with scholarly self-reflection and biographical narrative. Within both comparative social science and comparative law approaches there are ongoing debates about the value of purportedly objective, macro-sociological, bird's-eye view country case study comparisons and narrations of the development of socio-legal studies in different geographies.[8] By contrast, studies in scholarly self-reflection – represented by autobiographical and autoethnographical accounts – focus on the individual, typically subjective, experience. Our approach both builds upon and combines the approaches taken across these literatures, and represents an attempt to blend two levels of observation: the macro-, bird's-eye view of academic cultures and geographies, and the micro-level, introspective observation provided by scholarly self-reflection.

A. Comparative Socio-Legal Case Histories

As Roger Cotterell remarks, the 'comparative history of sociology of law is yet to be written, and to write it would certainly be a massive task'.[9] While an extensive body of scholarship exists that reflects on the nature of legal sociology, 'socio-legal studies' or 'law and society' approaches,[10] identifying what links these research fields remains a challenge. Defined mainly by their opposition to traditional doctrinal approaches and their interdisciplinary nature,[11] their relationship with the 'traditional' contributory academic disciplines, such as law,

[8] See for a discussion of the debate in the social sciences Lesley Bartlett and Frances Vavrus, *Rethinking Case Study Research: A Comparative Approach* (Abingdon, Taylor & Francis, 2016); on objectivity in comparativ law, see Günter Frankenberg, 'Critical Comparisons: Re-Thinking Comparative Law' in Maksymilian Del Mar, William Twining and Michael Giudice (eds), *Legal Theory and the Legal Academy* (Abingdon, Routledge, 2017).

[9] Roger Cotterell, 'The Place of a Stepchild: Notes on the Establishment of Modern Sociology of Law' in Håkan Hydén and others (eds), *Combining the Legal and the Social in Sociology of Law: An Homage to Reza Banakar* (Oxford, Hart Publishing, 2023) 47.

[10] Just a few classic examples of many: Richard L Abel, 'Law and Society: Project and Practice' (2010) 6 *Annual Review of Law and Social Science* 1; Carroll Seron, Susan Bibler Coutin and Pauline White Meeusen, 'Is There a Canon of Law and Society?' (2013) 9 *Annual Review of Law and Social Science* 287; Dermot Feenan (ed), *Exploring the 'Socio' of Socio-Legal Studies* (London, Palgrave Macmillan, 2013); Brian Z Tamanaha, *Realistic Socio-Legal Theory: Pragmatism and a Social Theory of Law* (Oxford, Clarendon Press, 1997).

[11] Naomi Creutzfeldt, 'Traditions of Studying the Social and the Legal' in Naomi Creutzfeldt, Marc Mason and Kirsten McConnachie (eds), *Routledge Handbook of Socio-Legal Theory and Methods* (Abingdon, Routledge, 2019).

sociology or political science, is very much dependent on local factors, as development of these disciplines has historically happened within the confines of the nation-state. The reason for this is that scientific discourses mainly emerged in, and were channelled through, nationally organised academic institutions, which provided the material grounds and resources for them in the form of academic employment. These institutions organise teaching and/or research in subdivisions that usually take the form of academic disciplines,[12] with the result that the way(s) in which these institutions and disciplines have developed has a profound impact on the type of knowledge that was and is being produced. At the same time, this development is historically highly contingent and generally little known or understood outwith the particular communities in question, or not at all. While there is a well-established line of research on the history of sociology in various countries,[13] there have been relatively few initiatives collecting single-country analyses on socio-legal studies, broadly defined.[14] Notable exceptions include a series in the *International Journal of Law in Context*[15] or occasional articles in the *Journal of Law and Society*,[16] but these have been largely factual and descriptive. Until now, there has been no attempt systematically to compare these case studies. Regarding both the history and contemporary circumstances of socio-legal studies, we are at the very beginning of such systematic comparison.

From a socio-legal perspective, the question is whether socio-legal comparative methodology[17] can be said to provide tools for the comparison of socio-legal trajectories themselves. We believe that it does and we employ the contributions in this volume in the joint endeavour of achieving and illustrating such a comparison. To this end, in section III, we suggest heuristic categories that could structure systematic comparisons.

Case studies usually tell histories in an 'objective' way, particularly if they are encyclopaedic. However, it is difficult to deny that any such attempt entails the need to make practical decisions on what to report and what to omit.[18]

[12] Paul Trowler, Murray Saunders and Veronica Bamber (eds), *Tribes and Territories in the 21st Century: Rethinking the Significance of Disciplines in Higher Education* (Abingdon, Routledge, 2012).

[13] See, for example the book series 'Sociology Transformed' (since 2014), edited by Holmwood and Turner (Springer).

[14] See R Treves and JF Glastra Van Loon (eds), *Norms and Actions: National Reports on Sociology of Law* (Dordrecht, Springer Netherlands, 1968) for an early compilation.

[15] See David Nelken, 'Law in Other Contexts: A New Initiative for the Journal' (2012) 8 *International Journal of Law in Context* 133, with contributions by Israël on France, Hammerslev and Madsen on Denmark, Machura on Germany and Murayama on Japan.

[16] With contributions by Campbell and Wiles on Britain (1975), Noreau and Arnaud on France (1998), Economides on New Zealand (2014), Bora on Germany (2016), Colson and Field on France (2016), Skąpska on Poland (2019) and Wheeler on the UK (2020).

[17] Naomi Creutzfeldt, Agnieszka Kubal and Fernanda Pirie, 'Introduction: Exploring the Comparative in Socio-Legal Studies' (2016) 12 *International Journal of Law in Context* 377.

[18] See Boaventura de Sousa Santos, 'Law: A Map of Misreading. Toward a Postmodern Conception of Law' (1987) 14(3) *Journal of Law and Society* 279–302.

That decision is necessarily a subjective choice, irrespective of whether decades of disciplinary history have to be squeezed into an article or can be examined in a book-length study. This is not necessarily a defect of country case studies, especially since the inherent subjectivity of any scholarly activity outside the methodologically rigorous 'hard sciences' is well understood and can be accounted for.[19] However, as we argue in the next section, if used in a conscious and transparent way, the subjectivity and social embeddedness of an author might also contribute to comparisons.

B. Scholarly Self-Reflection

As England has argued, '[t]he intersubjective nature of social life means that the researcher and the people being researched have shared meanings and we should seek methods that develop this advantage'.[20] In line with this, in recent years there has been a proliferation of literature on scholarly self-reflection,[21] a development that can also be observed for socio-legal studies. In particular, autoethnography[22] and studies of positionality in research[23] have attempted to provide methodological and theoretical underpinnings to this self-reflective practice. Against critiques that have dismissed self-reflective practices as unscientific, the contributions have demonstrated that such practices are a means of producing and unearthing knowledge that would otherwise either be hidden or skewed by a dogmatic view of scientific objectivity. Moreover, they show how research is 'a process not just a product',[24] one that is always socially embedded. In this regard, the process cannot be separated from the body and person of the researcher, nor detached from those professional identities that contribute both meaning and context, as well as often influencing the form and substance of the research being undertaken.

[19] This is not to say that subjective choices and biographical factors play no role in the 'hard sciences', as Science and Technology Studies, and most famously, Thomas Kuhn's work on the history of Physics have demonstrated in detail. However, this question does not concern us here since these factors are much more obvious (and acknowledged) for the Humanities and Social Sciences. On the 'scientificity' of socio-legal studies, see Susan S Silbey, 'What Makes a Social Science of Law? Doubling the Social in Socio-Legal Studies' in Dermot Feenan (ed), *Exploring the 'Socio' of Socio-Legal Studies* (London, Macmillan Education UK, 2013).

[20] Kim VL England, 'Getting Personal: Reflexivity, Positionality, and Feminist Research' (1994) 46 *The Professional Geographer* 80, 82.

[21] See, for example Alonzo M Flowers, 'Self-Reflection as a Critical Tool in the Life of an Early Career African American Male Scholar' in FA Bonner et al (eds), *Black Faculty in the Academy* (Abingdon, Routledge, 2014).

[22] Elaine Gregersen, 'Telling Stories about the Law School: Autoethnography and Legal Education' [2021] *The Law Teacher* 1.

[23] Lynette J Chua and Mark Fathi Massoud, *Out of Place: Fieldwork and Positionality in Law and Society* (Cambridge, Cambridge University Press, 2024).

[24] England (n 20) 82.

Although slightly different from the genre of scholarly biographical writing, that is, the narration of one's professional life-story, which – more often than not – cannot be separated from the personal life story, self-reflective writing shares some overlaps. The scholarly biographical genre typically comprises life histories of well-known intellectuals, in situations where the reading audience is most interested in the life of the person or persons themselves.[25] Usually not subject to any methodological control or restriction, these accounts are, in a sociological sense, most valuable for pointing to previously unknown historical facts and relational connections. Recent years have seen more academic engagement with scholarly life narration,[26] alongside increased scrutiny of its method; the interest in recording life stories of people who are relatively unknown – or even anonymous – lies in reconstructing prototypical trajectories (or deviation therefrom) of people who share certain features (gender, ethnicity, disability etc.),[27] and which very often concerns marginalised scholars.[28] In the area of socio-legal studies, a useful example is the *Journal of Law & Society*'s occasional series dealing with major books that have influenced well-known socio-legal scholars.[29]

However, although these reflexive perspectives are by now firmly established, they are by no means mainstream, only being applied or taught by a small minority of scholars. Accordingly, when we gave our contributors the task of *self-reflectively* questioning their work against the background of their respective disciplinary trajectories, we knew the extent of the challenge, and so deliberately left the theoretical and methodological approach underspecified to allow contributors the freedom to establish their own focus and choose their own methodology. Unsurprisingly, the methods they employed differed considerably, providing us with a rich variety of approaches that not only elevate this collected volume but also demonstrate the added value of this kind of blended perspective.

Marta Bucholc, for example, points to 'moments of continuity as well as those of inconsistency and contradiction inherent in the intellectual path of socio-legal studies in Poland', in order to 'demonstrate how they bear on methodological choices, research strategies, actions and omissions of scholars working in this field in Poland today'.[30] At the same time, she alerts us to the need to make transparent one's 'own situatedness, as a sociologist, as a lawyer

[25] Think of the autobiographies of Simone de Beauvoir or Betrand Russell.

[26] The term 'Auto/Biography' is in the title of a Routledge book series and a journal (*Auto/Biography Review*).

[27] Margaret K Willard-Traub, 'Scholarly Autobiography: An Alternative Intellectual Practice' (2007) 33 *Feminist Studies* 188.

[28] Robert J Nash and Sydnee Viray, 'The Who, What, and Why of Scholarly Personal Narrative Writing' (2013) 446 *Counterpoints* 1.

[29] See, for example, Mariana Valverde, 'Key Book in My Education: Hegel's *The Phenomenology of Spirit*' (2024) 51 *Journal of Law and Society* 28.

[30] Bucholc, p. 20.

and as a self-conscious socio-legal scholar' – demands for interdisciplinarity are of course in the interest of legal sociologists, but they may not be the panacea they are sometimes presented as. Balázs Fekete uses an apt image to express how he understood the task: to make

> the layer of a 'frozen' and lifeless view of socio-legal endeavours that takes shape from the summary of certain background information, historical trends, important names and relevant research outcomes – so to say a 'still life' in terms of visual arts … livelier by integrating some autobiographical points.[31]

Ole Hammerslev takes inspiration from Bourdieu's writings on scholarly self-analysis, pointing out that 'an analysis of your own position needs to be considered in relation to the field that has formed you and in which you are navigating and positioning yourself'.[32] For Liora Israël, the question 'from which standpoint are you speaking?' is more reminiscent of the 'critical political or psychoanalytical perspectives of the 1960s or 1970s than with the usual set of questions delivered in a book chapter today',[33] but she also notes that taking 'a reflexive perspective on one's career in the world of socio-legal studies' is useful to better understand the institutional development of the field. In her chapter, Revital Madar grapples with (non-)identification with socio-legal identity: hers is a 'contribut[ion] to socio-legal studies undertaken by an early-career scholar who is not a legal scholar nor a sociologist but whose matter is the law'.[34] Finally, Francisca Pou Giménez points out that the approach taken in this volume allows for the identification of those epistemic communities[35] that have nurtured her and her work, and 'the social, institutional and personal underpinnings of views that we have learned to aseptically portray as "fields", "currents", "schools" or even "theories"', providing 'the chance of rescuing some of these fields and currents from invisibility'.[36]

III. COMPARATIVE HEURISTICS

In this part, we introduce categories of phenomena that occur repeatedly in the chapter narratives. We do this through a heuristic framework of four 'clusters' as a tool for undertaking comparisons. This approach is the outcome of a collaborative effort at the Oñati workshop where, in a brainstorm session, participants shared their ideas about the different factors or phenomena that played a role in both their life stories and their disciplinary histories. Prior to the meeting, the editors had devised four clusters towards which we expected themes generated

[31] Fekete, p. 39.
[32] Hammerslev, p. 88.
[33] Israël, p. 105.
[34] Madar, p. 136.
[35] See section III.B.
[36] Pou Giménez, p. 151.

in the discussion to gravitate. The first cluster contained all of the factors directly connected to the individual biography of our authors. The second cluster concerned factors attributable to 'epistemic communities', which is to say, those groups in which the individual was embedded in their professional life, and with which they shared epistemic frameworks. The third cluster collected 'material' forces and structures, such as the immediate impact on the life of a scholar of institutional rules, power relationships and socio-economic conditions, for example, incentive structures for getting a job, or opportunities to secure funding for one's research. The fourth and final cluster encompassed the category of 'cultural' or 'contextual' factors, which are related to the production of both meaning and identity, and are typically the result of longer socio-historical developments.

We should be clear at this stage that the themes discussed in the following sections do not fit neatly into a strict classification, and nor is such categorisation our intention. Instead, the idea is that, even allowing for overlaps, each category plausibly connects to a roughly coherent body of theoretical literature *on the basis of which* one can make sense of the phenomena as they arise in each individual story. This heuristic is explicitly not tied to any single theoretical paradigm, but rather is open to different concepts, premises and hypotheses that might promise insights for the comparison.

In the following, we draw from themes that were collaboratively embedded in this framework, connect them to supporting theoretical literature and cite examples drawn from contributor chapters. Our aim is to demonstrate how the framework can be grounded in empirical observations, and to identify the potential of using socio-legal (and broader social-scientific) theories and methods to analyse the field itself.

A. Agency and Positionality: Scholar's Biographies

Although each individual academic trajectory is unique, there are a number of recurrent themes in a scholarly career path. Some of them describe a class of phenomena rather than something generalisable: for example, many of our participants mentioned the 'role of chance' affecting their academic trajectory, and we all know how serendipity can shape decisions taken in life.[37] Liora Israël's story is just one example of many:[38] having starting her career in French academia, where law was dominated by doctrinal approaches, Israël talks about how important the personal encounters with other prominent scholars were in

[37] Robert K Merton and Elinor G Barber, *The Travels and Adventures of Serendipity: A Study in Sociological Semantics and the Sociology of Science (1958)* (Princeton, Princeton University Press, 2004).

[38] Chapter 6.

forming her particular perspective and research interest. Israël also points to the importance of events that are specifically organised for young researchers, such as the Graduate Student Workshops of the Law and Society Association,[39] for fostering networks that can last over whole academic careers, and providing new perspectives on a field. The importance of both biographical coincidences and network-building is also stressed by Francisca Pou Giménez,[40] who, during her PhD at Yale, was introduced to a large community of Latin American graduate students of a similar age and, later, to a whole network of constitutional theorists from all over Latin America.[41]

A frequently occurring term in discussions of the role of subjectivity in the research process is 'positionality', which denotes the influence of one's own position in social relationships, and which is hypothesised to influence the research process and its outcomes. It has always been understood that 'that a researcher's social, cultural and subject positions (and other psychological processes) affect the questions they ask; how they frame them; the theories that they are drawn to; how they read',[42] but there is no straightforward answer as to how to align this with the scientific quest to provide 'objective' knowledge.[43] Perhaps unsurprisingly, positionality has more frequently and regularly been discussed in research that deals with gender, race/ethnic identity and sexuality.[44] As Revital Madar's chapter highlights, however, other social positions also need to be considered: given her North-African family background and her witnessing of militarised violence of Israel's occupation of Palestine. For her, law appeared more as a threat than a remedy.[45] Madar's account is one of questioning those categories and identities that academia creates and assigns to those who enter it – as she calls it, a 'net of unpositionalities'.[46]

Eva Kocher identifies as a feminist labour lawyer, but also as someone who initially started on the 'critical' side of the split between the sociology of law and critical legal studies in Germany, with the result that it took her around 20 years to start thinking about herself as a socio-legal scholar. Francisca Pou Giménez draws our attention to the role played by gender in both influencing one's academic career and being part of the formation of identity.

[39] The LSA Graduate Student Workshop at the LSA meeting in Miami 200X has also been crucial for Christian Boulanger in considering an academic career.

[40] Chapter 9.

[41] The 'Seminario en América Latina de Teoría Constitucional y Política'.

[42] Geraldine Pratt, 'Positionality' in Derek Gregory and others (eds), *The Dictionary of Human Geography* 5th edn (Oxford, Blackwell, 2009) 556.

[43] Jessica Soedirgo and Aarie Glas, 'Toward Active Reflexivity: Positionality and Practice in the Production of Knowledge' (2020) 53 *PS: Political Science & Politics* 527.

[44] See, for example, Mark Fathi Massoud, 'The Price of Positionality: Assessing the Benefits and Burdens of Self-Identification in Research Methods' (2022) 49 *Journal of Law and Society* 64.

[45] Madar, p 138.

[46] Madar, ibid.

For example, she argues that, in her experience, the socio-legal 'analysis of practice is sometimes damaging of the professional status of younger academics, many of them women, who are not awarded the prestige that accrues to practitioners of "high theory"'.[47]

B. Collective Sense-Making and Identity-Formation: Epistemic Communities and the Academic Habitus

The contributory role played by networks in terms of academic biographies has already been touched upon. This leads us to a well-covered theoretical concept, namely that of 'epistemic communities', and their role in forming individual scholars' understanding of the world and corresponding production of knowledge.[48] The concept originates from international relations scholarship, where epistemic communities have been defined as 'networks of knowledge-based experts' that help states in 'identify[ing] their interests, framing the issues for collective debate, proposing specific policies, and identifying salient points for negotiation'.[49] Since the early 1990s, however, the concept has been generalised to cover all kinds of professional networks operating through shared epistemological assumptions around a specific subject matter, such as lawyers and legal scholars, even encompassing sub-disciplines and expertise within the field of law.[50] The socio-legal community fits this description: a collection of individuals who share similar methodological and conceptual interests, and who use shared epistemic frameworks both to make sense of their observations and to build networks of collective agency in pursuing (what they perceive to be) common goals. A 'sub-discipline'[51] can be considered as such in circumstances where it has reached a certain degree of institutionalisation, or has attained the status of a 'movement'[52] or a 'research field',[53] where it is possible even to unite researchers across disciplines. Scholarly epistemic communities, it should be noted, can exist where there is no formal local institutionalisation of the field they study, as is the case with German critical legal studies, as

[47] Pou Giménez, p. 168.

[48] Kate Bulpin and Susan Molyneux-Hodgson, 'The Disciplining of Scientific Communities' (2013) 38 *Interdisciplinary Science Reviews* 91.

[49] Peter M Haas, 'Introduction: Epistemic Communities and International Policy Coordination' (1992) 46 *International Organization* 1, 2.

[50] Jen Hendry, 'The Double Fragmentation of Law: Legal System-Internal Differentiation and the Process of Europeanisation' in Daniel Augenstein (ed), *'Integration through Law' Revisited: The Making of the European Polity* (Farnham, Ashgate Publishing Ltd, 2013); Daniela Piana and Luca Verzelloni, 'Epistemic Communities Meet Communities of Practices' [2022] *Rivista di Digital Politics* 221.

[51] Pierre Guibentif, 'The Sociology of Law as a Sub-Discipline of Sociology' (2003) 1 *Portuguese Journal of Social Science* 175.

[52] Lawrence M Friedman, 'The Law and Society Movement' (1986) 38 *Stanford Law Review* 763.

[53] Kaijus Ervasti, 'Sociology of Law as a Multidisciplinary Field of Research' (2008) 53 *Scandinavian Studies In Law* 138.

mentioned above, being largely organic and bottom-up in their instantiation and continuation.[54]

Considering epistemic communities sociologically helps to avoid the 'great minds'-type of histories that concentrate on individual professors and their *oeuvre* of work, often disregarding the actual influence they had in terms of the local academic landscape. As Eva Kocher shows, Germany is a case in point: while many luminaries with impeccable and undisputed socio-legal credentials have been at German universities, the socio-legal community in Germany has remained relatively weak and fragmented.[55]

While this disconnect might appear strange, it is neither unusual nor surprising: the development of such a situated community cannot be seen as a linear and cumulative outcome of local intellectual history. In fact, as we will show below, it is necessary to acknowledge the impact of those material incentives and disincentives created by, inter alia, university hiring decisions, departmental policies, institutional *habitus*,[56] econo-political priorities and by funding body topic preferences. Moreover, developments are often not only local: as Liora Israël remarks, despite France having several 'so-called founding fathers of sociology …, the current landscape is probably more influenced by the pull of the US originated law and society tradition'.[57] This is to some degree also true for the German-speaking countries, with the caveat that the distinctively German Luhmannian tradition has and retains a significant influence there.

The empirical question that arises is how can epistemic communities be meaningfully differentiated from each other? Part of the answer certainly turns on the language factor: language proficiency facilitates inclusion and exclusion concerning bodies of literature, participation in conversations and local and global knowledge production. The global language of socio-legal studies is English, and Francisca Pou Giménez provides a salient example of what that can mean for a non-native speaker in the US.[58] There, whether or not one speaks the lingua franca natively provides or denies entry into the large market of the global anglosphere, and mobility within it. The chapters by Fekete, Hammerslev and Forić all describe the shift in in their home countries and regions from a conversation in the native languages within the local community to participation in the transnational and increasingly global English-language discussion. This step-change was not unmotivated: the practical appeal of external funding eligibility is supplemented by the prospect of a much larger audience for local knowledge production.

[54] This is not to say that epistemic communities are homogeneous – quite the opposite. Indeed, as the chapters in this collection show, the socio-legal community is characterised by a pluralism of normative commitments, theories and methods, but these are united by the view that a broader view than that taken by traditional legal jurisprudence, on one hand, and contemporary sociology, on the other, is both necessary and desirable.

[55] Kocher, p. 131.

[56] See below, nn 65–66.

[57] Madar, p. 105.

[58] Pou Gimenéz, p. 160.

This does not mean, however, that different national and regional socio-legal studies research is converging as a result of being part of an overarching English-language discourse. As the chapters in this book illustrate, there remain clear and distinctive differences, not to mention large and often unseen communities: for example, those arising from the aforementioned German-speaking countries. As Pou Gimenéz reminds us, 'the legal-academic communities of southern Europe are actually communities that bring together indistinguishably Europe and Latin America, at the impulse of the common use of Spanish'.[59]

Epistemic communities are the places within which scholarly identity is constantly (re)negotiated, not least because the question of which label is used in self-identification is a central thread in defining who is part of the community, and who is not, and in describing what the community is doing. For example, Balázs Fekete explains in his chapter that 'legal sociologists in Hungary tend to consider themselves as members of a closed scholarly group being distinct from similar scholarly associations and they are also convinced about having some specific research issues that only belong to them'.[60] By contrast, for Eva Kocher, this cannot be said about the fragmented German socio-legal community. She writes, 'it is one thing to address all socio-legal scholars in name; it is another thing to gather socio-legal researchers on family law matters, economic justice or labour law, and expect that they have common issues to talk about'.[61]

Revital Madar's chapter describes how she came to be identified – reluctantly – as a socio-legal scholar, and considers 'what this identification unveils concerning the law's capacity to colour other aspects of one's work'.[62] Such networks, it is important to note in terms of the concept of epistemic communities, are not static causal variables: indeed, the chapters by Forić, Hammerslev and Fekete all describe how the portrayed socio-legal communities have changed dramatically over the years, through political and generational change as well as through internationalisation. The chapter by Samir Forić traces the development of a socio-legal community in the Balkan countries, one within which he participated, and also stresses the importance of scholarly networks and epistemic community-building. Forić observed 'a gradual development of the discipline's distinctive identity – moving away from the narrow confines of legal theory where it was traditionally positioned, toward its own academic field that embeds the epistemic community no longer affiliated exclusively with law schools'.[63]

As some contributor chapters show, building and maintaining these communities is often supported by two complementary institutional structures: centres or institutes inside or outside the university, and professional associations.

[59] Pou Gimenéz, p. 152.
[60] ibid.
[61] Kocher, p. 133.
[62] Madar, p. 137.
[63] Forić, p. 62.

The institutions both contribute to the strengthening of socio-legal studies and are affected – positively or negatively – by how the community evolves over time. For example, Liora Israël points to the pivotal role of the Centre National de la Recherche Scientifique (CNRS) in France in promoting sociology of law research since the 1980s, by providing a space for an initial 'concentration of talents'.[64] Similarly in her chapter, Sally Wheeler points to the role of the Oxford Centre for Socio-Legal Studies in providing a central hub for the UK socio-legal community. Equally, university-based centres, such as those in Cardiff, Warwick and Sheffield, are places for socio-legal teaching and degree programmes, and – importantly for consolidation – for employment opportunities for early career researchers.[65]

Another concept that can be brought in to study the socialisation effects of epistemic communities is Bourdieu's notion of 'habitus', which denotes an observable pattern of dispositions and ways of behaviour, which has been acquired by being socialised into a specific social group.[66] Dezalay and Madsen define it as 'internalized schemes guiding agents' behaviour'[67] and apply it to the professional group of international lawyers; it has also been used to analyse legal professionals.[68] Balázs Fekete provides a vivid example in his chapter, illustrating the fact that reputational hierarchies between legal and socio-legal scholars 'is made explicit by their clothing', and remarking, a bit tongue-in-cheek, that the socio-legal habitus even includes being kind to early career colleagues.[69] Samir Forić, in his chapter, describes his journey from 'a doctrinal habitus – a cognitive scheme that orients thinking about and problem-solving of legal issues through the lens of legal doctrine' to a 'more theoretical, critical and reflective habitus', which he further developed into a 'socio-legal habitus that implies two types of engagement: first, active investment in the scholarship's field and, second, maintenance of the balance between external and internal perspectives of law'.[70] Eva Kocher also considers the 'lack of habitus and of integration in mainstream academia', which she believes enables a different means of dealing with knowledge production.[71]

[64] Israël, p. 110.

[65] Wheeler, p. 174.

[66] Pierre Bourdieu, *Outline of a Theory of Practice* (Cambridge, Cambridge University Press, 1977) 85.

For a socio-legal discussion and application of Bourdieu's *habitus*, see Jess Mant, 'Working Politically: Combining Socio-Legal Tools to Study Experiences of Law' in Jennifer Hendry, Naomi Creutzfeldt and Christian Boulanger (eds), 'Socio-Legal Studies in Germany and the UK: Theory and Methods', Special Issue (2020) 21(7) *German Law Journal* 1464–80.

[67] Yves Dezalay and Mikael Rask Madsen, 'The Force of Law and Lawyers: Pierre Bourdieu and the Reflexive Sociology of Law' (2012) 8 *Annual Review of Law and Social Science* 433, 442.

[68] James Thornton, 'Pierre Bourdieu's The Logic of Practice: Understanding the Working Practices of Lawyers' in Daniel Newman (ed), *Leading Works on the Legal Profession* (Abingdon, Routledge, 2024).

[69] Fekete, p. 47.

[70] Forić, p. 83.

[71] Kocher, p. 134.

C. Institutional and Political Economies of Academia

The third cluster discussed in the workshop concerned factors related to those institutional constraints and incentives that, in most cases, can be characterised as being external to the scientific domain itself. Most of these factors in one way or another have to do with finding employment within academia, and advancing professionally against a background of quantifiable metrics, such as research evaluation or external funding. These material forces affect both how epistemic communities evolve and how the academic habitus changes over time, but they are not part of either. In systems-theoretical terms we could say that, whereas epistemic communities and the academic habitus discussed thus far are part of the scientific system, such (institutional and career-related) operations belong to the functionally differentiated systems of the economy and of politics respectively, and merely 'irritate' the scientific system (where academic communications are 'understood').[72] Alternatively, were we to take a materialist perspective, these phenomena could be analysed relative to the political economy of higher education.[73]

As any socio-legal scholar knows, securing external funding plays an important role work, both in terms of the research that can be undertaken and professional advancement more generally. What needs to be studied in more detail is how and in what ways research funding affects the national, regional, and general development of socio-legal studies as a research field. Fekete notes that it is part of the measure of scholarly success,[74] while Hammerslev recalls that, to follow a career in the sociology of law in Denmark, he was guided towards both internationalisation and external funding.[75] Wheeler, by contrast, notes the UK peculiarity of governmental research evaluation to assess the quality of research, which then determines 'block grant' funding allocation to UK universities,[76] and highlights how socio-legal research is in fact more likely to attract funding than traditional doctrinal legal studies.

D. Historical Context and Trajectories

The final cluster discussed in the Oñati workshop revolved around the concept of 'context' in a sense separate from the other clusters discussed so far. Academic biographies, epistemic communities and institutional economies

[72] Niklas Luhmann, *Rechtssystem Und Rechtsdogmatik* (Kohlhammer, 1974) 13, 17; Niklas Luhmann, *Die Wissenschaft der Gesellschaft* (Wissenschaftliche Buchgesellschaft, 2002) 324.

[73] Tobias Schulze-Cleven and others, 'The New Political Economy of Higher Education: Between Distributional Conflicts and Discursive Stratification' (2017) 73 *Higher Education* 795.

[74] Fekete, p. 40.

[75] Hammerlev, p. 102.

[76] Wheeler, p. 182.

are all 'context' for doing socio-legal research, of course, but the factors we considered in the last cluster were more historical and 'long-durée' than the previously mentioned themes.[77] These factors were also able to encompass the socio-political environment within which the research took place, and which had a bearing on cohorts of scholars within a given area at a particular time. This concerns, for example, the existence of political regimes such as the Soviet empire in countries like Hungary, Poland or the former Yugoslavia, and the reverberations of colonialism which have had huge effects on countries like the UK, France, Spain and the Netherlands. The literature we draw upon here comes from political and historical sociology (of law):[78] it is fruitful to engage critically with classical comparative (social) histories of the legal profession and legal scholars[79] as well as the history of the development of social science disciplines at universities[80] to understand the impact of certain historical path dependencies on today's circumstances. At the same time, this should not lead to historically determinist accounts; sometimes certain conditions attributed to deep-historical or 'cultural' legacies can be of fairly recent origin.[81]

From this perspective, the most notable material factor is, as Samir Forić reminds us, the 'spatial dimension', which is apparent in terms of those national and regional 'developmental disparities that are reflective in the socio-legal trajectory'.[82] Another example is given by Bucholc, who argues that the early-twentieth-century political environment in Poland affected the way some of the classics of sociology of law were received in Polish socio-legal scholarship.[83] Fekete also reflects on the political and cultural proximity of Hungary to Germany, which has been a major influence.[84] Evidently political regimes also matter: as can clearly be seen in the chapters by Bucholc, Fekete and Forić, the communist systems of Poland, Hungary and the former Yugoslavia differed substantially, both between each other and over time, all of which had a

[77] Mathias Grote, 'What Could the "longue Durée" Mean for the History of Modern Sciences?' (Fondation Maison des sciences de l'homme, 2015) FMSH-WP-2015-98 https://shs.hal.science/halshs-01171257/document.

[78] Marta Bucholc, 'Historical Sociology of Law' in David McCallum (ed), *The Palgrave Handbook of the History of Human Sciences* (Singapore, Springer Nature Singapore, 2022); Paul Pierson, *Politics in Time: History, Institutions, and Social Analysis* (Princeton, Princeton University Press, 2004).

[79] For example, RC van Caenegem, *Judges, Legislators, and Professors: Chapters in European Legal History* (Cambridge, Cambridge University Press, 1987).

[80] Two examples from the literature using different 'looking glasses': Reza Banakar, 'Law Through Sociology's Looking Glass: Conflict and Competition in Sociological Studies of Law' in Ann Denis and Devorah Kalekin-Fishman (eds), *The ISA Handbook in Contemporary Sociology* (London, SAGE, 2009); Didier Fassin and George Steinmetz (eds), *The Social Sciences in the Looking Glass: Studies in the Production of Knowledge* (Durham NC, Duke University Press, 2023).

[81] EJ Hobsbawm and TO Ranger (eds), *The Invention of Tradition* (Cambridge, Cambridge University Press, 1983).

[82] Forić, p. 64.

[83] Bucholc, p. 21.

[84] Fekete, p. 41.

substantial impact on the ways in which socio-legal thinking could develop in a one-party state. In Germany, as Kocher points out, with 'the murder and the emigration of many socio-legal scholars with often socialist and/or Jewish backgrounds, German legal academia was cut off from the Weimar tradition after the Second World War'.[85]

IV. CONCLUSION

In this collected volume, we have made the case that valuable insights can be gained from exploring individuals' professional trajectories and disciplinary environment. Exploring the intersection of disciplinary and personal trajectories holds promise, both for studies of scholarly self-reflection and for the social history of ideas. This is where the macro-sociological meaning of 'trajectories' and the value of comparative-historical case studies comes in: we cannot understand phenomena observed in the socio-legal realm without tracing their historical genesis. This applies to easily observable, structural factors such as institutions or socio-economic conditions, as well as more fluid and difficult-to-measure variables, such as academic or legal 'cultures', mentalities, values and behavioural patterns.

By means of the heuristic framework outlined in this introductory chapter, we offer the reader a structure through which to understand and compare these trajectories. The four heuristics are: (1) individual biography; (2) epistemic communities; (3) institutional and economic forces, and (4) cultural/contextual factors. For the purpose of comparison, these heuristics allow us systematically to formulate questions and hypotheses, collect data and to present diverse trajectories in a manner that highlights both differences and parallels.

Future studies can extend the perspective to a wider set of cases, test our assumptions and extrapolate more stories at the intersection of disciplinary histories and scholarly biographies. It is not our intention that these chapters provide a comprehensive picture of a national academic legal culture. Indeed, we acknowledge that these chapters are necessarily only collections of particular perspectives, and ones that make no claim to being definitive. These reflections are indicative, not representative. We invite researchers to apply and test our heuristic in other settings and contexts, and to dive deeper into comparisons; the examples in our volume show that the following themes might be worth exploring in more detail.

Epistemic communities: We have seen that the existence of epistemic communities of scholars who identify with socio-legal approaches is a necessary but not a sufficient condition for the institutional success of socio-legal studies. Here,

[85] Kocher, p. 120.

the meaning of wider institutional structures, the academic career map, external funding and reputational capital can be explored.

Language: The transition to a global English-language epistemic community risks severing ties to local theory production, since the global discourse and its citation practices favour the 'big names' from the English-language literature at the expense of non-English authors, particularly if their works are untranslated. Here, a search for these internationally unheard national voices might paint an interesting picture and introduce to a wider audience stories that add richness to our understanding of the development of national epistemic communities and intellectual traditions.

The role of gender: Some authors discuss the role that gender played in their trajectories. Here, a more in-depth analysis and comparison would be helpful. For example, what different roles is played by gender across generations, across institutions, and across legal cultures?

'Black letter' law: One distinctive feature of socio-legal studies is that, in almost all cases, it derives its identity from its opposition to doctrinal scholarship. This opposition plays out very differently in each epistemic community, however. A particular challenge to the comparison of socio-legal trajectories is that need not only to be embedded in the histories of sociology, but also in histories of legal scholarship.

Finally, we hope that this predominantly Europe-focused collection is the first of many, and we invite readers to ponder how they might develop their own comparative inquiry into different socio-legal trajectories around the world.

2

The Comeback of Law: Theoretical Foundations and Research Traditions of Socio-Legal Studies in Poland after 1989

MARTA BUCHOLC*

In 2018, Zbigniew Cywiński, a sociologist of law based at the University of Warsaw, published a paper whose title is symptomatic for the self-perception of Polish socio-legal studies: *Petrazyckian Tradition in Polish Sociology of Law, or What Have We Gained By Not Referencing Ehrlich*.[1] Cywiński argued that Polish sociology of law was unique in the way it made use of the concepts and ideas of Leo Petrażycki as a source of inspiration for empirical studies of law. This, in the author's opinion, resulted in an innovative research programme focusing on legal culture and legal consciousness with highly original contributions to sociology of state and law. Nonetheless, while Cywiński argued that Polish sociology of law stood to gain by not referencing Ehrlich, it undoubtedly came at a price. By affirmatively mapping the history of Polish sociology of law on the Petrażycki-Ehrlich continuum, Cywiński provided a point of departure for a Strengths, Weaknesses, Opportunities and Threats analysis of the discipline. His paper is a good example of how reflection on theoretical sources and inspirations can feed into critical self-reflection – a task not unlike the one I am undertaking here.

I begin with an overview of the foundations of the main research traditions of socio-legal studies in Poland, starting with the interwar period (with a brief comment on the pre-1918 developments), moving towards the socialist era, and focusing specifically on the three post-1989 decades. My goal is to explore the

* I am very grateful to Marta Gospodarczyk and Grupa Mowa for their kind assistance with editing this chapter. The work on this chapter is funded by the Volkswagen Foundation (*Towards Illiberal Constitutionalism in East Central Europe: Historical Analysis in Comparative and Transnational Perspectives*).

[1] Z Cywiński, 'Tradycja petrażycjańska w polskiej socjologii prawa albo o tym, co zyskaliśmy, nie odwołując się do Ehrlicha' (2018) 74 *Studia Iuridica* 99–133.

interplay of the rich and long tradition of sociology of law in Poland and the contemporary research agendas in socio-legal studies. I insist on distinguishing the sociology of law (in Polish: *socjologia prawa*) from socio-legal studies, the latter having thus far no commonly accepted equivalent in Polish and most usually used in English. Although in daily academic circulation, the two expressions tend to be almost synonymous. I therefore follow Grażyna Skąpska in accepting, in the Polish context, the interchangeability of sociology of law and socio-legal studies, which I understand, broadly, to be the studies of law having an empirical component demonstrably anchored in the theories and methodologies of social sciences, as opposed to purely speculative philosophical reflection or legal dogmatics.[2]

I will point out the moments of continuity as well as those of inconsistency and contradiction inherent in the intellectual path of socio-legal studies in Poland in order to demonstrate how they bear on the methodological choices, research strategies, actions and omissions of scholars working in this field in Poland today. The first two parts of this chapter are entirely historical and rather general, since it would take up much more space than I have at my disposal to do justice to the history of sociology of law in Poland. Fortunately, many excellent authors, including those cited below, have covered large parts of this story in their work. In the following two parts, I discuss the genesis and the course of two processes that I argue are taking place now. The first is the ongoing turn of sociology of law towards a more comprehensive, inclusive and transdisciplinary approach to law – what might be called a 'return of the socio-legal'. The second process is the paradoxical rise of socio-legal studies triggered by the crisis of the rule of law in the country since 2015. In my conclusions, I will comment on how the two processes have reinforced each other with a possible side effect of expanding the Petrażycki-Ehrlich continuum.

I. GENEALOGICAL CONSIDERATIONS: SOCIOLOGY OF LAW BEFORE 1945

Not to focus too much on the vicissitudes of Poland, it is worthwhile to note that the period of the theoretical formation of sociology of law as a 'scholarly tradition' coincided with the disintegration and disappearance of the independent Polish (or, rather, Polish-Lithuanian) state at the end of the eighteenth century.[3] The following period of over a century of subjugation of divided formerly Polish-Lithuanian territories to the rule of Prussia (later Germany), Austria (later Austro-Hungary) and Russia is referred to in the historiography as the 'partitions'. Under the partitions, what used to be called 'Polish national

[2] Grażyna Skąpska, 'Socio-Legal Studies in Poland: Great Heritage, Empirical Accomplishments, Contemporary Challenges' (2019) 46 *Journal of Law and Society* 476–96, 476.

[3] M Deflem, *Sociology of Law: Visions of a Scholarly Tradition* (Cambridge, Cambridge University Press, 2008).

consciousness', as well as Polish culture and language, survived or even – occasionally – thrived. However, the fragmentation of territory resulted in a radically different experience of the law and state in each of the lands which became part of the three partitioning powers. As a result, after restoration of Polish statehood in 1918, the country was marked by legal pluralism to an extent unprecedented among modern European states, with a possible exception of the United Kingdom. Legal orders of the partitioning powers wrote over the palimpsest of old laws of the Polish-Lithuanian republic as well as the legal customs and informal norms in the highly regionally diverse, ethnically and religiously differentiated, predominantly rural country. At that time, it had been only slightly and selectively affected by industrial capitalism and bureaucratisation in the three distinct cultural versions. Manuela Boatcă has shown that Polish lands were a target of racialised, extractive colonial policy-making by the German Empire, and the same applies, albeit with some modifications, to the two other partitioning powers.[4]

I have argued that this state of Poland under partitions and after 1918 was one of the main reasons why some of the classics of sociology of law, including Max Weber and Emile Durkheim, did not resonate with Polish socio-legal scholarship.[5] The classics of sociology of law, as opposed to those of legal anthropology, tended to take state-made law as their point of departure for understanding any other form of law. Any thoughts on what we now call legal pluralism that they may have had were limited to historical cases and customary law, and not to the legal orders of colonial or decolonised territories, which is probably the optic best applied to Poland under and following the partitions. Such legal pluralism makes it more difficult to understand the reluctance of Polish sociologists of law to be inspired by the legacy of Eugen Ehrlich or the affine insights of the *Freirechtsschule* (Free Law School). The emergent new juridical field of Poland's society established in a new geographical space in 1918 was very closely related to German and, especially, Austro-Hungarian academia. Ehrlich's interest in *lebendes Recht* (living law) in law as it really is when operated by the people amongst themselves should not have been anything but inspiring for the lawmakers and practitioners of law striving for more uniformity and unification, both in the legal dogmatic sense and in the practice of jurisprudence and law enforcement. It would seem that the research program of Ehrlich should fit the bill, less owing to the frequently overrated empirical elements it contained than due to its acknowledgment of the inherent plurality of law.[6]

[4] M Boatcă, '"From the Standpoint of Germanism": A Postcolonial Critique of Weber's Theory of Race and Ethnicity' in J Go (ed), *Postcolonial* Sociology, *Political Power and Social Theory*, Vol. 24 (Bingley, Emerald Group Publishing, 2013) 55–80.

[5] M Bucholc, 'Dlaczego socjologia prawa Webera nie przyjęła się u nas?' (2015) V *Roczniki Historii Socjologii* 39–55.

[6] M Bucholc and M Komornik, 'Failed Emancipation Through Disciplinary Transgression: Eugen Ehrlich and the Emergence of Empirical Sociology of Law' (2019) 49 *Historyka Studia Metodologiczne* 15–39.

But, of course, the most direct explanation of why Polish sociology followed Leo Petrażycki rather than Ehrlich was the simple fact that the former came to work and teach in Poland after leaving Russia, thus becoming one of the founders of Poland's institutional sociology. This foundational moment accounts for what I would call the original ambiguity of Polish sociology of law. In 1919, Petrażycki was offered a newly established chair for sociology – the first one in Poland – by the Faculty of Law of the University of Warsaw.[7] Since legal theory was and remained his main interest, sociology of law was by that token associated with the academic structures and theoretical endeavours of legal academia. On the other hand, other founders of institutional sociology in Poland whose impact on the research interests of the following generations of academic sociologists was in many cases decisive, notably Florian Znaniecki and Stefan Czarnowski, had shown little interest in law. To an extent, the same can be said about political thinkers such as Ludwik Krzywicki or Stanisław Brzozowski, who contributed to the highly original social thought inspired by socialism and Marxism that had gained momentum since late nineteenth century and flourished in the interwar period. Despite their strong positions on social problems such as education, equality, or economic empowerment of the working classes, they tended to regard the legal and regulatory matters as secondary to structural and economic issues, which reduced the interest in any studies focusing on law as the main subject.

As a result, the landscape of early Polish institutional sociology seldom ranked law among the core interests. One consequence was that the sociology of law was institutionalised as a separated sociological subdiscipline relatively early. It was distinct enough from other kinds of sociology that there was little place to spare for law, and it stood apart by its early connection to legal academia. Another consequence was that as a subdiscipline, sociology of law was from the very beginning somewhat loosely linked to the research interests of sociology at large, and these interests were dictated by the intellectual and political agenda of the time. Not the least important factor was the predominantly theoretical and conceptual orientation strongly influenced by Petrażycki. As a result, Polish sociology of law was relatively ill-equipped to tackle the major issues which Polish society faced after 1918, since its ability to theorise the social, cultural and organisational consequences of the plurality of laws within a single sovereign nation state was limited. Clearly, much could have been gained by working with Ehrlich.

On the other hand, as Jacek Kurczewski observed,[8] the greatest potential of Petrażycki's concept of law was exactly the fact that it was not state-centred and inherently pluralist. However, it was never conceived as a theoretical foundation for an empirical research programme. For Petrażycki, legal pluralism was

[7] For more context, see M Bucholc, *Sociology in Poland: To Be Continued?* (London, Palgrave, 2016).

[8] J Kurczewski, 'Sociology of Law in Poland' (2001) 32(2) *The American Sociologist* 85–98, at 86.

an assumption and not a hypothesis. By the same token, however, Petrażyckian inspiration produced another serendipitous advantage. It focused on the mental, psychological, internal aspects of law, which related the sociological understanding of law to experiences and affective states of individual legal subjects. Law, according to Petrażycki, was therefore always so much more than whatever state-fixated and institution-bound lawyers said it was. This approach encompasses not only the bourgeois lawyers of the late nineteenth and early twentieth century, but any lawyers, anytime, anywhere. After 1945, when Poland's 20 years of interwar independence and six years of wartime trauma ended in the country being allotted to the Soviet bloc by the victorious allies, this advantage of accommodating a measure of methodological individualism within theory and theoretical sociology of law contributed to the preservation and positioning of Petrażycki's ideas as an alternative to the official Marxism in socialist Poland.

II. SOCIO-LEGAL STUDIES IN POLAND IN THE YEARS 1945–89

In a state that had lost its sovereignty (again), socio-legal studies took one of two turns. They either elaborated on those aspects of Petrażycki's theory which paved the way to the study of law beyond the focus on state as lawmaker, or they drew from the officially endorsed Marxist-Leninist ideology as it evolved over time, focusing on the structural aspects of law and state power. I will start with Petrażycki's tradition, which was chronologically older and, initially, much more strongly embedded in Polish socio-legal studies.

A. Petrażycki's Theory under Communism

The main agent of influence on whom the preservation of Petrażycki's legacy depended was Jerzy Lande. He had attended Petrażycki's classes in Saint Petersburg before the 1917 Revolution and later came to be a law professor at the Jagiellonian University in Cracow in 1929. There he played the role of Petrażycki's porte-parole in the academic community even before the latter's tragic death in 1931.[9] Even though some scholars argue that Lande was primarily a theorist of law and can hardly be regarded as a sociologist,[10] it was in sociology of law that he made his lasting mark. However, Lande's circle did not reproduce Petrażycki's almost exclusive inclination for the theoretical. Those students of Lande who took up Petrażycki's ideas, though mostly affiliated

[9] K Motyka, 'Socjologia prawa: Od Petrażyckiego do Podgóreckiego' in W Szymczak (ed), *100 lat socjologii w Katolickim Uniwersytecie Lubelskim Jana Pawła II. Idee – teorie – badania* (Lublin, TN KUL, 2018) 248.

[10] ibid 246.

with the law department in Cracow, tended towards the sociological more than the legal, and were, on the whole, much more practically oriented than their master.

The tradition of Petrażycki persevered into the 1960s and 1970s, when Marxist sociology of law took off. Adam Podgórecki, based in Warsaw, was the best-known internationally among the third-generation Petrażyckians trained by Lande in Cracow. His work was continued at the University of Warsaw by the next generation of socio-legal scholars, including, in particular, Jacek Kurczewski. Podgórecki was an ardent proponent of disciplinary identity of sociology of law.[11] He famously championed 'sociotechnique',[12] which can best be characterised as a practical science of social change, but he also contributed to the general theory of norms and organisations and to sociological theory of law. Kurczewski's doctoral thesis supervised by Podgórecki, defended in 1972, discussed the concept of pre-state law. At the Jagiellonian University in Cracow and at the Polish Academy of Sciences, Maria Borucka-Arctowa was another student of Lande who developed Petrażycki's ideas. She was the first woman in Poland to become a professor of law. She founded her own school of sociology of law and became a founding mother of an important branch of Polish sociology of law. She specialised in the studies of legal consciousness, images of law and motivational aspects of law-abiding behaviour, as well as (since the 1970s) legal socialisation and dispute resolution.[13]

Hanna Dębska so summarised the differences between Podgórecki's and Borucka-Arctowa's approaches to sociology of law:

> They draw on different strands of his [Petrażycki's] legacy – Podgórecki – primarily from the politics of law, Borucka-Arctova from legal consciousness – developing them *suo modo*. Both carry out empirical research in the teams they created, using, in principle, the same methods: Borucka-Arctowa on in-depth interviews, survey research …, while Podgórecki relies both on in-depth interviews, although he often points out their insufficiency, and on various survey methods, conducting, for example, research into the prestige of the law or the institution of divorce.[14]

The rivalry between the two lines of Petrażycki's legacy lasted after Podgórecki's emigration from Poland in 1977,[15] forced by the authorities' hostilities leading to closing his institute, which employed a stunning number of non-party researchers. Podgórecki became a highly respected and influential member of

[11] A Podgórecki, 'The Sociology of Law in Poland' in R Treves and JFG van Loon (eds), *Norms and Actions* (Dordrecht, Springer, 1968) 85–98.

[12] A Podgórecki, 'Sociotechnique' (1963) 8 *The Polish Sociological Bulletin* 47–57.

[13] G Skąpska, 'The Sociology of Law in Poland. Problems, Polemics, Social Commitment' (1987) 14(3) *Journal of Law and Society* 353–65, at 363.

[14] Hanna Dębska, 'Herezja w prawoznawstwie. Trajektoria polskiej socjologii prawa w XX wieku' in T Zarycki (ed), *Polskie nauki polityczne w perspektywie relacji władzy i zależności międzynarodowych* (Warsaw, Wydawnictwa Uniwersytetu Warszawskiego, 2022) 129 (original references omitted).

[15] Kurczewski, above n 8.

the international socio-legal community, much more internationally recognised than his competitor, especially in the socio-legal community, evidenced in part by the existence of the Isa RCSL Podgórecki Prize. Podgórecki was a co-founder of the Research Committee on Sociology of Law.[16] Dębska explains his success – as opposed to Borucka-Arctowa's – by pointing out that Podgórecki held not only a PhD in law but was also a trained sociologist.[17] This knowledge provided him access to both sociological theorising and more sophisticated methodologies, augmenting his chances of appealing to sociologists as well as legal theorists, thus gaining influence and institutional security in the field of law.[18] Podgórecki's international success was, therefore, an early premium on interdisciplinarity.

B. Marxist Influence on Sociology of Law under Communism

As far as Marxist influence in the late 1940s in academic legal scholarship is concerned, we face an apparent paradox.

On the one hand, at the outset of the new socialist statehood, it was very difficult to ensure legal training according to Marxist-Leninist ideological principles due to the simple lack of academic lawyers of Marxist persuasion. As a result, some notable figures of the pre-war legal academia and bar were able to survive the post-war years of Stalinist takeover despite their publicly known anti-Communist views or religious beliefs, and some Communist scholars were closely affined with the pronouncedly anti-Communist ones.[19] The Communist government found it relatively difficult to do without non-Communist scholars, which is probably one of the reasons why Polish academia never got Sovietised as much as many others in the Eastern Bloc.[20] This is not to say that the Stalinist era, which lasted until 1956 in Poland, was not a period of brutal and massive indoctrination and purges of the academic community – it was.[21] However, the Communist government's actions were not entirely successful, despite the emergence of 'legal-empirical research', a Marxist arrival using empirical research methods following Marxist assumptions in order to supplement dogmatic legal reasoning.[22] In fact, Skąpska argues that the empirical

[16] For more on Podgórecki's life, see A Kojder, 'Adam Podgórecki's "Vita Activa"' (1999) 126 *Polish Sociological Review* 323–30.

[17] Dębska, above n 14, 130.

[18] ibid, 130ff.

[19] M Bucholc, 'Juliusz Bardach and the Agenda of Socialist History of Law in Poland' in V Erkkila and H-P Haferkamp (eds), *Socialist Interpretations of Legal History* (London, Routledge, 2020).

[20] J Connelly, *Captive University: The Sovietization of East German, Czech, and Polish Higher Education, 1945–1956* (Chapel Hill, University of North Carolina Press, 2000).

[21] Hanna Dębska, *Homo academicus iuridicus. Geneza i struktura akademickiego pola prawnego w warunkach półperyferyjnych* (Unpublished doctoral dissertation at the University of Warsaw, University of Warsaw Repository, 2021) 117ff.

[22] Kurczewski, above n 8, 88.

turn was a direct reaction to the rigid dogmatism of Marxist legal studies in the 1950s.[23] Thus, Marxism fuelled two important streams of sociology of law: the Petrażyckian one indirectly and by opposition, and the legal-empirical by subversive affirmation.

On the other hand, the new authorities valued the political importance of the theory of law and state very highly and were attentive to whatever happened in legal academia. This occurred for the very same reasons as the lack of Marxist lawyers, which the new system sorely needed to ensure that the work of rebuilding the country after the war-time devastation would be conducted by an ideologically compliant state apparatus. Marxist theory of state and law became an obligatory course in legal education and a prestigious field of research, allowing for a new reshuffling of theoretical agendas with philosophy of law, theory of state institutions, theory of law and sociology of law all interplaying under a strong domination of theory.

The Marxist line of empirical studies of law and state developed steadily, but slowly. It was not an easy task to conduct empirical research that would stand the ideological tests of correctness based on Marxist historical determinism. Eventually, the main proponents of Marxist sociology of law came to be spread evenly between sociological and legal faculties of the country. Over time, an evolution took place in Marxist sociology of law that was somewhat similar to the processes undergoing in the Petrażycki's school. The interest in law, legal systems and state law-making expanded to include a general theory of organisations, institutions and intergroup relations. The best example of this line of development would be Stanisław Ehrlich, whose career began as a Stalinist philosopher of law in the late 1940s and ended as a theorist of interest groups and pluralism combining sociology with political sciences, and a target of an anti-Semitic campaign in 1968. Ehrlich was also an important member of International Political Science Association and a founder of IPSA Study Group on Problems of Socio-Political Pluralism.[24] Interestingly enough, Ehrlich was teaching a private seminar in the 1970s in which some of the future oppositionists and prominent contemporary right-wing politicians participated, including, famously, Jarosław Kaczyński.

On the whole, the Marxist line of sociology of law was much slower to develop an empirical agenda than the Petrażyckian one. Marxist thought tended to produce theory-heavy structural and institutional analyses in which law was but one of many variables. At the same time, this tendency created an opening for international networking and recognition, a side effect of the mode in which Marxist sociology developed in Poland coinciding with global theoretical trends. Polish Marxism was able to internationalise on this coincidence rather well, as shown by the reception of the works of Jerzy Wiatr and Włodzimierz

[23] Skąpska, above n 13, 353.

[24] For more on Ehrlich's life and views, see W Zomerski, 'Stanisław Ehrlich's Critique of Legal Dogmatics: Then and Now' (2020) 45(2–3) *Review of Central and East European Law* 314–33.

Wesołowski. Polish Marxism became an important part of the international debate on sociological theory, especially in the United States, drawing on Marx ever more strongly from the late 1950s. It contributed a fresh and interesting viewpoint from behind the Iron Curtain, carrying some empirical weight, notably due to the original Polish studies of social stratification.

C. Balance Sheet of the Communist Period

To sum up, the story of socio-legal studies in Poland between 1945 and 1989 comprises three parallel and interlinked historical processes. To begin with, legal dogmatic was much more firmly rooted in Marxism than socio-legal studies, but the Marxist foundation was lost almost entirely by the late 1970s, leaving the dogmatic part of law ideologically free-floating as of 1989. The Marxist inspiration in sociology seemed to be much more resilient and survived in 1989, and it gained Polish sociology a non-negligible measure of international recognition after Marxism returned in style in the West. However, Polish sociology of law did not benefit by this change of intellectual orientations as much as some other sociological subdisciplines, notably stratification studies, sociology of politics or organisations. As a consequence, the interest in law as a part of the sociological study of institutions, structures and organisations since the 1970s was gradually reduced towards 1989. In the meanwhile, socio-legal studies continuing Petrażycki's line were empirically oriented but not state-oriented. It prioritised socio-cultural and socio-psychological aspects of law, stressing the individual correlates of legal phenomena. As an end-result, Marxian inspirations in Polish sociology survived the fall of Communism and still hold their place in studies of structures and institutions. They are now (almost) freed from the odium of imposed ideological burden they once carried, and so were received anew to fit into the agendas of contemporary social scientists. However, in sociology of law, the role of Marxism was much less pronounced. Empirical studies of law were more closely attached to Petrażyckian line (which was anti-Marxist) and many sociologists of law were based at law faculties as self-proclaimed theorists of law and state. The latter lost any interest in Marxism they may have had early on, and consequently, since the 1970s, would produce little Marxist scholarship going much beyond lip service. In the two final decades of Communist rule, this historical dynamic forced sociology of law to go about reinventing its disciplinary identity.

III. 1989: THE EARLY PHASE OF THE TRANSFORMATION

In 1989, socio-legal studies in Poland could rely on a relatively large body of empirical studies of legal institutions and various cultural aspects of law, in particular, the studies of legal consciousness, which even became a kind of

Polish hallmark.[25] The most important figures in the field were relatively evenly distributed between law and sociology departments, with Warsaw and Cracow as two main centres, founded on the authority of central figures whose international standing also secured a degree of networking operable in 1989. This goes both for the Petrażyckian and the Marxist developmental lines, since both of them became well-established internationally before 1989, albeit relying on capital gathered in various international disciplinary fields (sociology, political science and law). Skąpska also argued that 'most of its proponents did not see their role as that of a detached observer'.[26] Social engagement and critical mindset were common to many Polish sociologists of law, notwithstanding their ideological differences.

Before 1989, some sociologists of law were active in the anti-Communist opposition and actively participated in the conceptual work on the future political and legal order of Poland. However, despite their engagement, Poland's transformation design and debate came to be dominated by the political and economic considerations that overshadowed the legal ones. I have argued that back in the late 1980s and early 1990s, law was conceived of as little more than a tool of what I called 'liberal pedagogy',[27] subservient to the goals of economic transformation. The law's internal dynamics and inertia, not to mention its own irreducible cultural effects, were entirely disregarded.

In a way, Poland seems to have missed the moment which Ralf Dahrendorf once so described:

> This is the hour of the lawyers. By that of course I do not mean the litigious advocates of American courts, nor the philologists of arcane texts in the Roman law tradition, but those who have the imagination and comparative experience to find a way out of the monopoly of the party and all subordinate monopolies too. This is the core issue, and it is not enough simply to remove the relevant article from existing constitutions.[28]

It was a situation not unlike the one after 1918, when the inertia of legal pluralism in the post-partition era was rarely thematised by the social sciences. The rewriting of laws took up so much effort that it left little imagination, be it legal or sociological, for any other exercise, including the understanding of the interplay of law, culture and society in a society undergoing a rapid and, in many ways, traumatic transformation.[29] Sociology in general, and its many subdisciplines institutionalising since 1970, was almost entirely dedicated to the study of transformation, and almost entirely concentrated on tracing the obstacles in

[25] M Fuszara, 'Sociology of Law in Poland' (1990) 11(1) *Zeitschrift für Rechtssoziologie* 42–50.

[26] Skąpska, above n 13, at 363.

[27] M Bucholc, 'Law and Liberal Pedagogy in a Post-Socialist Society: The Case of Poland' (2020) 18(3) *Journal of Modern European History* 324–34.

[28] R Dahrendorf, *Reflections on the Revolution in Europe* (New Jersey, Transaction Publishers, 2005) 22.

[29] P Sztompka, 'Cultural Trauma: The Other Face of Social Change' (2000) 3(4) *European Journal of Social Theory* 449–66.

the way of the country being efficiently transformed in the likeness of Western democratic market economies. Sociology of law was no exception.

Consequently, the main themes of socio-legal reflection in the late 1980s and 1990s continued focusing on the well-established set of research problems in a new framing. Legal consciousness, legal socialisation and cultural images of law were this time envisaged within the common framework of 'civilisational incompetence' of Polish society and rarely contested in the first transformation years.[30] It should also be noted that the study of the socio-cultural aspects of law rarely extended into the realm of cultural studies and their proper methods. Images and imaginaries were also frequently studied using quantitative, survey methods or with a strong quantitative component. Institutional aspects of the legal system were also researched, including pathologies such as corruption, abuse of power and various unintended consequences of legal change, whether in the executive or the judiciary. In general, the neo-institutional paradigm exercised a certain influence on socio-legal studies in Poland, mostly under the heading of social problems, following in Podgórecki's footsteps. Interestingly enough, while the transformation brought impulses for methodological and theoretical innovations in sociology at large, it was not so in sociology of law. There, the 1989 stock of theoretical inspirations largely remained unchanged into the late 1990s, even though the research themes came to include many of the subjects that used to be taboo before 1989 for political reasons, such as electoral law or peoples' opinions about public authorities.[31]

The instrumental and technical approach to the legal norms[32] contributed to the split between law and socio-legal studies. Sociology of law, initially spread between legal and sociological departments, came to associate with legal departments almost exclusively, and research on sociology of law in sociological departments became rare. This process revealed the growing distance between law and anything related to it, and other spheres of social life. It was an inevitable effect of the professionalisation of law, the expansion of the legal professions and the burst of economic opportunities awaiting law graduates. Poland may not have had its hour of lawyers in terms of inventing the democratic polity, but lawyers as agents of economic transformation certainly did play a crucial role in the 1990s.

This increasing attractivity of legal professions and the growth of the number of students of law was accompanied by an increase in the complexity of knowledge with which the law graduates were confronted. Studying law came to be viewed as a training that had to keep up with market demands and

[30] See P Sztopmka, 'Civilizational Incompetence: The Trap of Post-Communist Societies' (1993) 22(2) *Zeitschrift für Soziologie* 85–95.

[31] Fuszara, above n 25, at 43.

[32] With a possible exception of constitutional norms, as evidenced by the conflict over the value-framework of the new constitution in the 1990s, see E Hałas, 'Constructing the Identity of a Nation-State. Symbolic Conflict over the Preamble to the Constitution of the Third Republic of Poland' (2005) 149 *Polish Sociological Review* 49–67.

professional expectations more than with an academic standard. Again, this echoes the debates of the early 1920s and late 1940s when the either-or between academic and professional skills was sharpened by the systemic transformation and economic crisis. One visible sign of the market-professional orientation was the reduction of subjects not directly related to professional legal training, focusing strongly on dogmatics, in the legal curricula all over the country. Roman law and Latin, history of law, philosophy of law and sociology of law were reduced from obligatory to elective courses, their weight in the curriculum diminished, and the reproduction of scholarly ranks became threatened as the graduates aimed for more prestigious or practical specialisations.

The effect of European integration and accession was also far from favourable to socio-legal studies. Another huge corpus of concepts, norms and jurisprudence became part of obligatory curriculum and gained more and more relevance in legal practice, pushing out the educational contents that could be spared owing to their purely academic, non-professional nature. To give a particularly flagrant example of what this led to: professional ethics were left out of most university curricula entirely and delegated to the professional associations that took over the training of lawyers in Poland after five years of study.[33]

I hope the paradox of the early transformation period in socio-legal studies and legal education is clear by now. Whereas most of the sociologists turned to the study of the transformation with new theoretical tools, sociologists of law came to be closer bound with law departments where few new theories were forged and effort focussed mostly on the challenges of adaptation to what was seen as technical and external systemic requirements of market economy, democracy and European integration.

At the same time, sociologists of law were left almost entirely alone with law as a research subject, since it was omitted from sociological studies focusing on institutions, procedures and structures. Finally, sociology of law, relegated to law departments, was then relegated to the margins of legal education. Thus, its outreach among sociologists was limited and among lawyers, marginal. Socio-legal studies in Poland in the 1990s and early 2000s were confronted with a massive disciplinary resistance from the juristic field that was reoriented towards increasing professionalisation. This would also be the time when the immunity to critique of law in Polish legal academia consolidated.[34]

As a result of this situation, theoretical change in Polish sociology of law mostly occurred in the research areas which were of practical interest to lawyers

[33] For more on the legal professions in Poland, see K Gadowska, 'Poland. Opening Legal Professions' in RL Abel, O Hammerslev, H Sommerlad and U Schultz (eds), *Lawyers in 21st-Century Societies* (Cambridge, Hart Publishing, 2020) 309–30.

[34] See H Dębska, 'W okowach prawniczego sensus communis. O trudnościach uprawiania krytycznie zorientowanej socjologii prawa' (2014) 1(8) *Archiwum Filozofii Prawa i Filozofii Społecznej* 18–28.

as agents of the transformation, such as access to justice.[35] Other fields were left aside and only worked by very few and in relative isolation from academic teaching. This applies notably to critical legal studies (at the time this would mostly apply to feminist ones), law and literature or law and religion. The marginalisation of feminist critique of law was especially consequential, since reproductive rights turned out to be one of the most if not the most contentious subject very early into the transformation, and public opinion on abortion was extensively studied sociologically. Monika Płatek, pointing out the gender inequalities in the distribution of the benefits of the transformation, cited Petrażycki's call for equal rights for women.[36] Her voice – as those of other Polish feminists and gender scholars – remained unheard in society affected by what Agnieszka Graff and Elżbieta Korolczuk dubbed 'the anti-feminist backlash' long predating the fall of Communism.[37] This omission and marginalisation of the gender issue in the transformation processes had – I would argue – grave consequences not only for the country, but also for the next part of the history of socio-legal studies in Poland, starting in mid-2000.

The following words of Małgorzata Fuszara written in 1990, when read after more than 30 years, convey a strong sense of irony of history:

> Rapid social and political transformations and the accompanying legal changes create a unique opportunity for research in the field of sociology of law. New institutions emerge, legal consciousness is changed; legal education in previously forbidden spheres is introduced, as for example in the sphere of human rights. At the same time, censorship and other institutional obstacles that used to block research or publication of findings now ceased to exist.[38]

As it turned out, sociology of law not only had to struggle with the financial difficulties of conducting large-scale research under capitalism, which Fuszara mentions later in the same paragraph. This was a challenge that all social science in Poland faced. I should say that some of the obstacles to freedom of research and dissemination, though removed, would come back soon afterwards, though in a somewhat modified form. Some of the gains of the transformation, such as Poland's integration with global and European human rights order, were more fragile than could be expected. Most of all, however, the unique opportunity for sociology of law and socio-legal studies in general coincided with the circumstances which reduced their attraction for almost everyone – for fellow sociologists, for students and for policy-makers. Thus, I come to another paradox of socio-legal studies in Poland. A new impulse

[35] See eg J Winczorek and K Muszyński, *Small and Medium Enterprises, Law and Business Uncertainty and Justice* (London, Routledge, 2023).

[36] M Płatek, 'Hostages of Destiny: Gender Issues in Today's Poland' (2004) 76(1) *Feminist Review* 5–25.

[37] A Graff and E Korolczuk, *Anti-Gender Politics in the Populist Moment* (London, Routledge, 2022).

[38] Fuszara, above n 25, at 50.

for their development came from the very unexpected side, a side that set out to revisit and reject some of the most important components of the post-Communist transformation legacy.

IV. THE NATIONAL-CONSERVATIVE POLITICAL TURN AS A NEW IMPULSE FOR SOCIO-LEGAL STUDIES

The national-conservative turn after 2015 has been covered extensively in scholarship, the analyses often including the 2005–07 period when the national-conservative Prawo i Sprawiedliwość (PiS, Law and Justice) first came to rule the country for half a term, a prelude to its lasting domination of the political scene since 2015.[39] The unexpected change in Polish politics also created a revival of interest in Poland in a broad range of academic disciplines, from memory studies through gender and environmental studies. However, for socio-legal studies, the most important thing was that the change in Poland after 2015 was typically framed as – to put it somewhat vaguely – a problem with law or, as it may sometimes seem, the law's problem with politics, or, even, with society. What Skąpska calls a 'blatant abuse of binding law' summarises the dominant framing – and is also applied by myself in my many works on the subject.[40] After 2015, the law was there and the law was broken by the politicians, undefended or ineffectively defended by other politicians, by society, by international institutions, by civil society and by international public opinion. No wonder that interest in the mechanisms which make law susceptible to abuse and which could possibly endow it with resilience grew significantly. This happened alongside the – non-negligible – interest in justifying the abuse or arguing against it being abuse at all, which can also, ultimately and conditionally, stimulate an interest in law.

In 2016, when brainstorming the first of a series of articles we wrote for *Osteuropa*, Maciej Komornik and I first came up with the title 'The Whole Nation is Interpreting its Constitution', meant as a play on the afterwar call to action in rebuilding demolished Warsaw: 'The Whole Nation is Rebuilding its Capital'. The journal's diligent editors made us see how obscure our proposal would be for non-Polish readership, so we dropped it, but I somehow still feel attached to the idea. After 2015, everyone was suddenly interested in the constitution – what it says, how it says it, and how it can be read. Skąpska's pertinent research on constitutional consciousness of Polish society today shows that this interest has lasted and brought a certain rise in the sense of the importance

[39] M Krygier, 'The Challenge of Institutionalisation: Post-Communist "Transitions", Populism, and the Rule of Law' (2019) 15(3) *European Constitutional Law Review* 544–73; W Sadurski, *Poland's Constitutional Breakdown* (Oxford, Oxford University Press, 2019).

[40] G Skąpska, 'Constitutional Consciousness in a Society on the Verge of Democratic Collapse: The Case of Poland' (2023) 1(35) *Societas/Communitas* 43–72.

of the constitution, even though it cannot be trusted to be very deep, and is characterised by the typical ambivalence of the sense of importance of any abstract object in reference to public opinion.[41] The constitution and the constitutional crisis cannot, of course, be taken to stand *pars pro toto* for law as such. Nonetheless, the national-conservative government also took care to bring many other branches of law to public attention by generating contention and conflict, including but not limited to: reproductive rights, organisation of the judiciary, human rights, European law, environmental law, migration and asylum law, media law, parliamentary procedures, pension laws, social security laws, public health, electoral law, higher and general education law, memory laws and statutory regulation of state of emergency. All in all, I would see the developments since 2015 as a rising tide of popular interpretative effort, in which socio-legal scholars also participate.

The 2005–07 period (the first time PiS was in power) and the years after 2015 have demonstrated the link between values, worldviews and legal norms, which seemed to have been largely obfuscated since the constitutional debate of the 1990s. On the other hand, the haggling over the meaning of some provisions of laws and their binding effect have shown the limitations of legal reasoning. A demonstration was provided for the common-sensical view of lawyers as people who can argue just about anything. The view of law as a dogmatic domain of strict interpretation that is less common-sensical but frequently and eagerly reproduced by some legal scholars and legal professionals in general, became very hard to defend. Consequently, since 2021, it has become much more difficult to accept the dogmatic reasoning as the ultimate ambition in studies of law. This opens way for alternative, non-dogmatic ways to think and argue about the law. While it may conceivably be a challenge for the rule of law, since much juristic creativity has been directed at circumventing the limitations it poses on political action, it should also be an opportunity for socio-legal studies. In particular, the sociology of constitutions has certainly achieved an important reinforcement after 2015, since the understanding of constitutional order, real support for it and the extent to which this support was politically mobilizable suddenly became problems of primary importance for everyone, whatever their political views.

Another reason why the period since 2015 should provide a turning point in socio-legal studies is the fact that the legal change has disproportionately affected, both positively and negatively, socially weaker groups. These have included, at various times, women and pregnant persons, persons with disabilities, large families, LGBTIQ+ people, religious/worldview minorities, ethnic minorities, refugees and migrants, elderly and retired persons.

The debate on reproductive rights and human rights, especially after the restriction of abortion law in 2020, reinforced the debate on the status, binding

[41] Skąpska, above n 40.

force and sources of human rights.[42] Feminist legal scholarship, activist practice and sociological studies have repeatedly come together in the abortion debate, feeding into socio-legal scholarship on the subject.[43] The link between abortion law and the rule of law crisis – this most powerful impulse for socio-legal thinking since 2015 – was articulated by the European Court of Human Rights in *ML v Poland* (ECtHR, 14 December 2023).[44] This ruling can be construed as an indirect confirmation of the need for a more holistic approach to law and society in contemporary Poland where key contentious issues interplay strictly and reverberate at the international level.

Contentious politics around reproductive rights and the rule of law created a new sense of importance of social inequalities and revived reflection on the impact of the post-Communist transformation on inequalities, particularly on their gender dimension and the intersectionalities among gender, sexual orientation, class and place of residence. These developments I perceive – again – as an opening thus far little used in the scholarship. They allow for more critique of law from minority/marginal perspectives and for realignment of Polish socio-legal studies with the agendas of other societies experiencing similar problems in the East Central European region, in Europe in general but also, and most importantly, beyond. Notably, abortion debates and conflict around changing the abortion law in 2020 may conceivably have created women's mass movements as a new political actor.[45] That movement is supported by many socio-legal scholars, and it seems that the effects of feminist mobilisation in the socio-legal academic field are already there. Feminist and queer critique of law has arrived and is gaining momentum in Poland, both in the legal academia and in other social sciences.[46]

Other new openings for critical engagement with law stimulated by human rights considerations, thus far still incipient in the academia but very pronounced in the activist movements, were migrant and refugee rights, migration and

[42] M Bucholc and M Gospodarczyk, 'The Anti-Gender Offensive and the Right to Abortion in Poland' (forthcoming) *L'Homme. Europaïsche Zeitschrift für Feministische Geschichtswissenschaft*.

[43] A Śledzińska-Simon, 'Learning Lessons from the Populist Defeats: From Negative to Positive Constitutionalism' (2023) 32 *Social & Legal Studies* 893–910; K Kocemba, *Right-Wing Legal Mobilization Against Abortion. The Case of Poland* (MWP Working Paper, 2023) 2; K Sękowska-Kozłowska, 'The Istanbul Convention in Poland: Between the "War on Gender" and Legal Reform' in J Niemi, L Peroni and V Stoyanova (eds), *International Law and Violence Against Women*. (London, Routledge, 2020) 133–51.

[44] European Court of Human Rights, Application no 40119/21. See also Abortion Figurations, 'Video Blog 9: M.L. v. Poland' (Abortion Figurations, 12 April 2024) https://abortion-figurations.uw.edu.pl/video-blog-9-m-l-v-poland/.

[45] M Frąckowiak-Sochańska, M Zawodna-Stephan, A Żurek, M Brzozowska-Brywczyńska and A Nymś-Górna, 'Wstęp: Socjologiczne spojrzenie na Strajk Kobiet' (2022) 1 *Studia Socjologiczne* 5–7; B Hall, 'Gendering Resistance to Right-Wing Populism: Black Protest and a New Wave of Feminist Activism in Poland?' (2019) 10(63) *American Behavioral Scientist* 1497–515.

[46] See eg A Kościańska, 'Gender on Trial: Changes in Legal and Discursive Practices Concerning Sexual Violence in Poland from the 1970s to the Present' (2020) 50(1) *Ethnologia Europaea* 111–27.

asylum law and their intersection with human rights. The humanitarian crisis on the Belarussian border since 2020, with its related security considerations in view of the Russian anti-Ukrainian hostility, followed by an invasion of Ukraine by Russia in 2022, opened a new chapter in the history of migration and refugee policymaking in Poland. The corresponding legal debate is strongly marked by human rights references and arguments. The activist discourses, as well as social scientific studies, come explicitly to analyse and, as often as not, target law, in the basic dogmatic sense of the norms stipulated by treaties, statutes and regulations.[47] The convergence among migration studies, sociology of law, international law and human rights is clear for all to see.

Women's rights, rights of LGBTIQ persons, migrant rights, and all other cases for engagement with minority treatment and discrimination also feed into the new human rights discourses that bring new substance to legal critique. This shifts attention from domestic law to international interdependencies and increases the salience of human rights in socio-legal studies in Poland.

By the same token, the long-standing programme of studying legal consciousness and legal socialisation was enriched by the shift of attention towards international integration, especially European Union integration. It is – to the best of my belief – the first time the imaginary of European Union law has entered the empirical studies of law in Poland for good, since it is also the first time when the general public found the problems of the jurisdiction of the Court of Justice of the European Union or the European Court of Human Rights forced upon it by Polish political developments.

Last but not least in the years 2015–23, the national-conservative government had initiated a process of constructing a set of alternative/parallel institutions in many policy domains, including in legal education, although up until now, with little success if measured in absolute numbers. Nonetheless, the concept of legal education designed to realise a specific set of values (national belonging, patriotism, loyalty to the state, Christian morals) has been overtly advocated by the government. As well, the government has reinforced the criticisms of the value-stance of the legal elites supporting liberal democracy, whom the PiS wants abolished and replaced. I should say it may lead to a more critical approach to value-embeddedness of all professional and academic training. Simultaneously, it may support the revitalisation of the more academic variant of legal education, which would be beneficial for the self-reflection of law as an academic discipline and its opening to interdisciplinary dialogue. Another unintended consequence of the revealed situatedness of law and legal knowledge may, however, be a rise of engaged legal sciences. This would shed the veil of impartiality and academic distance to overtly follow political agendas – any

[47] See A Bodnar and A Grzelak, 'The Polish–Belarusian border crisis and the (lack of) European Union response' (2023) 28 *Białostockie Studia Prawnicze* 57–86; J Nizinkiewicz, 'Dr Machińska: Polska wyrzuca dzieci, kobiety w ciąży. Hańba na granicy' *Rzeczpospolita*, 30 January 2023.

political agenda. It should produce an expansion of sociological theorising into the field of the study of legal professions and legal knowledge, paving ways for new synergies between social sciences and law.

V. CONCLUSION

Poland is, of course, not the only European Union country, and definitely not the only country in the world, to have experienced a political and legal turn to the right that, in Poland's case, lasted from 2015 to 2023. Therefore, regional comparisons combining politics, law and culture offer another way out of methodological nationalism dictated by the limitations of the state legal system. It is a way for which history becomes indispensable by way of contextualisation, and this may help overcome the presentism of Polish socio-legal studies that had become established in the 1990s when the focus on transformation, adaptation and catching up obfuscated other concerns.

Undisputedly, since 2015, with the broad range of new impulses coming from the national-conservative political turn, Polish socio-legal studies did come out of the Petrażycki-Ehrlich dilemma. The study of cultural and psychological dimensions of law could be integrated with institutional analysis and with research of intra-systemic inconsistencies between the law in books and the law in action. It is also a period when the spirit of social engagement and social critique seems to be reinvigorated in socio-legal academia. Since the national-conservative turn manifested itself as a pathology of the legal system, it is reasonable to expect that the studies of Polish society of today will come back to law as a key problem of sociology – the centrality of law could hardly be more evident. On the other hand, the fact that reproductive rights, politics of history, religion and collective memory seem to occupy the central place in today's debates about law, state and politics, hope arises that cultural studies can be integrated into the socio-legal landscape more effectively. Finally, the relevance of European, regional and global frameworks for understanding the developments in Poland has by now become obvious – striving to account for the sub- and supra-national dimension of law paves way for socio-legal studies that would transcend the limits of the state-made legal system.

Since the beginning of my academic work in 2000, I have been a minor though active participant of many of the processes described above, and I had the privilege of meeting many of the scholars on whose expertise I rely on in this chapter. Over the years, my colleagues and I have done our best to contribute to the socio-legal work on women's rights, the rule of law and minority rights,[48] and we have contributed to putting the developments in Polish socio-legal studies in

[48] See M Bucholc (ed), *Established – Outsiders Relations in Poland: Reconfiguring Elias and Scotson* (London, Palgrave, 2024).

a broader comparative and historical context.[49] My feelings about the current comeback of law in social sciences, to which I am adding my share, are far from unambiguous – I expect and hope a lot, but I cannot shed the feeling of apprehension. I favour the trend toward interdisciplinarity and internationalisation of socio-legal studies, and I welcome the chance of law opening to sociological theorising, which I firmly believe is the best thing sociology has to offer other disciplines. I am, however, acutely aware that my own situatedness, as a sociologist, as a lawyer and as a self-conscious socio-legal scholar does not allow for a detached view of my own field, whether its history, or its perspectives for the future.

[49] N Trajanovski and J Szumski (eds), *Prawo, władza, pluralizmy. Myśląc ze Stanisławem Ehrlichem* (Warsaw, Scholar, forthcoming).

3

Socio-Legal Studies in Contemporary Hungarian Legal Scholarship: Successes and Challenges

BALÁZS FEKETE

IF I UNDERSTAND well the purpose of this book, its aim is to provide an insight into the various European traditions of socio-legal studies. In order to do so, the editors asked us to not simply sketch an introduction of the tradition we represent, but to also come up with some 'insider' points, too. These insights may animate the first layer of discussion concentrating on the description of the recent state of the art and the path leading there. With the help of this approach, the layer of a 'frozen' and lifeless view of socio-legal endeavours that takes shape from the summary of certain background information, historical trends, important names and relevant research outcomes – so to say a 'still life' in terms of visual arts – can be made livelier by integrating some autobiographical points.

Because of this unique goal, the structure of the chapter will be composed of two major sections. Part I will discuss the main features of the Hungarian socio-legal studies tradition, and it will also introduce the reader to the general conditions of Hungarian legal academia. I will argue that a Hungarian tradition of socio-legal studies has been in existence since the beginning of the twentieth century, and it has had a constant standing within the complex reality of Hungarian legal academia. In addition, Part I will present three milestones from the history of Hungarian socio-legal studies. The contemporary state of art will be studied in Part II, and it will also explain the main factors behind recent developments. Special emphasis will be given to contemporary research projects, findings and research tools. Further, the challenge of internationalisation and regional cooperation will be examined. Lastly, some autobiographical reflections will be included into the main text in italics as separate paragraphs where relevant. Hopefully, these more personal – therefore, not as objective and alienated as the conventional scholarly discussion – points and remarks can bring the reality of Hungarian socio-legal studies a bit closer to the foreign readers.

It should also be noted that both the structure and the argumentation of the chapter relies on a background thesis. This thesis is rather simple but important to be set forth directly. As compared to the previous periods, socio-legal studies has been rather successful in Hungary from the 2010s, and it is still on a promising track. That is, socio-legal studies seems to be blossoming nowadays, and if one tries to look behind the scenes, this is not as surprising as it may be at first glance.

To understand what is meant by success in this specific context – socio-legal studies in Hungary – reference has to be made to the contemporary story of the Hungarian law and literature movement. Law and literature studies was started by a small group of enthusiastic legal scholars in 2006 when the first 'Law and Literature Symposium' was held in Hungary.[1] At this time, law and literature[2] was an absolute novelty in the Hungarian legal academia. Although the idea of integrating literature into legal studies or applying literary insights to discuss legal issues had some precursors in the academic life of the interwar period,[3] it only achieved limited attention by legal scholars. Thus far, seven more Law and Literature Symposia have been organised, the last one in 2021, and follow-up journal special sections and edited volumes have been also published.[4] However, law and literature had almost no impact on legal education. Only some elective courses offered at a few faculties are exceptions, and the scholarly community behind it has been relatively small and closed, meaning that not too many new scholars entered this group. So, the scholarly discourse remained dominantly internal. Further, law and literature scholars were unable to attract external sources for funding such studies. Therefore, law and literature studies still lacks an institutional basis, such as a specific department, so scholarly cooperation has mostly been organised informally.

If one compares the contemporary story of socio-legal studies and law and literature in Hungary, some preconditions of 'scholarly success' may easily be identified. First, as will be presented later, socio-legal studies has been rather successful in institutionalisation – as legal sociology and, to some degree, legal anthropology – and is part of the law school curricula. It has its fixed place in legal theory departments. Second, socio-legal studies was able to attract external research funding sources from the national research funding agency, and that helped scholars carry out sophisticated empirical projects as well as support

[1] I H Szilágyi, 'Előszó. A Jog és Irodalom szimpózium előadásaihoz' (2007) 3 *Iustum Aequum Salutare* 7.

[2] See: JB White, *Heracles' Bow: Essays on the Rhetorics and Poetics of Law* (Madison, University of Wisconsin Press, 1985); I Ward, *Law and Literature: Possibilities and Perspectives* (Cambridge, Cambridge University Press, 1995) or M Aristodemu, *Law and Literature. Journeys from Her to Eternity* (Oxford, Oxford University Press, 2000).

[3] See: I H Szilágyi, 'Horváth Barna géniusza' (2007) 3 *Iustum Aequum Salutare* 31.

[4] For an overview, including all publication details, see: I H Szilágyi, 'Law and Literature in Hungary. An Introduction (2012) 53 *Acta Juridica Hungarica* 1; B Fekete, 'Jog és irodalom: csendes forradalom a magyar jogelméletben?' (2020) 31 *Korunk* 77.

academic mobility. Third, the broader legal academia and profession, though they regard these kinds of studies as 'different' from the settled positivist-dogmatic orientation, have continuously had an interest in socio-legal findings, which legitimised socio-legal studies broadly. Thus, success in this context predominantly means that socio-legal studies has been able to broaden its institutional positions, improve its financial position and participate meaningfully in the general legal scholarly discourse. And, obviously, these all would have been impossible without the continuous existence of an enduring multi-generational scholarly community dedicated to this way of legal studies.

I. A HUNGARIAN SOCIO-LEGAL STUDIES TRADITION?

The relevant literature points out that it makes sense to refer to various national traditions of socio-legal studies,[5] though both the scholarly attitude and the research methods of these studies seem to have a rather universal nature. Alternatively, leaving the frame of national interpretation, one may make a distinction between the North American and the European understanding of socio-legal research – critical versus secular[6] – as argued by Marc Hertogh. Socio-legal studies, although it shares a lot of common scholarly beliefs, convictions and substantive insights, has always been fragmented to some extent, mostly along national and linguistic or continental dividing lines.

From the perspective of the history of modern Hungarian legal scholarship, it can be argued that the tradition of Hungarian socio-legal studies has existed since the beginning of the twentieth century. The claim of studying the law with the help of sociological, ethnological or anthropological tools can be tracked back to the early years of that century.[7] Although Hungarian legal scholarship, in general, strongly subscribed to the German understanding of dogmatic or doctrinal legal scholarship,[8] other 'unconventional' methodological orientations also appeared in this era's Hungarian jurisprudence. The political and cultural proximity to German ideas stemmed from the fact that Hungary had been part of the Habsburg Empire within various constitutional settings[9] since

[5] See, eg: H Jennifer, N Creutzfeldt and C Boulanger, 'Socio-Legal Studies in Germany and the UK: Theory and Methods' (2020) 21 *German Law Journal* 1309.

[6] M Hertogh, *Nobody's Law. Legal Consciousness and Legal Alienation in Everyday Life* (London, Palgrave, 2018) 9–12; 78–79.

[7] See, eg: F Somló, *Der Güterverkehr in der Urgesellschaft* (Bruxelles, Misch & Thron, 1909) or J Baross, *Részleges jelentés az O.M.G.E. által a magyar parasztbirtokok öröklési módjaira vonatkozólag elrendelt adatgyűjtés eredményeiről* (Budapest, Uránia, 1905).

[8] See, eg: A Jakab, 'A Magyar alkotmányjog-tudomány története és jelenlegi helyzete' in A Jakab and A Menyhárd (eds), *A jog tudománya* (Budapest, HVG-ORAC, 2015) 159–92 and A Menyhárd, 'A polgári jog tudománya Magyarországon' in A Jakab, A Menyhárd (eds), *A jog tudománya* (Budapest, HVG-ORAC, 2015) 218–60.

[9] For a general introduction see: F Hörcher and T Lorman (eds), *A History of the Hungarian Constitution* (London, I.B. Tauris, 2020).

the seventeenth century. This implied that for the intellectual elite, including lawyers, the German language and culture were the main and general points of reference. Needless to say, the Hungarian socio-legal tradition has never been able to become a full component of the mainstream legal thinking – as it was always defined by the academic elite – but at least, it had a certain position, even if not too strong and influential, in the Hungarian legal academia from the early decades of the twentieth century. So, besides the ruling ideas of legal positivism or dogmatic orientation, the socio-legal approach of legal issues has also been legitimised.

Moreover, the existence of this socio-legal studies tradition is confirmed by the simple but telling fact that socio-legal studies has been carried out under three different political regimes – the interwar period, the Socialist era and the post-transitory period – during the twentieth century.[10] Obviously, the representatives of this tradition were not able to free themselves from the given era's political influences entirely. Nor were they unable to resist some political claims. For example, legal ethnology of the interwar period tried to reveal the 'unique Hungarian' spirit in contemporary Hungarian law,[11] or Socialist legal sociology worked hard on identifying those peculiar features of Socialist law that make it possible to overcome the deficiencies of bourgeois law.[12] But despite these external influences, socio-legal scholars maintained, and therefore enjoyed, broader or more limited scholarly and intellectual autonomy depending on the conditions of the given age. In addition, even if their opportunities to maintain foreign contacts were rather limited from the beginning of the Socialist era, they still preserved continuous attention towards foreign developments. When the strict Marxist-Leninist Socialist rulership started to soften to some extent, particularly after the failed revolution and freedom fight in 1956, Hungarian socio-legal scholars, including legal sociologists and ethnologists, decided to immediately reintegrate into the international scholarly community, mostly through publications and conference participation.[13]

In sum, the existence of the Hungarian socio-legal tradition seems to be, at least partly, independent from the nature of the actual political regimes. Thus, socio-legal studies in Hungary looks to have a certain internal academic coherence and institutional continuity, both being necessary for 'surviving' the challenges of the twentieth century. In broader terms, this tradition of socio-legal studies has always been characterised by a configuration of these four main

[10] For an insightful introductory discussion to Hungarian history with a special focus on the twentieth century see: B Cartledge, *The Will to Survive: A History of Hungary* (London, Timewell Press, 2006).

[11] L Papp, 'Népi szemlélet: magyarabb, szociálisabb jog' (1939) (July) *Magyar Élet* 10–12.

[12] K Kulcsár, *A jog nevelő szerepe a szocialista társadalomban* (Budapest, KJK, 1961).

[13] See, eg: E Tárkány Szücs 'Results and Tasks of Legal Ethnology in Europe' (1967) 1 *Ethnologia Europea* 195; K Kulcsár, 'La conaissance du droit en Hongrie' (1967) 18 *L'Année Sociologique* 429; K Kulcsár, 'Lay Participation in Organizational Decision Making' (1969) 17 *The Sociological Review* 151.

factors: (i) both sociological and ethnological/anthropological interest has been present in its scholarly orientation; (ii) the work of scholars has been guided by intensive attention to the foreign developments; (iii) there has never been an exclusive method, either qualitative or quantitative, that determined the research design, but a methodological openness and tolerance marked the Hungarian attitude; and (iv) the size of the socio-legal scholarly community was always relatively small, never more than 10–15 members, however, these scholars have been able to function as a full-fledged scholarly community. There has always existed a 'critical mass' of socio-legal scholars able to build up an intergenerational solidarity within the community – from inspiration to direct, with either personal or institutional help.

I think I could have never become interested in socio-legal issues without the impulses coming from the Hungarian socio-legal scholars' community. I was immediately fascinated by the classes of István H Szilágyi, who taught both legal sociology and legal anthropology when I was a law student at the beginning of the 2000s. As he built his socio-legal studies course on dominantly the French and Dutch scholarly traditions, his classes opened a window to a totally new, very different and so fascinating world as compared to the traditional materials of Hungarian legal education. To be honest, I felt that there was something in this new outlook that I could not find in conventional legal studies. In addition, I found a copy from András Sajó's Látszat és valóság a jogban *(Illusion and Reality in Law) in the library of the Department of Legal Theory by coincidence. This department too was managing socio-legal courses at that time, when I started to work as an assistant. I started to read it just for fun. At the beginning I was rather sceptical, but as I proceeded with it, I became really enthusiastic and this book convinced me that 'this is the way' to do legal studies. Of course, it took lots of time to find and build up my own scholarly identity. It is well known that I've never been a fast person, but the attractiveness of the community of socio-legal scholars was an indispensable stimulus for me.*

A. The Nature of Academic Culture in Legal Studies

The Hungarian Academy of Sciences was established in 1825 with the financial help of some reform-minded young noblemen. It earned a legal standing in 1827 and started to operate in 1830. Its very first task was to assist the development of a united and modern Hungarian language with special regard to the refinement of grammar. In addition, the academy began to organise scholarly meetings for its 'classes' – groups of scholars with a similar disciplinary interest – in order to increase the intensity of academic life.[14] Interestingly, one of these 'classes' from the very beginning was that of 'legal science' (*jogtudomány*). Thus, legal

[14] See: *History of the Hungarian Academy of Sciences* (official online publication) accessible at: https://mta.hu/data/MTA_Tortenete_ENG.pdf.

academia has had a long-lasting standing in the system of Hungarian academia. This early recognition of 'legal science' also implies that the academic status of legal scholarship has never been seriously questioned or doubted, as it has been regarded as one of the building blocks of Hungarian academic life during various historical periods of modern Hungarian history. Today, the academy has 11 'classes' and one of them, Section IX, Section of Economics and Law, brings together lawyers and economists. So legal studies still has a high standing in the structure of Hungarian academic life. It has to be mentioned that today's academy has much broader functions than earlier. In addition to its original goal to form a learned society, it also takes part in financing research activities through various grants and support programmes, and it awards the special title of 'Doctor of the Hungarian Academy of Sciences' which is the highest academic degree in the country.[15]

In addition to the Hungarian Academy of Sciences, the central agent of Hungarian scientific life, Hungarian legal academia is also composed of the community of Hungarian faculties of law. There are eight law schools in Hungary: three of them work in Budapest, while five of them are situated in the countryside. Considering institutional dynamics, the faculties of law had a 'blooming period' following the second half of the 1990s as, of these eight law schools, four were established in this period.[16] Due to various statutory requirements,[17] which otherwise codified the long-lasting tradition to a great extent, the curricula of faculties of law converge considerably, so the structure and materials of legal education are relatively similar to each other. This also implies that socio-legal studies has been taught at all these faculties either as a part of introductory or theoretical courses. At most of the faculties, the socio-legal scholars are integrated into those departments that are designated to teach theoretical and philosophical disciplines.[18]

Mine is a typical story of legal socialization: I studied legal studies in Hungary (1998–2003) and in Leuven (2006–2007), so I have no degree from either sociology or anthropology. But I also went through a strong socio-legal studies socialization at the Pázmány Péter Catholic University Faculty of Law where I studied general sociology, legal sociology and legal anthropology courses, and we also learnt lots of 'social theory of law' in the frame of legal theory classes.

[15] For details see: Zs Körtvélyesi, 'The Hungarian Academy of Sciences: An Overview' in A Jakab-Zs Körtvélyesi (eds), *A Magyar Tudományos Akadémia helyzete és reformlehetőségei/The Situation and Reform Opportunities of the Hungarian Academy of Sciences* (Budapest, Osiris 2017) 204–06.

[16] For a general introduction and overview see: B Fekete, 'Practice Elements in Hungarian Legal Education System' (2010) 51 *Acta Juridica Hungarica* 67.

[17] cf 18/2016. (VIII. 5.) EMMI rendelet *a felsőoktatási szakképzések, az alap- és mesterképzések képzési és kimenti követelményeről* 2. Jogász osztatlan szak (explicitly mentions legal sociology as 'basic knowledge relating to legal education').

[18] See: D Vukovic and B Fekete, 'Sociology of Law in The Region: from Histories of Socio-Legal Thinking to New Research and Teaching Agendas' (2015) 57 *Socilogija* 553.

The goal of this faculty was not to train 'legal technicians' simply – as the dean told us many times – but to send out 'well-educated lawyers' being conscious of the world, in the broadest sense, around them.

In general, Hungarian legal academia – the community of legal scholars at the academy and in the world of law schools – has always been dominated by the 'normative/doctrinal' approach, especially by its German version. This is due to the strong political and cultural connections of Hungary to the Habsburg Empire as well as to the prominent status of German language within the Hungarian elite during the seventeenth through nineteenth centuries. It may be argued, even if it is an obvious simplification, that the Hungarian legal academia had to be regarded as an affiliation of the German legal world in intellectual terms until the collapse of the Dual Monarchy (ie the Austro-Hungarian Monarchy) in 1918, and to a lesser extent, even in later periods.[19] There were some endeavours to soften or lighten this strong cultural dominance in legal scholarship from the last decades of the nineteenth century, especially in the field of comparative law, so a limited French and English influence can also be seen.[20] One cannot talk about an exclusive German influence on legal studies in Hungary, but this influence and impact has been broad and comprehensive. This situation has just started to change in the last 20 years when the English language, especially among younger scholars, acquired a similarly prestigious position. However, in historical terms, this a very new development.

The Hungarian legal academia shares, and has shared, the general features of these scholarly communities. It is hierarchical as well as conservative by nature. Conservativism can be understood in two but interrelated forms. First, it is conservative from a cultural perspective; it prefers traditional research issues and favours conventional approaches.[21] Second, its institutional attitude is also conservative; it overtly favours settled scholars with tenure as compared to young, early career researchers when financial and prestige issues are at stake. Nonetheless, the recent leadership of the academy has put a special emphasis on helping integrate early career researchers, with special regard to

[19] See: Catherine Dupré's thesis where she argues that the case law of the Hungarian Constitutional Court in its first years after 1989 had decisively been determined by the import of similar German case-law. See: C Dupré, *Importing the Law in Post-Communist Transitions: the Hungarian Constitutional Court and the Right to Human Dignity* (Oxford, Hart, 2003).

[20] For example, Maine's Ancient Law was translated to Hungarian as early as in 1875 by Ágost Pulszky, perhaps the first Hungarian socio-legal scholar. He also added a long postscript to the translation in which he discussed the relevance of Maine's work in a European context including the relevant French and German findings. HS Maine, *A jog őskora* (Budapest, Akadémia, 1875). Or, in 1943, Barna Horváth published a comprehensive monograph on English legal philosophy, the very first book in the Hungarian legal academia making accessible the insights of English jurisprudence to the Hungarian readership. B Horváth, *Angol jogelmélet* (Budapest, Magyar Tudományos Akadémia, 1943).

[21] cf M Oakeshott, 'On Being Conservative' in M Oakeshott, *Rationalism in Politics and Other Essays* (Indianapolis, Liberty Fund, 1991) 407–37.

women, and supporting their work through establishing various scholarship programmes[22] and specific research grants.[23]

The first individual department of legal sociology was established at the Eötvös Loránd Tudományegyetem Faculty of Law in 1987.[24] Departments of legal theory or jurisprudence started to offer courses in legal sociology from the 1990s. Practically all Hungarian faculties of law have a sociology of law course in their curricula in some form, either as compulsory or elective courses.[25] The teaching of legal sociology has two main forms today. So far, in harmony with the German intellectual legacy, legal sociology has mostly been taught in the form of plenary lectures (*Vorlesung*) as are most of the other subjects in legal education. One professor faces a bigger group of students and she or he explains subjects of legal sociology, generally without too much interaction with the audience. However, this dominantly one-way channel of teaching has changed to a more interactive form as some faculties decided to introduce seminars or smaller group elective classes of legal sociology. These seminars or small group classes are not as theory oriented as the plenary lectures that presented various chapters from the social theory of law. Instead, they provide room for teacher-student interaction and even inspire the students to carry out some micro-research projects as a requirement of the class.[26] The question of which form of teaching is used is answered by the traditions of the given law school, how this subject has been taught beforehand, as well as the available human and financial sources.

In sum, the socio-legal study of legal issues has been integrated into the institutional background of legal academia – a network consisting of the academy and its Institute for Legal Studies as well as the faculties of law – from the 1960s. Socio-legal studies is definitely an official part of 'the system', so it has a certain status and standing within legal academia. However, undeniably,

[22] See these scholarship and grant programmes: *Bolyai ösztöndíj* (mta.hu/bolyai-osztondij/bolyai-janos-kutatasi-osztondij-105319), *Prémium posztdoktori kutatói program* (mta.hu/mta-premium-posztdoktori-kutatoi-program_762).

[23] The 'Lendület program' (mta.hu/lendulet).

[24] One may argue that the establishment of this Legal Sociology Department was a final, and rather spectacular point of a longer and less visible story. Kálmán Kulcsár had already begun to teach a course of sociology in 1965 in the form of plenary lectures for law students, and the teaching of sociology was gradually broadened by integrating a second semester of sociology focusing on specialised ways of sociology, including legal sociology, and adding seminars and a discussion group into the curriculum. So in the first half of the 1980s, the teaching of sociology and sociological research had an impressive base at the ELTE faculty of law. For details: L Boros, 'A szociológiai oktatás megjelenése az Állam- és Jogelméleti Tanszéken' (manuscript) accessible at: http://tollelege.elte.hu/sites/default/files/articles/boros_laszlo-a_szociologiai_oktatas_megjelenese.pdf.

[25] Some textbooks used for teaching: M Bencze and E Vinnai, *Jogszociológiai előadások* (Debrecen, DU Press, 2012); I H Szilágyi, P Cserne and B Fekete, *Társadalmi-jogi kutatások* (Budapest, SZIT, 2012).

[26] At the ELTE Faculty of Law.

it has never been part of mainstream or 'orthodox' legal studies.[27] It also represents something 'different' from the conventional canon. Thus, a sociological interest in studying law has always been 'different' in the sense of intellectual orientation – something curious and divergent from the general patterns of the way a 'good' or a 'proper' legal scholar should think and work.

Some contemporary socio-legal scholars argue that this standing has improved in the last 20 years, and even legal scholars concentrating on a specific area of law have recognised the potential of such an approach.[28] Thus, I would argue that there is a tacit assumption among representatives of other more conventional fields of legal studies that legal sociology 'exists', and it may even be relevant for studying law. However, it remains something 'different' or 'unconventional' – at least if it is compared to the logic of specific legal disciplines.

Socio-legal scholars have never been the most renowned members of Hungarian legal academia. It's a fact that no one disputes, and it's not surprising as hierarchy in a group is always determined by the majority. Their 'difference' is even made explicit by their clothing – a 'typical' legal sociologist in Hungary would never wear a dark and formal suit with tie at an academic event, but only a dingy corduroy jacket with a scarf, if any. Additionally, their behaviour deviates from the typical legal scholar public code of conduct focused on formalities. They prefer to be direct and informal, and they can even be kind with younger colleagues. To be honest, as my personality is also rather oriented towards informality, and I'm always sceptical of existing settled hierarchies, I found this style of 'academic' behaviour inviting and I started to integrate into this circle happily. I did so even though I was also conscious that I would swiftly lose all the social and public benefits of a legal academic standing.

B. Milestones in the History of Socio-Legal Studies in Hungary

The Hungarian tradition of socio-legal studies, in the broadest sense, is composed of two main streams since the early years of the twentieth century: (i) an ethnological/anthropological one and (ii) a sociological approach, most frequently called 'legal sociology'. Obviously, the dividing line between these two approaches is not objective and solid. One may point out various examples of the cross-fertilisation of these areas and, sometimes, one single author can contribute to both fields.[29] But, this distinction still has a relevance when discussing the history of socio-legal studies in Hungary. This chapter will deal with the sociological approach, or legal sociology, as the author's expertise and

[27] cf P Legrand, *Negative Comparative Law* (Cambridge, Cambridge University Press, 2022) 47–103.

[28] Vukovic and Fekete (n 18) 556.

[29] As a good contemporary example see the oeuvre István H Szilágyi, who started as a legal anthropologist, but, later, he also participated in various legal sociology projects.

research interest is prominently associated with this approach.[30] For an overview of the history of 'legal sociology' in Hungary, three milestones have to be noted. Needless to say, the complete story is more complex, but the discussion of these milestones can reveal the main historical features of legal sociology in Hungary.

Before going into the details of the milestones, two founding myths[31] have also to be examined briefly in order to shed light on the broader intellectual orientation of Hungarian socio-legal studies. These founding myths are present at the establishment of any kind of scholarly community.[32] They have no direct impact on specific research findings as they are almost always invisible, not explicit and mostly tacit. Nonetheless, they orientate research activities by influencing the worldview and actions of scholars attached to the given scientific community. The first founding myth comes from a Weberian approach to scholarship as well from sociological positivism. That is, the members of Hungarian socio-legal tradition have continuously embraced the idea of a value-neutral scholarly orientation. Basically, they all thought themselves as scholars who were able to free themselves from their personal convictions and beliefs, at least to a decisive extent, and, therefore, they can provide a rather objective description of the issues – or facts – studied. They believed that scholarship can function in an objective way guided by a value-neutral scholarly attitude.

The second myth is related to disciplinary borders. In essence, the representatives of the Hungarian socio-legal tradition all implied that their field of study possesses solid boundaries. That is, they regarded legal sociology as a true discipline that can be delineated from other areas of study, such as private law or administrative law. This rigid view on disciplinary borders, mostly motivated by internal 'political' struggles within the legal academia, implied an extremely important idea. If legal sociology has solid and well-defined borders, making it different from other legal scholarly areas, it can also be argued that there should be certain scholarly topics that are exclusively the domain of the legal sociologist. Thus, legal sociological discourse is an autonomous one within the polyphony of legal scholarship, and it is predominantly the business of legal sociologists.

In sum, legal sociologists in Hungary tend to consider themselves as members of a closed scholarly group distinct from similar scholarly associations. They are convinced they have specific research issues that belong only to

[30] For the history of the ethnological approach see B Fekete, 'Legal Ethnology and Legal Anthropology in Hungary' in MC Foblets et al (eds), *The Oxford Handbook of Law and Anthropology* (Oxford, Oxford University Press, 2022) 233–61.

[31] I'm very grateful to Marta Bucholc who drew my attention to the role of founding myths in the process of establishment of socio-legal studies. M Bucholc, *Sociology in Poland. To Be Continued?* (London, Palgrave Macmillan, 2016) 1–13.

[32] Although Thomas Samuel Kuhn pointed it out in the context of natural sciences, his ideas on values as components of a scientific paradigm can explain well the role of these kind of abstract ideas in scientific and scholarly activities. See TS Kuhn, *The Structure of Scientific Revolutions. Second Edition* (Chicago, The University of Chicago Press, 1970) 184.

them. In addition, their attitude is deeply influenced by the idea of a positivist and value-neutral science providing an objective view on the phenomenon studied. Obviously, in the case of an individual scholar, the degree of influence of these founding myths can naturally vary, but none of them can escape them completely.[33]

i. Barna Horváth's Rechtssoziologie

The first Hungarian law professor who explicitly dedicated his work to a sociological study of legal phenomena was Barna Horváth, professor of the faculty of law at the universities of Szeged and Kolozsvár (Cluj), from 1929 to 1945. Horváth had a strong background in legal theory, especially in neo-Kantian legal philosophy, so he arrived at the field of socio-legal studies from legal philosophy.[34] However, he did not only try to create a solid theoretical basis for a sociological study of law on a neo-Kantian epistemological basis, but he also carried out the very first legal sociological fieldwork in the 1940s. To establish a sound theoretical foundation for legal sociology, he argued in his seminal work entitled *Rechtssoziologie*[35] – it may be surprising that the Hungarian translation from the original German was published only in 1995[36] – that *Sein* (Is) and *Sollen* (Ought) can be studied together. The strict separation of these spheres, as required by classic neo-Kantianism,[37] may be overstepped, and this brought about the birth of a qualitatively new approach to study legal phenomena.

This new approach, passionately advocated by Horváth, was called a synoptical approach. Horváth argued that it could enable the researcher to study facts and values in light of each other, meaning that law and reality did not have to be separated from each other anymore. Instead, they could be studied, analysed and discussed in the same, unitary scholarly framework. To illustrate the potential of such an approach to legal studies, the second part of *Rechtssoziologie* provides an in-depth discussion of five sociological and

[33] A good illustration of this attitude is the discussion in Kulcsár's *A jogszociológia problémái* (*Problems of Legal Sociology*). This monograph on the history of American and Continental legal sociology was published in 1960, and it has a clear Marxist character, as for instance the author argues for a strong Marxist critique of bourgeois authors. But it is also obvious that legal sociology is understood as a distinct field of legal studies and Kulcsár provides a very scholarly, and largely unbiased and descriptive presentation of the foreign authors discussed. Marxist-Leninist claims had an impact on this work, naturally, but they cannot overrule the general scholarly attitude expressed in the ideas of value-neutral description and autonomy of the field. K Kulcsár, *A jogszociológia problémái* (Budapest, Közgazdasági és jogi könyvkiadó, 1960).

[34] For a general study of Horváth's philosophy see: Á Zsidai, 'Die Erscheinung der Perspektive (Synoptische Rechtstheorie von Barna Horváth)' (2004) 44 *Annales Universitatis Scientiarum Budapestinensis de Rolando Eötvös Nominatae. Sectio Iuridica* 207.

[35] B Horváth, *Rechtssoziologie* (Berlin, Grunewald, 1934).

[36] B Horváth, *Jogszociológia* (Budapest, Osiris, 1995).

[37] As a good example see: H Kelsen, *Reine Rechtslehre* (Leipzig und Wien, Deuticke, 1934).

historical factors that have had a strong impact on the formation of modern law. In Horváth's understanding, these factors are economy, conflict (or war), power, knowledge and procedure.

Horváth was the first law professor in the history of modern Hungarian legal studies to carry out prima facie legal sociology fieldwork. He was particularly interested in the study of public opinion, and he published long studies on this issue.[38] For example, in a paper published in 1939, he discussed in detail the impact of mass media on the formation of public opinion. He also reviewed the methods of public opinion pooling with the help of some English and American sources and data.[39] In conclusion, he argued that an empirical study of public opinion is unavoidable if one has an intention to understand its internal dynamics.[40] As a practical point, Horváth also studied the convictions and beliefs of law students in Szeged, Hungary, at the beginning of the 1940s, with help of a survey method. Having analysed almost 400 questionnaires sent back by law students, Horváth could sketch the main personality traits of future lawyers. For example, the answers clearly pointed out that the great majority of the respondents could not accept the statement that 'the law is simply what power prescribes'.[41] Horváth's study from the 1940s first raised certain issues of legal consciousness; consequently, he can also be regarded as the forerunner of these kinds of studies in Hungary.

ii. Kulcsár's National Surveys

Due to the Soviet-backed Communist takeover of political power in 1949 and the comprehensive reorganisation of academic life in a Marxist-Leninist spirit, interest in studying the social functioning of law seemed to disappear in the 1950s. There had been expulsion of all those scholars who were regarded as 'problematic' by the new leaders of the Hungarian Academy of Sciences, such as Horváth who emigrated to the United States in 1949.[42] However, the relatively fast transformation of the legal order, from a bourgeois one to a new, socialist one, also implied the need to study the social context where these new legal provisions were intended to have an impact on the citizens' ordinary behaviour. This gave rise to the birth of socialist legal sociology represented by the path-breaking studies of Kálmán Kulcsár. Obviously, due to the denied-but-silently-respected legacy of Horváth, Kulcsár did not have to start from zero for methodology and fieldwork.

[38] B Horváth, *A közvélemény ellenőrzése* (Szeged, Magyar Királyi Ferencz József Tudományegyetem, 1939).

[39] ibid 48–59 and 60–62.

[40] ibid 62.

[41] B Horváth, 'A láthatatlan ember' (1942) 6 *Délvidéki Szemle* 231.

[42] On Horváth's oeuvre S Szászy, 'Barna Horváth in memoriam' (1974) 25 *Österreichische Zeitschrift für öffentliches Recht* 1.

At the beginning of the 1960s, a main issue for both the socialist legislator and politics of law was the question how the newly introduced socialist legal provisions – for example, a socialist Civil Code was enacted in 1959 – affected the everyday behaviour of citizens. In theory, these new legal provisions represented a novel and revolutionary attitude towards society, as they endorsed various Marxist-Leninist insights and, thereby, strived to serve the entirety of society in place of defending the privileges of the ruling class.[43] Their social impact was a crucial issue. Therefore, with a strong backing of the socialist academy, the young Kálmán Kulcsár designed and carried out a survey study in 1965 on the question how much the people knew about the new socialist provisions. This was regarded as the first step of such a research programme that intended to study the 'legal reality' of socialist Hungary. In addition, in a symbolic sense, this study by Kulcsár Kálmán, who became the director of the Institute of Sociology of the Hungarian Academy of Sciences in 1969, also marked the start of socialist legal sociology.[44]

From various aspects, Kulcsár's research has to be regarded as 'revolutionary'. In a theoretical sense, it accepted that the law has a limited capacity to shape the citizens' legal relationships, and its impact on social reality is not at all self-evident. In addition, knowledge of legal provisions has a central place in this issue, and understanding the question of how media transmit legal information and shape the content of law is of a crucial relevance. Kulcsár rejected the approach that supposed there was a direct communication between the abstract legislator and the mass of citizens.[45] Lastly, Kulcsár made a distinction between legal consciousness and legal knowledge. He argued that legal knowledge was a part of legal consciousness, and it meant the social level of knowledge of the law. Needless to say, social stratification could have a great influence on citizen's legal consciousness.[46] In addition, general legal knowledge had to be distinguished from the knowledge of specific areas of law, and these obviously may differ to some extent.

Methodologically, Kulcsár organised the very first survey study in the socialist age, and he designed a well-conceptualised questionnaire. The fieldwork was carried out by law students from three faculties. Although the sample was not representative in a strict geographical sense, Kulcsár intended to cover most of the settlement types in the country – the inhabitants of the capital Budapest, and some middle-sized cities and villages were added into the sample (n=1200).[47]

[43] For a theoretical study of socialist law see: I Szabó, *Jogelmélet* (Budapest, Közgazdasági és jogi könyvkiadó, 1977).

[44] It has to be noted that Kulcsár had a scholarship to study in the USA from 1965 to 1966. He was visiting fellow at Columbia University and the University of California Berkeley during this period. This fact can explain his expertise of American legal sociology and his attachment to this scholarly orientation as expressed in his various works.

[45] Cf J Griffiths, 'The Social Working of Legal Rules' (2003) 48 *Journal of Legal Pluralism* 1.

[46] K Kulcsár, *A jogismeret vizsgálata* (Budapest, MTA-JTI, 1967) 19.

[47] ibid 13–14.

As for the lack of strict representativeness, Kulcsár submitted that his aim was only to understand some differences in legal knowledge among the main classes of the Hungarian society.[48]

Based on the questionnaire, the factors that were expected to have an influence on the citizens' legal knowledge can easily be identified. First, Kulcsár put a serious emphasis on socio-demographic variables such as the type of settlement, gender, social position and profession. Additionally, the questionnaire addressed specific points that may also have some explanatory value with regard to legal knowledge. For example, social activity, reading legal texts, interaction with state bodies and some basic knowledge about politics were those factors that seemed to be relevant.[49]

By applying the method of scale calculation, data analysis concluded that the level of legal knowledge in the Hungarian society is 0.55, as compared to the ideal of 1 if all the people had answered every question correctly.[50] Some findings of Kulcsár are rather intriguing, even today. First, he points out that white collar workers – the elite of the society, the intellectuals – had the highest level of knowledge of law. This number, which represented the level of knowledge, decreased in the cases of blue-collar workers and agricultural workers. Thus, a positive correlation between social stratification and knowledge of law could be proven statistically. Second, the level of knowledge of various areas of law differed to a greater extent. People tended to be familiar with the provisions of criminal law the most, while the least known part of the legal order was that of public law including constitutional and administrative provisions. Third, Kulcsár asserted that gender had a decisive role in shaping the knowledge of law through gender specific social roles, and it resulted in a higher level of knowledge by males. Finally, certain channels of communicating legal provisions could also be identified. These were the texts of legal provisions, and maybe surprisingly, three-quarters of the respondents read legal provisions. In addition, case reporting in newspapers also tended to have an impact, and lastly, interpersonal discussion had a role in shaping the level of knowledge.

This research, carried out in 1965 and findings published in 1967, seems to have a special place in the history of Hungarian legal sociology. First, it proved convincingly that a socio-legal study can set forth conclusions relevant in academic and political senses. It legitimised this field of knowledge even if

[48] ibid 12.

[49] ibid 29–30.

[50] 'The ideal level of legal knowledge, when all the respondents answer every question correctly, is 1, and the real level will show how far the number of the right answers approaches the ideal level. The actual level will always be less than 1. The actual level of knowledge is obtained by dividing the number of wrong answers by the number of all questions and subtracting the quotient from 1.' B Fekete and I H Szilágyi, 'Knowledge and Opinion about Law (KOL) Research in Socialist Hungary' (2017) 58 *Hungarian Journal of Legal Studies* 331.

official Marxism-Leninism was rather sceptical to sociology as a 'bourgeois science'.[51] Second, due to its well-elaborated hypotheses and methodological choices, it paved the way for future studies also addressing the place of law in the socialist society. Lastly, Kulcsár, as an influential personality of the socialist legal academia, could help younger scholars to find their way in this new field of study even if the conservative legal academia was rather sceptical towards this sociological wizardry.

iii. Sajó on Illusion and Reality in Law

The heyday of socialist legal sociology was definitely the 1980s with special emphasis on the publication of András Sajó's *Látszat és valóság a jogban* (*Illusion and Reality in Law*).[52] Besides Kulcsár, who became one of the strongmen of Hungarian legal academia in the 1980s, the younger András Sajó, research fellow of the Institute of Legal Studies, became a key personality of legal sociology in this period. He had carried out various group studies focusing on people's legal consciousness,[53] and, as summary, he published a monograph on the general state of legal culture in the late-Kádárian country.

Sajó's *Illusion and Reality* is certainly a masterpiece of Hungarian legal sociology. It discusses the main areas of socialist law – civil law, administrative law and penal law – by applying a well-developed socio-legal toolkit. In addition, Sajó's published some short stories and even a novel in this period, he had a certain reputation as a man of letters,[54] too. His *Illusion and Reality* included two chapters with a non-scholarly character. These chapters presented two different discourses – a not so friendly, but tense and partly ironical one in which the 'legal sociologist' seeks to convince the 'legislator' and the 'judge' that a socio-legal approach to law makes some sense; and the other one depicts a dialogue between the 'legal sociologist' and a zen 'master' about the role of law in life. Both chapters try to prove the relevance of a socio-legal orientation for the broader, not only lawyerly, audience with help of literary tools. Thus, Sajó's book was a unique endeavour in its time as it alloyed professional socio-legal research with literature, and it is still unique in the field of Hungarian legal studies.

The main thesis of this unconventional monograph can be summarised as follows. Normally, both people and government expect that the law has a great impact on society itself and especially on everyday behaviour. This point is generally confirmed by socio-legal research. But it is argued by Sajó that the

[51] cf Z Fleck, 'Szocialista jogelmélet és szociológia' (2004) 45 *Világosság* 65.

[52] A Sajó, *Látszat és valóság a jogban* (Budapest, KJK, 1986).

[53] eg: A Sajó, 'Jogi nézetek az egyéni tudatban' (1976) 19 *Állam- és Jogtudomány* 419 or A Sajó, 'A jogi nézetek rendszere a gazdasági vezetők jogtudatában' (1981) 24 *Állam- és Jogtudomány* 608.

[54] eg: A Sajó, *Útmutató az elkárhozáshoz* (Budapest, Kozmosz, 1982); A Sajó, *Karácsonyi merénylet* (Budapest, Magvető, 1979).

law plays a much lesser role in the everyday life of the 1980s socialist Hungary, and this points to a higher level of legal alienation.[55] Hence, the legal consciousness in Hungary is deeply pervaded by legal alienation. This point goes back to historical roots; for example, sociographies from the interwar period depict a very similar situation regarding the everyday relationship to the law.[56] Thus, legal alienation seems to be a regime-independent feature of Hungarian legal culture.

In addition to an in-depth discussion of survey data, Sajó contributed to the theoretical approach of legal consciousness. As a first step, he criticises widely the previous knowledge about law studies – compared to *Knowledge and Opinion about Law* studies in the 1970s[57] – as they were carried out mostly by Kulcsár. Sajó argues that the study of the issue of how much the citizens know about some legal provisions is simply inadequate to study the social reality of law. In his eyes, this is mostly due to the fact that popular knowledge about law is rather casual. It lacks lawyerly systematisation, is fragmented to a greater extent and has highly situated meaning that it is centred on specific situations, not on abstract concepts. In addition, everyday social practice may easily overstep specific legal provisions as social normative practices originate from other sources. For instance, customs or substantive justice claims also have a strong influence on everyday behaviour.[58] In sum, Sajó is rather sceptical about the utility of simply studying the general or abstract level of knowledge about law.

Sajó argues further, to consider more seriously the so-called evaluative and emotional-volitional dimensions of legal consciousness. The evaluative dimension means the extent that people accept the law as a measure for various kinds of behaviour has to be studied. People may consider law as a measure to assess their own acts, to evaluate others' acts or to understand a specific situation. By raising these points in the Hungarian legal discourse, Sajó established a conversation to reflect on various attitudes toward the law.[59] Emotions may also play a crucial role in shaping legal consciousness according to Sajó's perspective. For example, emotions have the potential to shape knowledge about the law as they orient the individual, or they may encourage the individual to act in case of a legal claim. The issues of legal consciousness cannot properly be understood without reflecting on the role of emotions, especially if the motivations of human actions are at stake.

In essence, with the help of data analysis and the integration of these novel theoretical insights, Sajó depicts quite a depressing picture of the late-Kádárian

[55] cf Hertogh (n 6) 49–60.

[56] See: Sajó (n 52) 343–45 (see also endnote 16 in the book).

[57] See: A Podgorecki et al, *Knowledge and Opinion about Law* (London, Martin Robertson, 1973).

[58] Sajó (n 52) 274–78.

[59] ibid 278–80.

legal culture. Basically, he argues that law is not part of the social culture – it has not been properly integrated into it. Law only plays an external role, if any. Citizens rarely turn to the law on their own intention, as they try to settle their issues with the help of non-legal normative commitments. Legal provisions are mentioned exclusively if one of the parties would like to invoke the authority of the state in order to strengthen his or her position.[60] The situation is especially discouraging if a dispute with a state organ or body is at stake. According to the popular view, legal points cannot simply work here. But 'begging, the gestures of clemency seeking loyalty and references to fairness (not so much on the merits), or, at most, on equality are asserted'[61] rather than a legally conscious attitude.

II. THE MOST SUCCESSFUL YEARS OF LEGAL SOCIOLOGY IN HUNGARY: FROM 2010 ONWARDS

A. A General Overview

As was mentioned earlier, the thesis of this chapter is that the recent years, let's say from 2010, are a successful period in the history of the Hungarian socio-legal tradition. This success comes from the constellations of various factors naturally, but – in my eyes – there has been one specific factor that decisively contributed to it. Basically, the financial context of socio-legal studies changed dramatically, as certain projects – and the research teams behind them – were able to win funding from the government research funding agency – currently: National Research, Development, and Innovation Office – in a rather competitive environment. With the support of these grants, it has become possible to carry out various nation-wide surveys, finance larger scale qualitative research projects and establish fix-term positions to help the younger generation of scholars. Today, socio-legal studies seems to be a relatively well-funded area of legal studies in Hungary.

From 2012 to 2021, four research projects addressing socio-legal issues won research grants from the governmental research funding agency. These were: *Legal Culture in Hungary* (2012–2016) (NKFIH 105552); *Normative Arguments in Everyday Use* (2013–2017) (NKFIH 109439); *Lack of Rights Consciousness in the Legal Cultures of Central Europe and Balkans: Myth or Reality?* (2017–2021) (NKFIH FK 125520); and *Novelties of Criminal Law in Legal Consciousness* (2017–2020) (NKFIH 125378). This list of government-funded projects has just broadened as two other socio-legal studies projects got funding in 2022. One of them focuses on cultural prerequisites of rule of law (*Support for the*

[60] ibid 309.
[61] ibid 311.

Rule of Law: The Cultural Preconditions of a Strong and Stable Rule of Law (2022–2026) (NKFIH 143831)), while the other is devoted to the relationship between democratic elements in the citizens' behaviour and their relation to law (*Democratic Acts and Relation to the Law in a Family History Background* (2022–2026) (NKFIH 143092)). All in all, the financial context seems to be rather favourable for socio-legal studies, broadly understood, in these days. This has to be compared to the general belief that even if the strengthening of research and development activities has been a crucial area in governmental policies since 2010, the budgetary sources allocated to it has not drastically been increased in this period.

I was also one of these grant-holders (my project: Lack of Rights Consciousness in the Legal Cultures of Central-Europe and Balkans: Myth or Reality?*). I should admit, the management of this project was an indispensable experience in my professional life as it helped me to make a further step in improving my academic capacities. At the beginning of the project, including the preparation of the project proposal, I was rather naïve, I think. I thought that outcomes of these kinds of projects were only dependent on scholarly excellence. However, I had to realize almost immediately that we need not only good scholarly capacities, but some administration and management skills are more than necessary to carry out the project successfully. In addition, I also had to learn how to build up a well-functioning research team and how to manage the 'human dimension' of its work. So, all in all, it was a formative experience for me.*

B. The Main Findings in the Contemporary Period

This is the list of the major issues studied from 2010 by Hungarian legal sociology. They demonstrate the main points of the contemporary orientation.

(i) Knowledge about law studies comparing the pre- and post-transitory situation. This kind of research relied on the findings of Kulcsár from the 1960s as a starting point. The findings pointed out that the general level of knowledge about the law has increased in the last 50 years. This change is pre-eminently due to the fact that public education has considerably been broadened during the latter period.[62]

(ii) The study of general features of Hungarian legal culture. For example, data analysis showed that two main features are a high level of general

[62] B Fekete and Gy Gajdsuchek, 'Changes in Knowledge About Law in Hungary in the Past Half Century' (2015) 57 *Sociologija* 620; Gy Gajdsuchek and B Fekete, 'A magyar lakosság jogismerete az elmúlt fél évszázadban és ma – Összehasonlító elemzés Kulcsár Kálmán 1965-ös empirikus kutatása alapján' (2015) 5 *Pro Futuro* 11; Gy Gajdsuchek and B Fekete, 'A jogismeretet befolyásoló társadalmi tényezők elemzése' (2015) 5 Pro Futuro 71.

punitiveness[63] and a widespread legal alienation.[64] In some cases, these kinds of studies tried to compare certain features of Hungarian legal culture to those of other countries; for example, comparing to the data of the Netherlands and Serbia to broaden the interpretive room for the Hungarian findings.[65]

(iii) The legal consciousness of marginalised people. With the help of qualitative tools, analysis of more than 40 life story interviews revealed that legal points have had only a marginal role, if any, in everyday life. However, the findings also showed that the relationship to the law may have an impact on the formation of individual identities.[66]

(iv) Role of rights in everyday conflict settlement in Hungary. Because rights have a key role in dogmatic legal thinking, a comparative study tried to analyse everyday conflicts. In essence the findings showed that popular thinking is still pervaded by legal alienation. Most people are unable to effectively use the language of rights, but the person's higher level of income and education may make a slightly more likely rights-conscious attitude to conflict settlement.[67]

(v) The state of the Hungarian legal culture. A socio-psychological study analysed longitudinal data collected from the 2010s. It addressed the study of the impact of political convictions and 'just world' beliefs on mass legal attitudes. The principal finding showed that the respondent's party's political beliefs – if a person has a pro- or anti-government attitude in general – can decisively influence the opinion about the state of legal order.[68]

(vi) New criminal law provisions. Since 2010, the government enacted various new provisions – for example, occasional lowering of the age limit of criminal responsibility for crimes against property – to enhance some punitive claims having broad societal support. The impact of some of these provisions on legal consciousness and the general state of punitiveness in the Hungarian legal culture were examined in detail. The authors argued that

[63] I H Szilágyi and Gy Gajduschek, 'Nevelés és büntetés' in I H Szilágyi (ed), *Jogtudat-kutatások Magyarországon 1967–2017* (Budapest, Pázmány Press, 2018) 221–37.

[64] B Fekete and P Róbert, 'Understanding Hungarian Attitudes Toward Law in an International Context' available at SSRN 3120933 (2018) (ssrn.com/abstract=3120933).

[65] Gy Gajduschek, 'Wild East and Civilised West? Some Indicators of Legal Culture in Hungary, Serbia, and the Netherlands' (2019) 60 *Jahrbuch für Ostrecht* 165.

[66] Z Fleck et al, *A jogtudat narratív értelmezése* (Budapest, ELTE Eötvös, 2017).

[67] B Fekete, A Bartha, Gy Gajduschek and F Gulya, 'Rights Consciousness in Hungary and Some Comparative Remarks. Could an Increasing Level of Rights Consciousness Challenge the Autocratic Tradition?' (2022) 47 *Review of Central and East European Law* 220; B Fekete, 'Rights Consciousness in Hungary: What is Behind the Numbers? Lessons of a Focus Group Study' in R Cotterrell et al (eds), *Remembering Reza Banakar* (Oxford, Hart 2022) 173–88.

[68] I H Szilágyi, L Kelemen and SG Hall, *Changing Legal and Civic Culture in an Illiberal Democracy. A Social Psychological Survey of the Hungarian Legal System* (London, Routledge, 2022).

the individual's willingness to punish has a decisive influence on the assessment of these new provisions.[69]

C. Methods Applied and the Rise of Qualitative Research Tools

A main component of Kulcsár's legacy is that he established the tradition of carrying out national questionnaire surveys for studying the social context of law. Quantitative methods, including mathematical-statistical analysis, had been the ruling paradigm for Hungarian legal sociology until recently. However, from 2010, qualitative research tools have also appeared in the toolbox of socio-legal scholars. Besides the settled quantitative methodology, interviews,[70] life story interviews[71] and focus groups[72] have also been used to get closer to those layers of citizens' attitudes toward law that are inaccessible because of the apparent deficiencies of mathematical or statistical generalisations. In addition, using the tools of document analysis, the practice of police bodies reporting on everyday cases for the courts in various proceedings has been studied.[73]

D. Two New Trends: Changing Publication Habits and Strengthening Regional Cooperation

Lastly, two new trends have to be discussed. Prior to 2010, almost all socio-legal publications were published in Hungarian academic journals or in edited volumes in Hungarian. The communication of the Hungarian socio-legal community was rather introverted and primarily addressed the domestic readership. However, this situation has begun to change gradually, as some findings have also been published in English in addition to the original Hungarian publications. Needless to say, this process of making the Hungarian socio-legal tradition bilingual led to some changes in the thinking of socio-legal scholars of the country.

First of all, these English publications opened up the opportunity for external reflection, enabling foreign scholars to start a discussion with their Hungarian colleagues. These discussions are ongoing, and naturally they shape

[69] M Hollán and T Venczel, 'Age Limits of Criminal Responsibility for Property Offences. A New Empirical Research on Legal Consciousness in Hungary' (2019) 60 *Hungarian Journal of Legal Studies* 381; M Hollán and T Venczel, 'A hivatali vesztegetés büntetendősége a jogtudatban: ismeretek és vélemények' (2020) 10 *Pro Futuro* 9.

[70] F Gulya, 'A jogosultságtudat kvalitatív megközelítése: a szakértői interjúk tanulságai' *JTI Blog*, 2020 (jog.tk.hu/blog/2020/03/a-szakertoi-interjuk-tanulsagai).

[71] Fleck et al (n 65).

[72] Fekete (n 66).

[73] E Vinnai, 'A diskurzus kötött rendje. Kihallgatás és jegyzőkönyvezés a magyar büntetőeljárásban' in Szabó M (ed), *Nyelvében a jog. Nyelvhasználat a jogi eljárásban* (Miskolc, Bíbor Kiadó, 2010) 153–91.

the Hungarian socio-legal scholars' understanding of their own problems. So, the space for reflection has broadened considerably. Second, the start of English publications also helped to improve the domestic academic standards as the Hungarian authors have to face the publication requirements of international journals and foreign editors. These 'encounters' have already provided lots of impulses for the internal development of legal sociology and helped the reception of many foreign insights.

In my case, the role of international professional influences, with special regard to mentoring, cannot be underestimated. Dave Cowan, Marie-Claire Foblets, Marc Hertogh, David Nelken and Ulrike Schultz have been those persons for whom I can only be very grateful as they helped me to integrate into the 'international socio-legal studies community'. Retrospectively, the most crucial influence was that they convinced me that my perspective and my findings are relevant and interesting for the international community of socio-legal scholars. This was an indispensable support as I've always been rather doubtful on the real value of my scholarly activities. The huge amount of positive feedback I got from them, and from some other scholars, too, made me believe that my contribution can have a say, even if I come from a peripheral country where these kind of studies are manifestly underrated.

The second recent trend sees Hungarian socio-legal scholars participating in some regional academic co-operations. These events[74] and projects[75] were inspired by the idea that regional legal cultures have been facing rather similar challenges, even if the national ways of development have had their own unique features, naturally. So, there may be some chance that a regional socio-legal studies hub will take shape in the near future and the regional scholars will be able to articulate their own research interests and issues more efficiently than before.

This has been my understanding and interpretation of the story of socio-legal studies in Hungary. Needless to say, other scholars may present quite a different story, though I believe that a partial convergence might occur with special regard to the main personalities and major contemporary findings. But this does not change the fact that this chapter is mine, so the responsibility for its content is also mine. One may point out that references to the contemporary political situation and climate – sometimes described as democratic backlash, erosion of rule of law, or an autocratic turn – are missing completely. And this is a valid point. But as someone who has been socialised into this tradition, I believe that a story of a field of study can be written without being explicit on our political preferences.

[74] See: Vukovic and Fekete (n 18) 549–52.

[75] See: B Fekete (ed), 'Rights Consciousness and Legal Cultures in Central and Eastern Europe' (special section) (2019) 60 *Jahrbuch für Ostrecht* 161–251.

4

Sociology of Law in the Western Balkans: Instrumentality, Liminality and Beyond

SAMIR FORIĆ

SOCIO-LEGAL SCHOLARSHIP IN the Western Balkans region has been on an upward trajectory since the 1990s, particularly in the last decade.[1] This is manifested in different areas, such as induction of university courses of sociology of law in both legal and sociological education programs, production of textbooks, monographs and papers, national and inter-regional research projects and organisation of international conferences. The upturn is the outcome of processes such as globalisation, internationalisation, Europeanisation and innovation of the university-level programmes that paved the way for introduction of English-written literary sources and cooperation with socio-legal scholars from abroad, namely from Central and Western Europe. The research field of law and society or sociology of law – as it is traditionally termed in continental Europe – solidified and affirmed its disciplinary identity through three different networking events in three regional capital cities between 2014 and 2016.

On 21 November 2014, the Faculty of Law in Belgrade hosted the conference 'Citizens, Societies and Legal Systems: Law and Society in Central and Southeastern Europe'. It featured scholars from Serbia, Hungary and Slovenia whose papers were published in a special issue of *Sociology*, one of the longest-running regional sociological journals, and the first issue to promote sociology of law specifically.[2] On 28 and 29 May 2015, the Faculty of Political Sciences in Sarajevo hosted the 'Second International Workshop on Law and Ideology: Memories of Struggle, Struggles of Memories', featuring international and

[1] The term 'Western Balkans' or 'Western Balkans region' I use here is a geographical one, not a geopolitical one, and is comprised of the following countries: Slovenia, Croatia, Serbia, Bosnia and Herzegovina, Montenegro, North Macedonia, Albania, and Kosovo--in adherence to United Nations Security Council Resolution 1244 (10 June 1999).

[2] D Vuković and B Fekete, 'Sociology of Law in the Region: From Histories of Socio-Legal Thinking to Research and Teaching Agendas' (2015) 4 *Sociologija* 550, at 545.

regional scholars whose presentations were focused on the nexus of law and memory.[3] Finally, on 1 and 2 December 2016, the Faculty of Law in Zagreb hosted the international conference 'Society, Law, Legal Culture' marking the 110th anniversary of the faculty's Chair of Sociology, the oldest one in the region. The latter conference remains the most important one to this day, both in terms of its thematic scope (focused explicitly on sociology of law), size (around 50 participants from the region but also from Central Europe) and impact. One such impact concerns networking between scholars from Croatia, Serbia and Bosnia and Herzegovina (BiH) who joined forces in 2017 and conducted comparative empirical research on the legal profession in the respective countries in 2018.[4]

As a participant in these events, bar the first one in Belgrade, and a scholar belonging to the younger generation who succeeded their teaching posts from predecessors whose proficiency in English was limited and who did little to innovate the sociology of law syllabi, I witnessed a gradual development of the discipline's distinctive identity. I saw it move away from the narrow confines of legal theory where it was traditionally positioned and evolve toward its own academic field that embeds an epistemic community no longer affiliated exclusively with law schools. Now, regional socio-legal scholarship finds itself in a position to challenge but also to subvert the conditions that hampered its development for a long period of time and move beyond them.

The hampering conditions are those of instrumentality and liminality. The first evaluates the socio-legal body of knowledge and purview in terms of its utility for legal scholarship and doctrinal legal education. The second understands anything claiming to be socio-legal as inherently problematic. Neatness of a disciplinary border dividing law and other social sciences, seems to drive

[3] R Mańko and M Stambulski, 'Law and Ideology: Critical Explorations' (2015) 5 *Wroclaw Review of Law, Administration and Economics* 1, at 3.

[4] Research project 'Lawyers and Legal Profession in Serbia, Croatia and Bosnia and Herzegovina' was conducted by Danilo Vuković and Valerija Dabetić from the Faculty of Law in Belgrade, Marko Mrakovčić from the Faculty of Law in Rijeka, and Samir Forić from the Faculty of Political Science in Sarajevo. It was conducted without institutional support and surveyed around 1,500 lawyers from three countries. Principal findings were presented at the Research Committee for Sociology of Law meeting in Lisbon in September 2018. Subsequently, results were partially published in the following works: M Mrakovčić and D Vuković, 'Stavovi pripadnika pravničkih profesija o pravosuđu u Hrvatskoj i Srbiji' (2019) 56 *Politička misao* 75; D Vuković, V Dabetić and S Forić, 'Serbia and Bosnia and Herzegovina: Challenges of Liberalisation and Democratic Consolidation' in RL Abel, O Hammerslev, H Sommerland and U Schultz (eds), *Lawyers in 21st Century Societies: vol. 1: National Reports* (London, Hart, 2020); D Vuković and M Mrakovčić, 'Legitimacy, Independence and Impartiality: How Serbian and Croatian Legal Professionals Assess Their Judiciaries?' (2022) 74 *Europe-Asia Studies* 945, 967; and in doctoral theses by S Forić, *Strategije profesionalizacije u procesu institucionalizacije prava u Bosni i Hercegovini nakon Daytonskog mirovnog sporazuma, doktorska disertacija* (Sarajevo, Fakultet političkih nauka Univerziteta u Sarajevu, 2019) and B Dabetić, *Izazovi konsolidacije sudstva kao nezavisne grane vlasti u Srbiji na početku 21. veka*, doktorska disertacija (Beograd, Univerziteta u Beogradu – Pravni fakultet, 2023). Unfortunately, due to the lack institutional support and formal networking of regional scholars, it remains the only such academic endeavour so far.

sociology to instinctively withdraw from any legal academic subject and question the validity of socio-legal scholarship as a branch of specialised sociology. The conditions are reflective of wider political, social and academic processes in which the regional socio-legal trajectory was halted – and almost brought to its tragic end – after the glorious early days when socio-legal scholarship was the driving force behind the rise of both legal and sociological scholarship. Even if the potency of such conditions has been reduced in the wake of the most recent developments, they remain prominent and should not be understated or ignored.

Regional socio-legal scholarship has traditionally been entangled with law both institutionally and disciplinarily. Its development was, and to an extent still is, proportional to that of legal scholarship. The latter tries to broaden its scope by including theoretical (in the sense of social sciences, for example, criminology, economics, gender studies), philosophical and sociological dimensions of law as its own tenets. Legal scholarship retains its disciplinary monopoly over every and all academic legal subjects, while, simultaneously, trying to integrate them. It epistemologically condenses them to fit the narrow and practically oriented doctrinal model of scholarship, legal education and professional training. The doctrinal model, present in almost all continental Europe, maintains no need for jurisprudence and optimises socio-legal scholarship as 'sociology of law'. Its primary purpose is to provide intellectual legitimacy to legal scholarship. Its secondary purpose is to broaden the perspectives of legal inquiry. This differs from the other modes of optimisation in socio-legal scholarship. For instance, in the United Kingdom, it assumes the form of socio-legal studies. The primary purpose of the latter is not validatory, but practical, aligning with the problem-solving orientation of legal scholarship.

Hence, sociology of law retains academic value in relation to its validatory performance. Its value is first and foremost an instrumental one. Still, innovations in legal education that have expanded its thematic focus to social issues that relate to law (Europeanisation, gender, transitional justice, etc) incite the demand for expertise that is not purely doctrinal. In the process, they pave a way for greater disciplinary autonomy of sociology of law.

Sociology itself, on the other hand, ever since its emancipation from the law schools in the 1950s and 1960s, developed without taking interest in issues relating to the law, state and social control. While general sociology dealt with the most general and profound issues of its time (mostly social change: modernisation, socialist revolution, post-socialist transformation, and globalisation; and social structure), branches of specialised sociologies dealt with specific social institutions and social problems. But it did not consider the institution of law nor the problem of social control. It relinquished them to law. The approach is consistent for both theoretical and empirical sociological scholarship. Hence, sociology of law was approached as an inherently problematic node in the network of social science scholarship. It was the object of disdain inviting inevitable conflicts over disciplinary ownership and authority between sociology and law, leading to its confinement in a liminal disciplinary space. Still, expansion of sociology's scope and establishment of new specialised branches, on the premises of paradigmatic openness, interdisciplinary and transdisciplinary engagement, saw sociology of law introduced as a course in sociology study programmes and a subject of interest at sociological research institutes, albeit to a limited extent.

In relation to these fundamental conditions of instrumentality and liminality, the regional socio-legal trajectory can be seen spanning three distinctive phases: inception phase – where there are no such conditions; encapsulation phase – where such conditions emerge; and emancipation phase – where such conditions may be transcended. This chapter is, for the most part, devoted to the historical trajectory comprised of these three phases. However, the spatial trajectory is highlighted whenever possible due to the inner regional developmental disparities that are reflective in the socio-legal trajectory. Deeper comprehension of the trajectory would not be possible without considering the spatial dimension which is why it features first in the following section, serving also as a window of contextualisation. The second section aims for fuller comprehension of the scholarship's trajectory in total by focusing on my own academic trajectory in the field, as it illustrates some of the most recent developments. Finally, the chapter concludes with a summary and one final reflection on conditions of instrumentality and liminality. It ends on a positive note by identifying not only positive developments that go beyond these conditions but identifying an existence of precondition of the scholarship – existence of scholars.

I. TRAJECTORY OF THE SOCIO-LEGAL SCHOLARSHIP IN THE WESTERN BALKANS

A. The Spatial Dimension of Trajectory: The Landscape of Disparity

Historically, the wider region of the Balkan peninsula has served as a border between so-called Western and Eastern civilisations. This is mainly presented by Austrian and Hungarian monarchies on the west and the Ottoman Empire on the east with their respective belief systems, cultures and legal traditions. This was particularly the case with the Western Balkans region that has, in its modern history, experienced various processes of social and political change. In terms of the latter, in the late nineteenth century, territories of today's Slovenia, Croatia, Bosnia and Herzegovina and the northern Serbian region of Vojvodina were parts of the Austro-Hungarian monarchy. The Kingdom of Serbia and the Principality of Montenegro were independent states, while today's Northern Macedonia and Albania were a part of the Ottoman Empire. In the early twentieth century, following the Balkan Wars and World

War One, all countries except Albania who gained independence in 1912 formed the first Yugoslav state (1918–29 Kingdom of Serbs, Croats, and Slovenes, 1929–41 Kingdom of Yugoslavia). This was succeeded by the second Yugoslav state after the events of World War Two (1945–63 Federal People's Republic of Yugoslavia, 1963–92 Socialist Federal Republic of Yugoslavia). The last decade of the twentieth century was one of turmoil, crises and wars in Croatia, Bosnia and Herzegovina and Kosovo following the dissolution of the second Yugoslav state. There was then the subsequent emergence of independent states and their respective development tied with Euro-Atlantic integration processes.[5] As for social change, industrialisation and modernisation processes were taking place from the mid-nineteenth until mid-twentieth centuries. This was followed by the post-World War Two socialist revolution in whole region, and that was followed with the late-twentieth century processes of post-socialist democratic transition, economic liberalisation and globalisation. However, the processes and their respective developments, were both temporally and spatially uneven. The fact of unevenness has over time created socio-economic and political disparities that are reflected in the present-day state of political, legal and economic integration of the region to the European Union.

B. The North-South Divide of the Trajectory

Aggregated disparities showcase the north and south regional divide manifested, *inter alia*, in the socio-legal trajectory. In the region's north, the first books that include a systemic overview of global socio-legal theories and introduce prominent scholars such as Ehrlich, Podgórecki, Black, Luhmann and Treves were published in Ljubljana and Novi Sad, two major cities in the region's far north.[6] Belgrade and Zagreb have traditionally been two of the most important centres for socio-legal scholarship, especially the former. While Zagreb was the first regional centre to host a chair of sociology in the early twentieth century, Belgrade has remained a central hub from the early 1930s until the present day, which is not surprising given that it was a capital of both iterations

[5] Slovenia, Croatia, and North Macedonia (1991), Bosnia and Herzegovina (1992), Serbia and Montenegro (2006) and Kosovo (2008). Nowadays, the region is entrenched into Euro-Atlantic integration processes as Slovenia (since 2004) and Croatia (since 2013) are members of the European Union (and the North Atlantic Treaty Organisation, NATO), Montenegro, Albania, and North Macedonia (all NATO members) and Serbia are in the European-Union-accession negotiation process, Bosnia and Herzegovina is a candidate country and Kosovo a potential candidate.

[6] A Igličar, *Teme iz sociologije prava* (Ljubljana, Uradni list Republike Slovenije, 1991); A Molnar, *Društvo i pravo: istorija klasičnih sociološkopravnih teorija. Knj. 1, Francuska, Rusija (SSSR), Engleska, SAD* (Novi Sad, Visio Mundi Academic Press, 1994); A Molnar, *Društvo i pravo: istorija klasičnih sociološkopravnih teorija. Knj. 2, Skandinavija, Nemačka, Austrija* (Novi Sad, Visio Mundi Academic Press, 1994).

of the Yugoslav state. The only two research centres that engage with socio-legal scholarship are also located in the region's north: The Institute for Sociological and Criminological Research in Belgrade and the Institute for Criminological Research in Ljubljana.[7]

While sociology of law has been traditionally present in the north and continues its development based on the authority of esteemed scholars, longevity and existing institutional capacity, in the south, it is only emerging relatively recently, and its trajectory is taking a quite peculiar turn. The first notable peculiarity concerns the trend of expansion of socio-legal education outside of the traditional institutional confines of law schools. The second concerns academic production of education materials in sociology of law. Regarding the expansion of educational institutions, Sarajevo, Eastern Sarajevo, Banja Luka, Niš and Tirana host sociology of law university courses both in the law schools and in the departments of sociology (at faculties of political science in Sarajevo, Banja Luka; faculties of philosophy in Eastern Sarajevo, Niš; and Faculty of Social Sciences in Tirana). Regarding educational materials, notable socio-legal literature of international renown was exclusively published in Podgorica.[8] Also, production of textbooks has been on the rise for the past 15 years, thereby placing the southern production centres such as Skopje,[9] Eastern Sarajevo,[10] Banja Luka,[11] Tirana,[12] Prishtina[13] and Kičevo[14] on the regional socio-legal map.

One of the reasons the socio-legal trajectory had lagged in the region's south, beside the absence of scholars, tradition and capacity, concerns what Fatmir Zanaj describes as 'historical prejudice toward sociology that traces

[7] Institute for Criminological and Sociological Research in Belgrade was established in 1971 following the institutional merger of the Institute for Criminological and Criminal Justice Research and the Institute for Sociology. It is highly productive in terms of its publications (both journals: *Proceedings* and the *Review for Criminology and Criminal Law*, are published tri-annually) that cover socio-legal adjacent topics (social deviance, social control, application of criminal law, ecology, family law, etc). The Institute for Criminology at the Faculty of Law in Ljubljana was established in 1954, as the first of its kind in former Yugoslavia, and soon became independent. One of their ongoing projects concerns a criminological and socio-legal analysis of the rise of illiberal democracies.

[8] Jean Carbonnier's *Legal Sociology* was translated from French in 1992, Georges Gurvitch's *Sociology of Law* from English in 1997, Leon Petrażycki's *Theory of Law and Morals* from Russian in 1999 and Vincenzo Ferrari's *Law and Society* from Italian in 2011.

[9] T Čokverski, *Sociologija na pravoto (opštestvo i pravo)* (Skopje, Studentski zbor: Praven fakultet, 1996); Đ Tonovski, *Sociologija na pravoto* (Skopje, FON Univerzitet, 2008).

[10] Z Nikolić, *Uvod u sociologiju prava* (Istočno Sarajevo, Pravni fakultet Pale Univerziteta u Istočnom Sarajevu, 2008).

[11] B Kovačević, *Društvena uloga prava: uvod u sociologiju prava* (Banja Luka, Defendologija centar za sigurosna, sociološka i kriminološka istraživanja, 2010); I Šijaković and D Vilić, *Sociologija za pravnike* (Banja Luka, Udruženje sociologa Banja Luka, 2013).

[12] F Zanaj, *Sociologjia e së Drejtës* (Tiranë, 'Naim' Publishing House, 2010).

[13] B Sadikaj, *Sociologjia e së Drejtës* (Prishtina, Prishtina University Press, 2010).

[14] A Jovanoski, *Sociologija na pravo* (Kičevo, Univerzitet 'Sv. Kliment Ohridski' – Bitola, Praven fakultet Kičevo, 2021).

back to the communist times'.[15] The prejudice did not only delay the emergence of socio-legal scholarship. It also meant that the growing supply of legal education and subsequent induction of sociology of law courses in its curricula saw the teaching responsibilities for these courses assigned to lecturers who 'are almost exclusively lawyers, without any scientific sociological training'.[16] The general attitude to sociology and the state of affairs in regard to socio-legal teachers' academic background, do perhaps speak more about the local experience of sociology under communism in Albania, quite different from sociology under socialism in former Yugoslavia.[17] But the truth is that sociology in the whole region was associated with Marxism, especially in the region's south, and that it bore a stigma of the ideology of the past in the post-socialist aftermath.[18] Once sociology was free of this stigma, namely since the 2005 Bologna reforms in higher education, it pursued the path of its reinvention that bred conditions under which the liminality dilemma for sociology of law could be challenged. However, the other part of Zanaj's remark highlights the instrumentality condition. Sociology of law, when taught exclusively by legal scholars, is considered viable only so far as it fits the doctrinal model, that is, where it can supplement doctrinal legal scholarship and provide it with some theoretical legitimacy.

The peculiarity of the regional socio-legal trajectory has a sound spatial reference, painting a broad picture of the scholarship region-wide, but also reflecting developmental disparities. For example, developments can be traced back to the region's south, owing to the fact that it represented a fieldwork for pioneering socio-legal research. Still, the establishment of the scholarship occurred in the north, as did two of the totals of three developmental phases of the trajectory: the inception phase lasting from late-nineteenth century to 1950s, followed by the encapsulation phase until mid-1980s. The south gained traction only recently, its relevancy is linked to the emancipation phase lasting from the mid-1980s onwards.

[15] F Zanaj, 'What Consequences, in Relation to the Reforms in the Area of Law, Would the Deserved Expansion in the Study of the Field of Sociology of Law in Albania Bring?' (2015) 4 (2, S2) *Academic Journal of Interdisciplinary Studies* 165.

[16] ibid. This statement applies to many law schools in the region, namely those outside of traditional centres, and originates from the regional traditional model of academic recruitment and trajectory where socio-legal teachers were selected from the pool of legal scholars. Still, the major regional centres of legal education such as Belgrade, Zagreb, Rijeka, Banja Luka, Sarajevo and Kičevo recruit these teachers from the pool of sociologists (see A Ždralović, 'Sociologija (prava) u pravničkom obrazovanju' (2021) 54(SI) *Godišnjak Pravnog fakulteta Univerziteta u Sarajevu* 92f).

[17] See M Duller, 'Yugoslav Sociology: Political Autonomy Under a Single-Party Regime' in A Hincu and V Karády (eds), *Social Sciences in the 'Other' Europe since 1945* (Budapest, Pasts, Inc., Central European University, 2018); I Spasić, J Pešić and M Babović, *Sociology in Serbia: A Fragile Discipline* (Cham, Palgrave Macmillan, 2022).

[18] Spasić et al (n 17) 75.

II. HISTORICAL DIMENSION OF SOCIO-LEGAL TRAJECTORY

A. The Inception Phase (1874–mid-1940s)

Socio-legal scholarship in the Western Balkans predates the institutionalisation of sociology and is, in its entirety, associated with the pioneer in sociology and one of the great legal scholars – Baltazar Bogišić. As an international scholar and professor of legal history in Odessa, he was commissioned by Montenegrin Prince Nikola Petrović to lead the project of codification of private law in 1873 that resulted with the General Property Code for the Principality of Montenegro in 1888. Having obtained his PhDs in philosophy (1862) and in law and political science (1864) in Vienna, he coordinated the codification project from Paris, where he also maintained correspondence with Oxford based scholars such as Henry Sumner Maine, Fredrick Pollock, and Paul Vinogradoff, all prominent comparativists of the era.[19] Maine used Bogišić's work on the Southern Slav extended family (*zadruga*), an analysis deemed as truly socio-legal as the one by Vrban,[20] when comparing it to the *rajapoot* institute in India.[21] Bogišić's monumental work *Miscellany of the Current Legal Customs of South Slavs* from 1874, along with related works focused on regional legal customs and the methodology of data collection, comprise a rich body of work that has continually been a subject of consideration, reflection, and inspiration for regional academia.[22] Looking into the survey questions and their answers reveal a genuine sociological interest, which is quite evident in the part on criminal law, for example, the structure and frequency of crime, social background of the victims of suicide, and function of honour and shame in relation to punishment.[23] Tomica Nikičević, in the Foreword of the referenced book, maintains that Bogišić's approach was to research law in its juxtaposition with social reality, expressed through customs.[24] Bogišić was a member and in 1902 served as a president of René Worms' International Institute of Sociology in Paris.[25] He also strived to include sociology in legal education during his tenure at the Faculty of Law in Odessa.[26]

[19] D Čepulo, 'West to East – East to West: Baltazar Bogišić and the English School of Historical and Comparative Jurisprudence (H. S. Maine, F. Pollock, P. Vinogradoff)' in Z Pokrovac (ed), *Rechtswissenschaft in Osteuropa: Studien zum 19. und frühen 20. Jahrhundert* (Frankfurt, Klostermann Verlag, 2010).

[20] D Vrban, *Sociologija prava: uvod i izvorišne osnove* (Zagreb, Golden marketing-Tehnička knjiga, 2006) 53ff.

[21] Z Rašović, *Knjaz Nikola i Valtazar Bogišić. Knj 1, Biografije, rodoslovi, testamenti, referati, zakonopisanje* (Podgorica, Udruženje pravnika Crne Gore, 2021) 290.

[22] cf Čepulo (n 19); Rašović (n 21).

[23] V Bogišić, *Izabrana djela (I–IV). Tom III, Pravni običaji u Crnoj Gori, Hercegovini i Albaniji* (Podgorica, CID; Beograd, Službeni list SCG, 2004) 353–60.

[24] ibid viii.

[25] Spasić et al (n 17) 13.

[26] D Vuković, *Društvo i pravo: uvod u sociologiju prava* (Beograd, Univerzitet u Beogradu – Pravni fakultet, 2021) 25.

Two key themes in Bogišić's work were rural life and law. These themes gradually drifted apart, however, as rural sociology and sociology of law developed as the first two specialised sociologies in the first part of the twentieth century. Rural sociology was the focus of Zagreb-based scholars such as Dinko Tomašić and Rudolf Bičanić. Except for Belgrade-based Sreten Vukosavljević, sociology of law was the focus of the younger generation of scholars gathered around the 'founding father of Serbian sociology' Slobodan Jovanović.[27] The scholars in question were working at the Belgrade Law School, most of them received some part of higher education in France. The most prominent were Đorđe Tasić, Jovan Đorđević, Radomir D Lukić, Dragoslav Todorović and Svetozar S Marković. Tasić and Đorđević offered a special course in sociology and directed the Sociology and Philosophy of Law Seminar for doctoral students in the late 1930s with Lukić joining them in 1940.[28]

Tasić was the most influential socio-legal scholar in the interwar period. His trajectory showcases the scholarship's trajectory in this phase, as it was marked by the convergence of law and sociology. The story resembles that of early socio-legal scholarship in France, and that was, along with the one in Germany, the most influential for the region.[29] Still, while the French case was one of true convergence, the region's case was the inception of sociology in law.[30] Sociology was first institutionalised in law schools in Zagreb in 1906 and later in Belgrade in 1935.[31] In 1931, the royal decree was passed requiring all law departments in Yugoslav universities to include chairs and courses in sociology. An amended version specified general sociology and statistics as core courses in legal studies, and legal sociology as an elective course.[32] Tasić established the first regional sociological association in 1935 and launched *Sociological Review* in 1938, the first of its kind and modelled after the famous French journal *Année sociologique*.[33] The fact that only one issue was published reflects the

[27] Spasić et al (n 17) 19; E Maksimović, 'O procesima sociološkopravne nauke u Jugoslaviji' in DM Mitrović (ed), *Teorija, filozofija i sociologija prava: prilozi sa naučnog skupa "Jugoslovenska teorija, filozofija i sociologija prava u prošlosti i danas", Bečići 15-18. maj 1997* (Beograd, Pravni fakultet, 2017) 150.

[28] Spasić et al (n 17) 20. Đorđević was the first post-war dean of the Belgrade's Law School and chairman of the Constitutional Court of the socialist Yugoslavia, but he gradually moved into political science and established the Faculty of Political Science in Belgrade in 1968 (Spasić et al (n 17) 55).

[29] ibid 24.

[30] S Forić, 'Tekovine Durkheimove društveno-pravne misli' (2016) 3–4 *Dijalog – Časopis za filozofiju i društvena pitanja* 67, 70ff.

[31] The Chair for Criminal Science and Sociology was the first chair for sociology in the Austro-Hungarian monarchy, formed at Zagreb Law School 1906. It was renamed the Chair for Sociology and Statistics in 1936, and the Chair of Sociology in 1967 (S Ravlić, 'Sociologija i pravni studij u Hrvatskoj – uz povijest Katedre za sociologiju' in D Krbec (ed), *Hrvatska sociologija: razvoj i perspective* (Zagreb, Hrvatsko sociološko društvo, 2008) 61). The Chair for Sociology at the Belgrade Law School was formed in 1935 and was integrated into the Chair for Theory, Philosophy and Sociology of Law following the higher educational reforms in the 1960s (Spasić et al (n 17) 55).

[32] Spasić et al (n 17) 20.

[33] Society for Philosophy and Sociology of Law was renamed three years later as Society for Sociology and Social Sciences (Spasić et al (n 17) 22).

tragic developments of the obliteration of the first Yugoslav state in 1941 and the execution of Tasić by the occupying German forces in 1943. Other sociologists, like Slobodan Jovanović and Mirko Kosić went into exile, while others, like Todorović and Đorđević, discontinued their interest in sociology of law marking the end of the inception era.[34]

Tasić's background was public law, international law, and legal philosophy but 'his own intellectual evolution was pointed in the sociological direction' at least a decade prior to his early death.[35] His trajectory was similar to that of some of the most influential French scholars in the region, who were themselves influenced by Émile Durkheim, namely Léon Duguit, Maurice Hauriou and François Gény. Duguit's work on the transformation of public law (*Les transformations du droit public*, 1913) was translated into Serbian in 1929. It inspired the legal duality paradigm, the scholarship's leading paradigm of this phase that even survived into the next one. The paradigm concerns the issue of the social origin of the creation of law and differentiates between state-created, formal and positive law, and social law that originates spontaneously from coordinated social action.[36] Božidar S Marković, inspired by the named authors, but also by Ehrlich's distinction of social and state norms and by Gurvitch's distinction of social and state law, became a major proponent of this paradigm. He framed it in two forms: as a duality of sociological and state norms,[37] and duality of positive law.[38]

The other paradigm in socio-legal scholarship, discovery of law in social facts, was theorised as the sociological method in law. It has the longest continuity in regional scholarship and attracts the interest of scholars to this very day. Its first major proponent was Tasić who was succeeded by Radomir D Lukić. In his inaugural lecture from 1940 *On the Concept of Sociology of Law*, Lukić made two assertions that would go to form a cornerstone of socio-legal scholarship in the next phase of development. First, he asserted that sociology is to deal with facts and explain them via empirical and causal-explicative laws. Second, he asserted that the sociological method in law, namely legal interpretation, is to be understood as normative.[39] This second assertion presents a break from Tasić's understanding of the sociological method as non-normative.[40] Another

[34] Vuković and Fekete (n 2) 558.

[35] Spasić et al (n 17) 24.

[36] cf S Bovan, *Osnovi sociologije prava*, peto izdanje (Beograd, Univerzitet u Beogradu – Pravni fakultet, 2020) 165f.

[37] BS Marković, 'O sociološkom i etatističkom normativitetu u pravu' in RD Lukić (ed), IV *Zbornik za teoriju prava* (Beograd, Srpska akademija nauka i umetnosti, 1990).

[38] BS Marković, 'O dualitetu pozitivnog prava' in DM Mitrović (ed), *Stvaranje prava / Treći skup Jugoslovenskog udruženja za teoriju, filozofiju i sociologiju prava, Miločer 24–25. septembar 1999* (Beograd, Jugoslovensko udruženje za teoriju, filozofiju i sociologiju prava: Savet projekta Konstituisanje Srbije kao pravne države, Centar za publikacije Pravnog fakulteta, 2000).

[39] RD Lukić, 'O pojmu sociologije prava' (1941) 42(3) *Arhiv za pravne i društvene nauke* 183, 189.

[40] ALj Mitrović, 'Sociological Method in the Face of the Challenges of Legal Practice' in S Miladinović and A Vuković (eds), *In Honor of Professor Đorđe Tasić: Life, Works and Echoes* (Belgrade, Serbian Sociological Association, 2023) 49.

break, implicated by this assertation, concerned the methodology of socio-legal research. Tasić, much as other sociologists of that time, insisted that sociology should be both theoretical and empirical engagement, and he practised that conviction.[41] On the other hand, Lukić engaged in sociology only theoretically, even if he himself claimed that the approach that favours office-work rather than fieldwork hindered development of sociology in Yugoslavia.[42]

To summarise, the inception phase marks the emergence of socio-legal scholarship that predates institutionalisation of sociology, carried out by Baltazar Bogišić whose work inspired successive generations. The emergence and development of sociology occurred in law schools. The sociology of law was, in many respects, a predecessor of general sociology, owing much of its inception to legal scholars whose personal trajectories lead them from law toward sociology. Such development was favoured by the state, since law schools were traditional bastions of political, legal and social order, operating in the time when many different national, ethnic and class-groups found themselves in a self-governing polity. That era's turn of events raised important social questions of integration and order.[43] Also, such development favoured legal scholarship, as sociology provided it with broader theoretical legitimacy by being a dominant social science of the era.[44] In the field there were no other occupants bar one, so there was no need for border-marking. Hence, the development of non-dogmatic ideas and perspectives was unrestrained. The upward trajectory was best showcased in the existence of a cadre composed of a devoted community of scholars whose recruitment and engagement were of an institutional design. The cadre was established by the late 1930s but the events of World War Two and an immediate ideological break with sociology practically obliterated the cadre. The lack of a cadre or a lack of precondition of scholarship was reported as a root cause that hindered development of socio-legal scholarship in the mid-1960s.[45] This fact, along with emerging conditions of instrumentality and liminality, marked the beginning of the encapsulation phase of the trajectory.

B. The Encapsulation Phase (1950s–mid-1980s)

The following phase of socio-legal trajectory can be divided into two stages: the early and the late one. Also, differentiation can be made between a soft and hard encapsulation. The former type coincides with the early, while the

[41] Spasić et al (n 17): 25; Vuković and Fekete (n 2) 577.

[42] RD Lukić, *Osnovi sociologije*, osamnaesto izdanje (Beograd, Zavod za udžbenike i nastavna sredstva, 1994) 133.

[43] Ravlić (n 31) 60.

[44] ibid.

[45] O Mandić, 'The Sociology of Law in Development of Sociology in Yugoslavia' in R Treves and JF Glastra Van Loon (eds), *Norms and Actions: National Reports on Sociology of Law* (Hague, Martinus Nijhoff, 1968) 120.

latter coincides with the late stage. Following the establishment of the second Yugoslav state, sociology of law found itself encapsulated in the broader framework of general legal science comprised of theory (legal theory, philosophy, and sociology of law) and doctrine (legal science). Theory, on one hand, provided legal scholarship with broader academic legitimacy. On the other hand, theory embedded legal scholarship into the dominant Marxist or historical materialism paradigm, and in line with the official Yugoslav doctrine of socialist self-management.

The encapsulation, namely its soft variant, had institutional and epistemological expressions. Following the legal education reform in the early 1950s, the Belgrade law school clustered theory, philosophy and sociology of law into a singular department. Shortly thereafter, the Yugoslav Association for Theory, Philosophy and Sociology of Law was established in 1957.[46] Another example of institutional encapsulation could be seen in the composition of The Working Group 'Law and Society – Fundamental Research', a section of the Yugoslav Academy of Science and Arts.[47] It comprised only legal theorists and legal philosophers but no sociologists. Notably, sociologists were absent from the 28th meeting in 1984 devoted to the relation of legal science and sociology.[48]

Sociology in legal education existed without being properly named (identified) while the university course of sociology of law was absent from the curricula.[49] There was one textbook on sociology of law by Rudolf Legradić from 1965, but its content bore no semblance to what one would ordinarily associate with the discipline, not in terms of scholars, concepts, ideas, approaches nor themes, which is not surprising giving the book's subtitle was 'General Theory of Law'.[50] The situation was quite different with one textbook for the

[46] The other law schools in the country, mostly due to the fact of lack of a cadre and their establishment occurring in the late 1950s, and during 1960s and 1970s, clustered theory, philosophy, and sociology of law into chairs for public and international law. Zagreb law school retained its Chair for Sociology and Statistics, renamed as Chair for Sociology in 1967.

[47] The available information on the Working Group shows that it existed from 1979 until 1989 and that it published five editions of the Yearbook *Law and Society*, between 1982 and 1989. Ivan Padjen was its secretary from 1989 until 1983 (I Padjen, 'Teorija prava u socijalističkoj Jugoslaviji' (2013) 13 *Hrvatska i komparativna javna uprava* 1200.

[48] I Padjen, *Metodologija prava: pravo i susjedne discipline* (Rijeka, Pravni fakultet Sveučilišta u Rijeci, 2015) 117.

[49] ibid, 128. Instead, the sociological courses were titled as: 'Basics of Science of Society', 'Introduction to Science of Society', 'Science of Society', 'Introduction to Social Sciences', 'Theory of Law and State', 'Introduction to Legal Science of Law and State', and 'Basics of Marxism' (cf B Kašić, 'Sociologija i historijski materijalizam. Prijepor jednog vremena' (1989) 20 *Revija za sociologiju* 68; Ždralović (n 16) 91).

[50] cf Maksimović (n 27) 150. In the Foreword, Legradić states that the textbook is based upon the lectures he gave to students of faculties of economics in Zagreb and Belgrade between 1958 and 1964, and that it represents an attempt of 'dialectical synthesis of social phenomena such as morals, law, and the state, from their objective laws of development' (R Legradić, *Sociologija prava* (Beograd, Savremena administracija, 1965) III). Also, see note 95 for the second, but much lesser-known, textbook by Todor I Podgorac.

course on the theory of law and state (official title for a course on sociology) in the Zagreb law school, published in 1964. *Structure of Law* by Berislav Perić featured sociology of law in the part devoted to sociological theories of law. It included an overview of Gurvitch's ideas and a 'solidaristic' strand of theories inspired by Durkheim and advocated by Duguit, Hauriou and Gierke.[51]

In the early stage of encapsulation, some of the socio-legal concepts from the previous inception phase managed to survive, albeit as vestiges, but they were adjusted to fit the official political and social doctrine. Social law was conceptualised as autonomous law that exists in coherence with the state law, to the extent where difference practically disappears.[52] The sociological method was now considered not only as normative, but even dogmatic – meaning that its use for doctrinal law was purely instrumental and directed inwards, not outwards.[53] The encapsulation was a backdrop to emerging conditions of instrumentality and liminality that turned the socio-legal trajectory downwards and almost lead to its complete disappearance – up until the twilight of the socialist era. While instrumentality concerned the relationship between sociology of law and law, liminality concerned the relationship between sociology of law and sociology. Both were tied with the development of sociology in socialist Yugoslavia that saw the emergence of two core centres: one affiliated with faculties of philosophy, which started hosting sociology as a study programme in the early 1950s, and the other affiliated with law schools, represented by two prominent figures: Radomir D Lukić and Oleg Mandić.[54]

Lukić and Mandić, based in the Belgrade and Zagreb law schools, respectively, were the most prominent socio-legal scholars, and their respective textbooks in sociology were widely used in socialist Yugoslavia's legal education. Mandić was one of the original members of the Research Committee on Sociology of Law (RCSL), launched in Washington DC in 1962, representing Yugoslavia.[55] The most important developments in the early stage are summarised in his report *The Sociology of Law in Development of Sociology in Yugoslavia*.[56] There he emphasised the distinction between Yugoslav and USSR styles of historical materialism. The former he rendered as open and respective of sociology as a social science in its own right; the latter rendered as dogmatic and closed to such recognition. He also claimed that law in the socialist countries plays a dynamic role of fortifying revolution by laws that provide and impose changes upon the social system.[57] Mandić noted that sociology was

[51] B Perić, *Struktura prava*, dvanaesto izdanje (Zagreb, Informator, 1994) 159–229.

[52] Legradić (n 50) 251ff.

[53] O Mandić, 'Sociologijski metod i pravna dinamika' in RD Lukić (ed), *Međunarodni simpozij o metodologiji pravnih nauka* (Beograd, Srpska Akademija nauka i umetnosti, 1973) 35ff.

[54] Spasić et al (n 17) 42f.

[55] R Treves and JF Glastra Van Loon (eds), *Norms and Actions: National Reports on Sociology of Law* (Hague, Martinus Nijhoff, 1968) 2.

[56] Mandić (n 45) 117–22.

[57] ibid 117, 121.

expunged from the overall system of social science for being a 'bourgeois ideology' in 1947 and made a great comeback in 1953. Sociology was then followed by immediate institutionalisation as a compulsory course in all the faculties of social sciences and the establishment of specialised research institutes tasked with the development of specialised sociologies. Demand for sociology, conceived by the state to be a vehicle for advancing socialism in the country, far exceeded its supply, namely in terms of lacking a cadre. This was especially the case for sociology of law.[58] Mandić reported on jurists that examined problems from both a juridical and a sociological standpoint, but there were 'no systematic empirical studies that could collect data to be analysed and serve a basis for generalisations'.[59] The absence of empirical research and the sole theoretical focus led Mandić to conclude that the scholarship was, at best, the precursor of sociology of law in Yugoslavia.[60]

Interestingly, Mandić's (1968) report omits to mention Jože Goričar, another legal scholar turned sociologist dubbed as the founder of Slovenian sociology and sociology of law.[61] Based in the Ljubljana Law School, he maintained a personal relationship with Gurvitch, who visited Yugoslavia on several occasions in the late 1950s and early 1960s to observe the performance of self-management social relations and law.[62] Goričar's socio-legal scholarship was based on Durkheim's and Gurvitch's works and focused on the relationship between social relations and the autonomous law that governed them. He concluded that the self-management or autonomous law was ineffective for its lack of sanction, thereby not fulfilling functions of social integration and social control.[63] In the mid-1970s, his approach to sociology of law broke with the dominant one. He claimed that it should focus on transitional occurrences between different forms of social behaviour (obligatory, desirable and permissible actions) and norms (legal norms, customs and habits), and treat law as the dependent variable defined by social conditions, thereby emerging as a specialised sociology.[64] Unfortunately, Goričar's ideas and observations occurred in the wake of arising developments in legal theory that mark the transition between soft and hard encapsulation variant (or between early and late stage). His focus on Gurvitch led him away from the dominant Marxist paradigms in social sciences which is why they gained no traction in legal or in sociological scholarship. They were completely ignored by his fellows, except another socio-legal scholar, Ljubljana Faculty of Philosophy-based Anton Žun.

[58] ibid 118ff.
[59] ibid 120.
[60] ibid 121.
[61] A Igličar, 'Jože Goričar na stišču prava in sociologije' (2007) 44 *Teorija in praksa* 500, 507.
[62] ibid 504.
[63] ibid 505ff; J Goričar, 'Pravna nauka i sociologija prava (o nekim opštim metodološkim pitanjima)' in RD Lukić (ed), *Međunarodni simpozij o metodologiji pravnih nauka* (Beograd, Srpska Akademija nauka i umetnosti, 1973) 143.
[64] Goričar (n 63); Igličar (n 61) 503ff.

The late stage of encapsulation began in the late 1960s and early 1970s. The period is marked by the synthesis of Marxist theory of law and state with ideas of pure law by Hans Kelsen. This is best exemplified by the book of Sarajevo-based legal theorist and philosopher Zdravko Grebo (1979), neatly titled *Marx and Kelsen*.[65] The so-called 'Kelsenian turn' in Yugoslav legal scholarship is attributed to Radomir Lukić as the leading legal theorist of the socialist era whose books were canonical and used in universities all over Yugoslavia.[66] The 'Kelsenian turn' played a role in distancing from the Soviet model of the General Theory of Law and State and provided 'Western legitimacy to these views'.[67] It also moved legal scholarship to reinforce formalism under the guise of legal positivism. 'The formalism and rigid textual positivist of this phase of the socialist legal tradition tended to also be wrongfully identified with legal positivism and personified with Hans Kelsen'.[68] This development had negative implications toward sociology of law as it reduced both the discipline and its crucial concepts to mere nominal categories, namely: (social) facts and (social) relations.

Transformation of concepts to mere buzzwords employed in the legal-theoretical discourse showcased an epistemological encapsulation of sociology of law. It was further aided by purification attempts, based on the Kelsenian distinction of causal social sciences such as sociology and normative social science such as law,[69] that gained the form of an anti-sociologisation thesis. For instance, in his paper advocating the said thesis from 1983, presented at the 18th meeting of the Working Group 'Law and Society – Fundamental Research', Ivan Padjen maintained the position of the uselessness of sociology of law for legal science because 'social facts are inherently normative'.[70] Since sociology cannot provide answers about the efficacy of legal systems, and due to its own shortcomings, resistance to 'sociologisation' – an attempt to add special sociologies to positive legal disciplines – is imperative. It invokes 'sociologisation of normative

[65] Z Grebo, *Marx i Kelsen: kritička analiza Kelsenove kritike naučne osnovanosti Marxovog shvatanja društva, države i prava* (Sarajevo, "Svjetlost": Novinsko-izdavačka organizacija Službeni list SRBiH: Republički zavod za javnu upravu, 1979). Denis Preshova and Nenad Markovikj in 'Old Patterns Die Hard – The Idiosyncrasies of the Yugoslav Legal Tradition and the Problem of Continuity in the Western Balkans' in C Cercel, A Mercescu and MM Sadowski (eds), *Law, Culture and Identity in Central and Eastern Europe: Comparative Engagement* (Abingdon, Oxon/New York, NJ, Routledge, 2024) at 123 claim that the 'specific origin of the acceptance of Kelsen's theory remains unclear and it was never proclaimed an official position by legal authorities in the country, it was following the political departure from the Soviet influence, which found its reflection at the academic level as well'. But it is worth noting that Kelen's *General Theory of Law and State* was translated into Serbian in 1951 in Belgrade, while his paper *On Borders between Legal and Sociological Method* was translated even earlier, in 1927 in Belgrade.

[66] F Karčić, *A Study on Legal Formalism in Former Yugoslavia and its Successor States* (Center for Integrity in the Defence Sector report No. 1/2020, 2020 and Preshova and Markovikj (n 65) 123f.

[67] Preshova and Markovikj (n 65) 124.

[68] ibid.

[69] H Kelsen, *Pure Theory of Law* (Clark, NJ, The Lawbook Exchange, Ltd., 2005) 85ff.

[70] Padjen (n 48) 87.

legal science'.[71] The following year, during the 28th meeting of the said working group, Padjen claimed that, due to its methodological shortcomings, sociology of law can only be viable if it is 'theoretically and methodologically structured as sociology of social action', but that discipline is actually 'itself a normative legal science'.[72] For Padjen, the only way for sociology and legal science to move closer to each other was to include sociology into the integrative legal science and to introduce sociology of law as the linking academic discipline between legal theory and sociology.[73]

Padjen's remarks showcase the extreme of hard encapsulation variant as it negates even the nominal existence of sociology of law and sees it only as a prospect that requires a completely different organisation of legal and sociological education.[74] He emphasised 'integrative legal science' but was very critical toward its main proponent, Nikola Visković.[75] As a legal scholar based in the Split law school, Visković's approach to sociology of law may be considered as an example of the soft encapsulation variant. In his book *Concept of Law*, Visković advocated for integral legal theory based on the classical Weberian division of labour in law between normative legal science concerned with norms, philosophy of law concerned with values and sociology of law concerned with social relations.[76] His ideas were, by far, as legal theoretical scholarship is concerned, the most benevolent toward sociology of law. He recognised the viability of the discipline in dealing with social relations as concrete pre-normative relations that, along with values and norms, constitute the legal order, a concept broader than the legal system constituted solely by legal norms.[77] Despite the originality of his book and vast number of references that also include works by Weber, Durkheim, Gurvitch, Carbonnier, Treves and Bobbio, it was subject to staunch criticism like that of Padjen and by the leading figure in the field, Radomir D Lukić, who rejected them as reductive and deviant from the dominant theoretical legal scholarship.[78]

The socialist era saw both legal scholarship and sociology thrive, namely due to their practical purpose of driving social, cultural, political and legal modernisation of the country.[79] Still, their respective trajectories could not have

[71] ibid 88.
[72] ibid 126.
[73] ibid 128.
[74] ibid.
[75] ibid 88, 94, 121.
[76] N Visković, *Pojam prava: prilog integralnoj teoriji prava*, drugo dopunjeno izdanje (Split, Logos, 1981) 41.
[77] ibid 68–98.
[78] RD Lukić, 'Normativnost prava' (1991) 39 *Anali pravnog Fakulteta u Beogradu* 191ff.
[79] Duller (n 17) 175. In his analysis of the public role of sociology in the socialist Yugoslavia, Matthias Duller asserts that 'sociology stood close to the socialist project to which it aimed to contribute and whose general ideological premises it shared', and that 'the Yugoslav government endorsed a massive expansion of the higher education system, in which the social sciences played an uncommonly large role' (ibid 179).

been more separate, negatively impacting socio-legal scholarship. Sociology of law was organisationally clustered with legal theory and legal philosophy and was practically absorbed by the former. Its confines marked the only place where it could exist, even though that existence became only nominal, and even that was at stake during the late stage of encapsulation. On the other hand, sociology had no interest in academic legal subjects and developed special branches related to problems of labour, family, gender, religion, but not to the problem of social control as a problem of shared interest between law and sociology. The development exacerbated conditions of instrumentality and liminality. Still, despite this development, socio-legal scholarship managed to reappear, totally unexpectedly, and subsequently emancipate itself, riding on the wave of changes that saw the end to the Cold War, but also to Yugoslavia.

C. The Emancipation Phase (mid-1980s Onward)

The twilight of socialist Yugoslavia that began in the mid-1980s saw publication of three books that represented a radical break with the tradition marked by encapsulation. Two of these were published in Belgrade in the same year. Ivan Janković, attorney at law with a PhD in sociology, published a book (1985) on the death penalty in Yugoslavia which continues to be exemplary socio-legal and criminological research to this day.[80] Uglješa Zvekić's book (1985) on the profession of judges was even more influential, inspiring a generation of younger scholars of explicit socio-legal orientation in the late 2010s.[81] The book exemplifies empirical socio-legal research and is theoretically founded upon works in the sociology of professions and sociology of organisation – even though it was defended as a doctoral thesis at the Belgrade Law School in 1983. In Zagreb, the book on social regulation by Eugen Pusić (1989), the founder of the aforementioned Working Group 'Law and Society', appeared and featured the first systemic overview of Weber's, Luhmann's and Habermas's socio-legal ideas.[82]

[80] I Janković, *Smrt u prisustvu vlasti* (Beograd, Istraživačko-izdavački centar SSO Srbije, 1985).

[81] U Zvekić, *Profesija sudija: sociološka analiza* (Beograd, Institut za kriminološka i sociološka istraživanja, 1985).

[82] E Pusić, *Društvena regulacija: granice znanosti i iskustva* (Zagreb, Globus, Pravni fakultet Sveučilišta, Centar za stručno usavršavanje i saradnju sa udruženim radom, 1989).

The book also features a subheading about sociology of law in the Introduction, explicitly affirming its existence while highlighting its liminality condition. Pusić remarks that there is a problem facing sociology of law limiting its ambition to be a discipline in its own right. In the gap between questions whether sociology of law is a supplementary discipline in legal scholarship, or is it a part of sociology, 'sociology of law lives some kind of borrowed existence like a tree growing from the old wall of jurisprudence, splashed by rising river of sociology' (Pusić, ibid, 10). The liminality appears as an 'emotional drama played around the border marking' exacerbated by general legal theory's suspicion that sociology of law infringes on its disciplinarian territory (ibid).

The trajectory in these early days was spontaneous and fragmented, but that changed in the 1990s with the publication of books that integrated the socio-legal body of knowledge in the form of systemic theoretical overviews.[83] Also, as noted above, some classical socio-legal books by Carbonnier, Gurvitch and Petrażycki were translated into Serbian and published in Podgorica between 1992 and 1999. The trajectory also attained organisational form with the Belgrade Law School introducing a socio-legal specialisation in postgraduate studies in the mid-1990s.[84] Additionally, the Yugoslav Society for Theory, Philosophy and Sociology of Law in Belgrade started implementing the state-run project of modernising the legal system and constituting it on the basis of rule of law, hence transforming its nominal to real status with a clear public function perspective. The project resulted in six highly important publications. Namely, three edited volumes by Dragan M Mitrović,[85] and three interconnected monographs authored by Lukić's successor Jugoslav Stanković.[86] The latter trilogy, titled *Basics of General Sociology of Law*, integrated and organised the socio-legal body of knowledge in three major units: law and sociological method and

[83] Igličar (n 6); Molnar, *Društvo i pravo Knj. 1* (n 6); Molnar, *Društvo i pravo Knj. 2* (n 6). In terms of scope and attention to detail in providing historical overview of socio-legal scholarship worldwide, Aleksandar Molnar's two volumes of *Law and Society: History of Classical Socio-Legal Theories*, remains unrivalled in the region. The first volume (*Knj. 1*) covers France, United Soviet Socialist Republic (USSR), England and the United States, while the second (*Knj. 2*) covers Scandinavia, Germany and Austria. His doctoral thesis, *Constitution of Sociology of Law*, was defended at the Faculty of Philosophy in Belgrade in 1992, marking the symbolic ending of the liminality condition. Unfortunately, Aleksandar Molnar's trajectory moved outside of the field toward fields of sociology and political science (Vuković and Fekete (n 2) 557).

[84] Maksimović (n 50) 150.

[85] DM Mitrović (ed), *Teorija, filozofija i sociologija prava: prilozi sa naučnog skupa "Jugoslovenska teorija, filozofija i sociologija prava u prošlosti i danas", Bečići 15–18. maj 1997* (Beograd, Pravni fakultet, 1997); DM Mitrović (ed), *Teorija, filozofija i sociologija prava u svetu: stanje problemi, izazovi / Drugi skup Jugoslovenskog udruženja za teoriju, filozofiju i sociologiju prava, Miločer 14–17. maj 1998* (Beograd, Jugoslovensko udruženje za teoriju, filozofiju i sociologiju prava: Savet projekta Konstituisanje Srbije kao pravne države: Centar za publikacije Pravnog fakulteta, 1998); DM Mitrović (ed), *Stvaranje prava / Treći skup Jugoslovenskog udruženja za teoriju, filozofiju i sociologiju prava, Miločer 24–25. septembar 1999* (Beograd, Jugoslovensko udruženje za teoriju, filozofiju i sociologiju prava: Savet projekta Konstituisanje Srbije kao pravne države: Centar za publikacije Pravnog fakulteta, 2000).

[86] The first edited volume (Mitrović 1997, n 85) features three socio-legal papers: *Legal Sociology and Contemporary Social Change* by Radivoj Stevanov (pp 79–90), *Legal Thought of Valtazar Bogišić* by Čedomir Bogićević (pp 123–30), and *On the Processes of Socio-Legal Science in Yugoslavia* by Eva Maksimović (pp 147–50). The second (Mitrović 1998, n 85) features five papers: *Sociology of Law in Poland* by Todor Podgorac (pp 41–65), *Legal Efficiency* by Jugoslav Stanković (pp 67–86), *Law and Culture: Legal Culture* by Agneš Kartag-Odri (pp 201–10), *Controversies of Sociology of Law* by Stanislav Dimitrijević (pp 211–18), and *Two Directions in Sociology of Law: Socio-Centric and Legal-Centric* by Eva Maksimović (pp 219–34). The third volume (Mitrović 2000, n 85) features four papers: *On Duality of Positive Law* by Božidar S. Marković (pp 9–19), *Distributive Function of Law and Creation of Law* by Saša Bovan (pp 192–207), *General Principles of Creation of Law* by Eva Maksimović (pp 209–19), and *Sociological Understanding of Đorđe Tasić's Creation of Law* by Staniša Dimitrijević (pp 259–68).

the sociological concept of law;[87] creation of law;[88] and application of law and the subject of sociology of law.[89]

The following decade saw the trajectory moving upwards with the backdrop of the Bologna reforms in higher education in the mid-2000s. Reforms introduced socio-legal courses either as elective courses of sociology of law or as compulsory courses of sociology with sociology of law. The trend instituted the further production of textbook literature in the 2000s and 2010s. Their order of appearance, both temporally and spatially, reflects the general trajectory of development of the Western Balkans manifested in the north-south divide. Since the textbooks published in the south are listed above, I will proceed to list those published in the north, starting with Slovenia, followed by Croatia and Serbia.

In Ljubljana, Albin Igličar, successor to Jože Goričar, published the textbook *Introduction to Sociology of Law* in 1986, followed by *Themes from Sociology of Law* in 1991, *Sociology of Law* in 2004 and *Perspectives in Sociology of Law* in 2009.[90] In 2014, he published an updated version of the reader (the first one appeared in 1980) *Law and Society: Reader in Sociology of Law*, featuring selected works by him and by Ehrlich, Goričar, Gurvitch, Habermas, Luhmann, Weber and Žun. A new edition of his *Perspectives on Sociology of Law*, co-authored with his successor Tilen Štajnpihler Božič, was published in 2020 and updated in 2022.

In Zagreb, Eugen Pusić's successor Josip Kregar published the first edition of the *Introduction to Sociology* textbook in 2005 that also included socio-legal topics. A revised edition was published in 2013 and the new textbook *General Sociology with the Introduction to Sociology of Law* was published in 2020, followed by a second edition the following year.[91] In Osijek, Duško Vrban published *Sociology of Law: Introduction and Basics* in 2006.[92] The book was

[87] J Stanković, *Osnovi opšte sociologije prava. Deo 1, Pravo i sociološki metod, sociološki pojam prava* (Beograd, Savet projekta Konstituisanje Srbije kao pravne države u uslovima tranzicije: Centar za publikacije Pravnog Fakulteta Univerziteta, 1996).

[88] J Stanković, *Osnovi opšte sociologije prava. Deo 2, Stvaranje prava* (Beograd, Savet projekta Konstituisanje Srbije kao pravne države: Centar za publikacije Pravnog Fakulteta Univerziteta, 1998).

[89] J Stanković, *Osnovi opšte sociologije prava. Deo 3, Primena prava, predmet sociologije prava* (Beograd, Pravni fakultet Univerziteta, 2000).

[90] *Introduction to Sociology of Law* in 1986, followed by *Themes from Sociology of Law* in 1991, *Sociology of Law* in 2004 and *Perspectives in Sociology of Law* in 2009.

[91] Since the late 2000s, the Chair for Sociology at the Faculty of Law in Zagreb is comprised of scholars with background in sociology and political science, whose interests are reflected in the chapters of the textbook they co-authored. The textbook includes two explicitly socio-legal topics: *Sociology of Law* by Josip Kregar (S Zrinščak, J Kregar, D Sekulić, S Ravlić, K Grubišić, D Čepo, A Petručišić and M Čehulić, *Opća sociologija sa sociologijom prava*, drugo izdanje (Zagreb, Pravni fakultet Sveučilišta u Zagrebu, 2021) 107–44, and *Legal Culture* by Slaven Ravlić and Mateja Čehulić (ibid, 145–76).

[92] D Vrban, *Sociologija prava: uvod i izvorišne osnove* (Zagreb, Golden marketing-Tehnička knjiga, 2006).

and still is in wide regional use for sociology of law courses, either as compulsory or additional reading. Vrban was succeeded by Josip Berdica who published *Law and Society: Introduction to the Interdisciplinary Approach* in 2023.[93]

In Belgrade, Milovan M Mitrović published the textbook *Introduction to Sociology and Sociology of Law* in 2006,[94] following the introduction of the same-titled course one year earlier.[95] The second edition, co-authored by Saša Bovan, followed the structure where the first part covered sociological topics, while the second part covered socio-legal ones.[96] Mitrović published the new textbook *Basics of Sociology of Law* in 2018, co-authored by Danilo Vuković, while Bovan published his own textbook of the same title in 2014, with the most recent edition published in 2023.[97] Finally, a new textbook by Danilo Vuković, *Society and Law: Introduction to Sociology of Law*, was first published in 2021.[98]

Besides textbooks, several other books appeared in the last two decades: *Paradigmatic Origins of Sociology of Law* by Saša Bovan in 2004, *Essays on the Theory, Philosophy, and Sociology of Law* by Marko Dokić in 2012, *The Outline of Sociology of Law* by Albin Igličar in 2013 (the first one and only one so far to be published outside of the region – in Saarbrucken, and in English), *Citizens in the Collectivist Ideology: Socio-legal Analysis of the Position of 'Others' in Bosnia and Herzegovina* by Amila Ždralović and Admira Sitnić in 2013[99] and *Legal State and Shadowed Order: Law, Institutions, and Social Resistance* in Serbia by Danilo Vuković in 2022.[100] Edited volumes devoted to two socio-legal scholars were also published: in Zagreb, devoted to Josip Kregar, and in Belgrade, devoted to Đorđe Tasić.[101]

[93] J Berdica, *Društvo i pravo: uvod u interdisciplinarni pristup* (Zagreb, Novi informator, 2023).

[94] MM Mitrović, Uvod u sociologiju i sociologiju prava (Beograd: Pravni fakultet, Službeni glasnik, 2006).

[95] Insight into a *Serbian Cooperative Online Bibliographical System and Service* (COBBIS) reveals many other textbooks published in various cities in Serbia like Novi Sad, Kragujevac, Kosovska Mitrovica and Belgrade, between 2000 and 2014. With wordcount limitation in mind, I have decided to only include those published by the authors from the Belgrade law school. One noteworthy author appearing in this list was Todor I Podgorac. He published *Selections from the Sociology of Law: Review Guide* in 1967 but since I was not able to obtain the copy of the reader, I opted to omit it from my analysis.

[96] MM Mitrović and S Bovan, *Osnovi sociologije i sociologije prava* (Beograd, Pravni fakultet Univerziteta, Službeni glasnik, 2009).

[97] S Bovan, *Osnovi sociologije prava* (Beograd, Pravni fakultet Univerziteta, Centar za izdavaštvo, 2023).

[98] D Vuković, *Društvo i pravo: uvod u sociologiju prava* (Beograd, Univerzitet u Beogradu – Pravni fakultet, 2021).

[99] A Sitnić and A Ždralović, *Građani/ke u kolektivističkoj ideologiji: sociološko-pravna analiza položaja 'Ostalih' u Bosni i Hercegovini* (Sarajevo, Centar za političke studije, 2013).

[100] D Vuković, *Pravna država i poredak u senci: pravo institucije i društveni otpor u Srbiji* (Novi Sad, Mediterran Publishing, 2022).

[101] G Gardašević, V Gotovac and S Zrinščak (eds), *Pravo i društvo: Liber amicorum Josip Kregar* (Zagreb, Pravni fakultet Sveučilišta u Zagrebu, 2022); S Miladinović and A Vuković (eds), *In Honor of Professor Đorđe Tasić: Life, Works and Echoes* (Belgrade, Serbian Sociological Association, 2023).

Regional socio-legal production accounts for almost 20 textbooks and more than 20 other publications (monographs, studies, readers, edited volumes), not counting earlier editions and versions, along with many papers published in local and international journals. Taken together with the expansion of sociology of law in higher education, including both legal and sociological, and projects and conferences, the regional socio-legal trajectory is evidently on the rise. In the phase lasting for the past four decades, sociology of law managed to be emancipated both in institutional and disciplinary senses. The former is showcased by the growing presence of sociology of law in the curricula all over the region and in affirming sociological perspective in postgraduate legal education.[102] The latter is showcased by emancipation of sociology of law from legal theory, as well as by increased interest of legal theory for sociology of law and recognition of its innate value beyond the instrumentality condition.[103]

To end this section, it is worth noting the topics that draw the interest of regional socio-legal scholarship in the emancipation phase. As mentioned earlier, topics of creation and application of law, and sociological method in law, dominated the field between the late 1990s and early 2010s. Since then, focus shifted toward two core areas: (a) judiciary and legal professions, and (b) law and culture, legal culture.[104] In the next section I describe my personal academic

[102] Zagreb Law School offers postgraduate studies in criminal law sciences that include courses on gender-based violence, law and film, LGBTQ+ law and politics and several criminological courses. Belgrade Law School offers specialisation in theory of law and state, philosophy, and sociology of law in its doctoral program with courses on sociology of law, legal culture, social change and law, sociological analysis of legal profession, and sociological method in application of law. Sarajevo Law School offers postgraduate study in law and gender with courses on gender theory, LGBTQ+ persons' rights and liberties, and various gender equality and law courses.

[103] Two doctoral theses are exemplary, and both were defended in Sarajevo. The first one, by Vjekoslav Miličić (V Miličić, Posebne metode u metodologiji prava i stvaranje prava, doktorska disertacija (Sarajevo, Pravni fakultet Univerziteta u Sarajevu, 1990), is focused on legal methodology and draws from Visković's integral theory of law. It analyses sociological method in legal interpretation and creation of law and asserts its position as one of modernising legal theory in late socialist Yugoslavia. The second one, by Damir Banović (D Banović, *Savremena sociološko-pravna teorija kao kritika pravnog pozitivma*, doktorska disertacija (Sarajevo, Pravni fakultet Univerziteta u Sarajevu, 2018), analyses contemporary socio-legal theory as a critique of legal positivism and asserts it as reflexive theory that stands between analytical approach and sociological understanding, hence possessing a great value for contemporary legal theory. Banović's thesis is the first one in Bosnia and Herzegovina that analyses ideas by Eugen Ehrlich, William Twinning, Roger Cotterrel, Denis Galligan and Bryan Z Tamanaha.

[104] For the core area on judiciary and legal professions see: Vuković and Mrakovčić (n 4); Forić (n 4); S Forić, 'Judicial Professions in Contemporary Bosnia and Herzegovina – Overview and Analysis of the Selected Features' (2022) 6 *Bosnian Studies – Journal for Research of Bosnian Thought and Culture* 50; Vuković, Dabetić and Forić (n 4); T Marinković, 'Judicial Culture and the Role of Judges in Developing the Law in Serbia' *Research Chapter No. 22/2021*, Project Working Paper Series 2021; D Preshova, 'Judicial Culture and Role of Judges in Developing the Law in North Macedonia' *Research Chapter No. 23/2021*, Project Working Paper Series 2021; D Čepo and M Čehulić, 'Pravosuđe u Hrvatskoj: problem, strategije, učinci' in Đ Gardašević, V Gotovac and S Zrinščak (eds), *Pravo i društvo: Liber amicorum Josip Kregar* (Zagreb, Pravni fakultet Sveučilišta u Zagrebu, 2022); V Duković, *Pravna država i poredak u senci: pravo institucije i društveni otpor u Srbiji* (Novi Sad: Mediterran Publishing, 2022); Mračković and Vuković (2022); B Spaić and

trajectory aiming to highlight the most recent developments of socio-legal scholarship in the emancipation phase, and to make the understanding of the trajectory more comprehensive.

III. PERSONAL ACADEMIC (SOCIO-LEGAL) TRAJECTORY

Essentially, my academic trajectory is one from law toward sociology, and is reflective of my educational background, academic career and research interests. The trajectory is also reflective of what might be dubbed as my 'socio-legal' habitus.

I received my higher education entirely at the University of Sarajevo where I enrolled in legal studies at Sarajevo Law School and international relations at the Faculty of Political Sciences. From the latter, I obtained a Bachelor of Arts degree in political science in 2008, and from the former I obtained a Bachelor of Arts degree in law in 2009. My trajectory henceforth moved toward sociology. At the Faculty of Political Sciences' Department of Sociology, I was a teaching assistant and obtained a Master of Arts degree, all in 2011. In 2019, I was promoted to an assistant professor position after completing my doctoral studies at said department.

During my legal studies, I was on the path of developing a doctrinal habitus – a cognitive scheme that orients thinking about and problem-solving of legal issues through the lens of legal doctrine, instituting somewhat of a technical mindset. I also experienced the instrumentality condition firsthand.

M Đorđević, 'Less is More? On Number of Judges and Organization of Judiciary' (2022) 7 *Pravni zapisi* 421; M Đorđević, 'Između sudstva i advokature – profesionalne preferencije studenata prava u Srbiji' (2022) 56 *Sociološki pregled* 680; V Dabetić, 'Biti ili ne biti advokat? Korporativizacija advokature kao odustajanje od njenog tradicionalnog profesionalnog smisla' in V Radović (ed), *Usklađivanje poslovnog prava Srbije sa pravom Evropske unije* (Beograd, Univerzitet u Beogradu – Pravni fakultet, 2023); Dabetić (n 4).

For the core area on law and culture, and legal culture see: D Vuković, 'Pravna kultura i primena zakona: sociološko-pravna analiza primene zakona u Srbiji' (2011) 60 *Pravni život – list za pravna pitanja i praksu* 656; S Forić, 'Specifičnosti društva i prava u Japanu' (2012) 1 *Sarajevski žurnal za društvena pitanja* 137; N Bardoshi, 'Legal Dynamics in a Border Area: Between Customary Law and State Law' (2013) 1 *Journal of Legal Anthropology* 314; G Črpić, 'Sociološki aspekti obiteljsko-pravnih instituta, pravna kultura i obiteljskopravni instituti' (2017) 7 *Godišnjak Akademije pravnih znanosti Hrvatske* 1; M Čehulić, 'Perspectives of Legal Culture: A Systemic Literature Overview' (2021) 51 *Revija za sociologiju* 87; M Čehulić, *Obilježja pravne kulture u Hrvatskoj*, doktorska disertacija (Zagreb, Sveučilište u Zagrebu – Filozofski fakultet, 2021); L Bubalo, 'An Introduction to the Legal Cultures of Bosnia and Herzegovina, Croatia, and Serbia (Western Balkan)' in S Koch and MM Kjølstad (eds), *Handbook on Legal Cultures* (Cham, Springer, 2023); S Forić, M Dokić and D Vuković-Ćalasan, 'Historical Trajectories and Shared Destiny as a Basis for Common Legal Identity: The Cases of Bosnia and Herzegovina and Montenegro' in C Cercel, A Mercescu and MM Sadowski (eds), *Law, Culture and Identity in Central and Eastern Europe: Comparative Engagement* (Abingdon, Oxon/New York, NJ, Routledge, 2024); R Demneri and A Punev, 'The Ever-Blurred Features of the Rule of Law: Albania and Bulgaria' in C Cercel, A Mercescu and MM Sadowski (eds), *Law, Culture and Identity in Central and Eastern Europe: Comparative Engagement* (Abingdon, Oxon/New York, NJ, Routledge, 2024).

My predecessor and mentor Ivo M Tomić, a socio-legal scholar of philosophical inclination, deemed my other studies positive and encouraged me to continue them in sociology. My other professors had a quite different attitude, discouraging those studies and scorning any attempts to introduce broader perspectives (political or sociological) to the doctrinal issues, deeming them transgressive. My choice to pursue an academic career outside of law was regarded as a waste of talent. The general perception toward sociology of law has changed over the last 15 years.

My other studies, namely in sociology, set me on a path to develop a more theoretical, critical and reflective habitus. Subsequently, I developed a socio-legal habitus, that implies two types of engagement: (a) active investment in the scholarship's field, and (b) trying to maintain the balance between external and internal perspectives of law. The first part of engagement led me to experience the liminality condition firsthand. In the start of my academic career, I found myself in an estranged environment – where I was the estranged one. My professor was employed by the Sarajevo law school and his only involvement in the Department of Sociology was in teaching a course on sociology of law – introduced in the mid-2000s as an elective course. His absence, in terms of full-time department membership, coupled with the fact that I only enrolled to sociology studies at the Master of Arts level and was only assigned to provide teaching assistance to the course in sociology of law, meant that my presence in the sociology department was deemed intrusive. As 'that lawyer kid' who possessed only a Master of Arts diploma in sociology, I aroused suspicion rather than trust. Suspicion was not directed only toward me but towards the course in general due to the traditional disdain of sociology for anything that concerns law. The relationships gradually warmed and I was also assigned to courses on sociology of religion and introduction to sociology. Still, the sense of alienation emanating from the liminality condition only strengthened my resolution to develop as a socio-legal scholar. And I did so by actively investing myself into the field through the usual scholarly activities such as researching, networking and innovating the course's syllabus.

My first paper about the law, society and legal culture in Japan managed to reduce the said suspicion and arouse some academic interest.[105] My second paper addressed the problem sociology of law faces in terms of its epistemological and institutional-disciplinary borders with both sociology and law as institutional domains of knowledge.[106] The paper managed to pique an interest from the broader sociological community in my home country, as it was seen as a fresh take on the matter. The ideas from the paper were refined and comprised the conceptual core of my doctoral dissertation that dealt with the

[105] Forić (2012) (n 103).

[106] S Forić, 'Sociology of Law and the Problem of Normative Closure of Legal Discourse' (2014) 4(7) *Sociological Discourse* 137, 156.

legal professions in contemporary Bosnia and Herzegovina. I provided an analysis of social action of the professional groups revolving around judiciary (judges, prosecutors and attorneys at law) in the process of the early 2000s overall legal and judicial reforms.[107]

The dissertation was an outcome of both researching and networking. The latter led to my visit to the Department of Sociology of Law at Lund University on two separate occasions in 2017, where I had access to library resources lacking in the regional libraries. It was an opportunity to consult with my host colleagues, especially the late Reza Banakar whose works inspired the dissertation in the first place. One year later, I was invited to participate in the regional comparative research on legal professions in Croatia, Serbia and Bosnia and Herzegovina mentioned above. The principal findings were presented at the Research Committee in Sociology of Law Meeting in Lisbon in 2018 and published in Richard A. Abel and other's edition of *Lawyers in 21st Century Societies. Volume I: National Reports*.[108]

My visits to Lund and subsequent networking yielded even more beneficial results. The exchange of ideas with my fellow hosts and students facilitated innovations in the syllabus of the course on sociology of law, in terms of content, teaching methods and literature. It also led to the proposal of a course on sociology of deviance and social control, developed in cooperation with Ida Nafstad. The proposal was accepted, and the course was introduced as compulsory at the Master of Arts study program in 2019. The addition of a new, and by the accounts of my departmental colleagues, more 'sociological' course, along with the sociology of law course gaining compulsory status several years earlier, aided in affirmation of my status and recognition by my immediate academic community. During my Lund stay, I was influenced by the dominant school of thought of that time, the normative-based approach proposed by Håkan Hydén. I wrote a paper about the approach in which I analysed its role in process of the sociology of law department's path to institutional independence and revitalisation of the scholarship in Scandinavia.[109] A thematic unit on norms and normativity was introduced in the sociology of law syllabus. It has proved to be quite suitable for students of sociology, since they are more equipped to study social rather than legal norms. In addition, it presents the opportunity for the students in sociology to sharpen their empirical research skills given that the

[107] Forić 2019 (n 4).

[108] Vuković, Dabetić and Forić (n 4).

[109] S Forić, 'Normativno razmatranje društva i pristup zasnovan na normama: primjer nordijske škole sociologije prava' in M Čamo and A Osmić (eds), *Pola stoljeća sociologije u Bosni i Hercegovini* (Sarajevo, Fakultet političkih nauka Univerziteta u Sarajevu, 2020) 89–124. I chose to write the paper in the local language (Bosnian, Croat, Serbian) so it would be easier for the regional readers to access its content. The idea of the paper was to introduce the development of socio-legal scholarship in the European North, to analyse, in Bourdieu terminology, the emergence of the particular field of study and its agents such as Håkan Hydén, and to introduce the basic precepts of the norm-based approach: concepts, methods, theoretical and analytical framework and practical application.

norm-based approach corresponds to the inductive methodology that they learn during their final year of the Bachelor of Arts study in Sarajevo.

IV. CONCLUSION

The Western Balkans region is a site of pioneering socio-legal research that only came into full fruition some 60 years after the publication of Bogišić's book *Miscellany of the Current Legal Customs of South Slavs* from 1874. This monumental publication serves as a starting point and primal reference in terms of importance, and not simply chronology, for the academic constitution of regional socio-legal scholarship. The trajectory of the scholarship was dissected into three historical phases. In the first or inception phase, sociology of law was, together with rural sociology, a framework for institutionalisation of general sociology and its subsequent development, mostly owing to the work of Đorđe Tasić. This fact, coupled with Bogišić's historical importance for social sciences in general and particularly law, substantiates the claim that socio-legal scholarship was avantgarde in that early era (between late 1800s and early 1940s).

Still, the tectonic change to which the region was subjected shifted the trajectory downwards. In the following phase, lasting from the early 1950s and mid-1980s, sociology of law found itself in a state of encapsulation. Its institutional clustering with legal theory and philosophy led to its epistemological assimilation. It was reduced to mere nominal existence and even that borrowed type of existence was subjected to a condition of instrumentality, a built-in evaluation mechanism whose ultimate outcome was that sociology of law was deemed unnecessary. These academic developments reflected wider political and ideological trends in which legal scholarship turned into a hegemony – diminishing toward non-normative, non-dogmatic ideas and dismissive toward those aiming to, both theoretically and empirically, examine the relation between law and society, as highlighted by cases of Visković and Goričar respectively. On the other side of town, sociology, revitalised and entrusted with an important public role of advancing the socialist self-management path, completely ignored its earlier trajectory and abstained from treating state, law, and social control as its academic subjects, as if they were monopolised by legal scholarship. This development bred a condition of liminality for sociology of law, denouncing the discipline's sociological identity.

Both conditions survived the end of the Yugoslav state. However, new development such as globalisation, internalisation and modernisation of higher education, contributed to the emancipation of sociology of law, where it found itself in the position to effectively challenge and even subvert those conditions. The emancipation is reflective of the upward trajectory of the scholarship, manifesting in its introduction to curricula both in and legal and sociological education. It is also manifesting in unprecedented levels of academic production, encompassing textbooks, monographs, edited volumes and papers. The ongoing innovation of educational programmes both in law and sociology, along with the increasing demand for interdisciplinary scholarship, inter-regional and trans-regional cooperation should further expand the field to up-and-coming scholars. It is already comprised of the mid and younger generation as it stands, constituting cadres in their respective affiliated institutions.[110] Almost 60 years ago, Mandić identified lack of cadres as a root cause of regional socio-legal underdevelopment, dubbing it as lack of supply in relation to the growing demand. At this point in time, one could argue that the supply and the demand are not that unevenly matched. The prospects of socio-legal scholarship in the region provide reason for optimism.

[110] It is worth noting that these cadres are not only present region-wide, but that their composition reflect the trends of present-day gender balance that is evident in both legal and sociological scholarship. Moreover, regional socio-legal scholarship is gradually becoming more feminised, with rising scholars such as Kristina Čufar (Ljubljana), Mateja Čehulić (Zagreb), Valerija Dabetić and Milica Đorđević (Belgrade) and Aleksandra Lj. Mitrović (Kosovska Mitrovica), all below 30 years of age.

5

Outline of a Danish Socio-Legal Trajectory Interconnected with Sociology of Law in Norway and Sweden

OLE HAMMERSLEV

> 'To understand is first to understand the field with which and against which one has been formed.'[1]

> '[R]eflexive analysis must consider successively position in the social space, position in the field and position in the scholastic universe. How, without surrendering to narcissistic self-indulgence, can one apply this programme to oneself and perform the sociology of oneself, one's self-socioanalysis, given that such an analysis can only be a starting-point and that the sociology of the object that I am, the objectivation of my point of view, is a necessarily collective task?'[2]

It would be tempting to claim that sociology of law in Denmark to a large extent developed through shadowboxing with Alf Ross's concept of law and his focus on judicial behaviour.[3] Theoretically, his Scandinavian legal realism concept of law and his focus on judicial behaviour inspired the first Danish socio-legal studies. Both Theodor Geiger's theoretical development of sociology of law and Verner Goldschmidt et al's studies on judicial behaviour in Greenland developed in dialogues with and with inspiration from Ross's work.[4] Ross reviewed and went into discussions with these early Danish socio-legal

[1] P Bourdieu, *Sketch for a Self-Analysis* (Chicago, University of Chicago Press, 2008) 4.

[2] P Bourdieu, *Science of Science and Reflexivity* (Cambridge, Polity Press, 2004) 94.

[3] Alf Ross was a distinguished Danish legal philosopher and scholar. As a leading figure in Scandinavian legal realism, Ross championed the empirical study of law, focusing on its practical applications rather than abstract or theoretical concepts. His seminal work, *On Law and Justice* (London, Stevens and Sons, 1958), offers a critical analysis of traditional legal theory and introduces a new framework grounded in realistic and empirical methodologies.

[4] T Geiger, *Vorstudien zu einer Soziologie des Rechts* (Berlin, Duncker & Humblot, 1947); V Goldschmidt, P Lindegaard and AW Bentzon, *Betænkning afgivet af den juridiske ekspedition til Grønland 1948–1949* (København, Statsministeriet, 1950).

studies,[5] just as he went into dialogue with the founder of Norwegian sociology of law, Vilhelm Aubert.[6] These dialogues, inter alia, inspired the professor in Sociology of Law at Aarhus University, Jørgen Dalberg-Larsen.[7] Dalberg-Larsen stimulated my generation of (the few) Danish socio-legal scholars to move into the sociology of law. We came from law and read Dalberg-Larsen's textbook on sociology of law.[8] Thus Dalberg-Larsen's understanding of sociology of law shaped our initial comprehension of the topic with its theoretical focus on the mainly European classics, such as Max Weber, Karl Marx, Jürgen Habermas and Niklas Luhmann, and empirical focus on public legal institutions and legal professionals – and very often mostly in a national or Nordic setting.[9]

This historical legacy and formation of the field conditioned the possibilities of my socio-legal practices when I entered the field around the millennium as a PhD student. This paper outlines my trajectory in relation to the development of the socio-legal field in Scandinavia. By doing this, my trajectory exemplifies the development of the conditioned 'space of possible' relating to scholarly practices, such as the importance of internationalisation, change of publication strategies and importance of external funding.[10]

First, the chapter discusses how it methodologically relies on Bourdieu's 'Why the Social Sciences Must Take Themselves as Their Object' and *Sketch for a Self-Analysis*.[11] Second, the chapter reflects on outlining the field of sociology of law in Scandinavia from around the millennium. Next it goes into an analysis of my trajectory starting with my position as PhD student, then my postdoc period and finally to my affiliation with the Department of Criminology and Sociology of Law at the University of Oslo in Norway and my move to the Sociology of Law Department at Lund University in Sweden.

I. METHODOLOGY

This chapter takes a backdrop against the Bourdieusian sociological tools and devices of how to write self-trajectories. According to Bourdieu,[12] an analysis of your own position needs to be considered in relation to the field that has formed you and in which you are navigating and positioning yourself. Linking

[5] T Geiger, 'Svar til Professor Alf Ross' [1946] *Juristen* 309–24; A Ross, 'Om begrebet 'gældende ret' hos Theodor Geiger' (1950) 63 *Tidsskrift for Rettsvitenskap* 242–72.

[6] A Ross, 'Review of: *En lov i søkelyset*' [1953] *Juristen* 367–72.

[7] J Dalberg-Larsen, 'Alf Ross and the Sociology of Law' (2005) 48 *Scandinavian Studies in Law* 39–50.

[8] J Dalberg-Larsen, *Lovene og Livet* (København, Jurist- og Økonomforbundets Forlag, 1999).

[9] Dalberg-Larsen's focus in his textbooks (J Dalberg-Larsen, *Retssociologi – problemstillinger og teorier* (København, Akademisk Forlag, 1973); Dalberg-Larsen (n 8)) was to a large degree inspired by Aubert's understanding of the topic (V Aubert, *Rettssosiologi* (Oslo, Universitetsforlaget, 1982).

[10] Bourdieu (n 2) (on a variety of such signifiers, see eg S Machura, 'Milestones and Directions: Socio-Legal Studies in Germany and the United Kingdom' (2020) 21 *German Law Journal* 1318–31.

[11] Bourdieu (n 2), (n 1).

[12] ibid.

Bourdieu's writings on self-analysis with his writings on 'Who Created the Creator' and 'The Biographic Illusion',[13] it is crucial to understand the position one can obtain and develop in the field by focusing on the historical and interlinked developments of the field.

Yet, when examining one's trajectory from a specific position in the field – or positionality with specific outlook, network, institutional affiliations, resources and scholarly traditions – it is inevitable that the story of the trajectory is particular. Nonetheless, it becomes possible to reconstruct the field through biographies and literature of the key persons who have developed the field's institutions, journals and scientific infrastructure, on the one hand, and on the other, those who have shaped the field in terms of concepts, theories and focus, inclusive of textbooks devising and defining the understandings of the field's doxa. Thus, the perspectives and the narrative will automatically focus on dominating persons and thus exclude and/or marginalise other scholars.

The data, which the chapter is based on, are biographies of key persons in the field, key persons' own writings about the structures of the field, institutional information, textbooks and other publications. Moreover, it relies on personal conversations with different scholars in the field. Thus, the chapter surveys qualitatively the interconnected histories of the development of the socio-legal trajectories in Scandinavia.

II. MY TRAJECTORY

To understand my own trajectory, it is necessary to outline the potential room for action by outlining the trajectory of the socio-legal field I entered as a PhD student at the Department of Sociology, University of Copenhagen around the millennium. At the time, sociology of law was marginalised in Denmark. Specifically, in terms of the individual researcher's position at their respective departments, it was represented by very few scholars and was spread out at different universities and struggled to get attention among students and legal scholars. Sociology of law was an adjunct to law and only very sporadically treated in sociology, which can be illustrated by the fact that it neither played a role, if mentioned at all, in Danish textbooks in sociology, nor was it in the curricula in sociology even when reading the sociological classics.

The socio-legal studies conducted in the 1980s and 1990s generally focused on theoretical issues, particularly criticising the dominating positivistic concept of law with a few exceptions.[14] Sociology of law, it was argued, was a part of

[13] P Bourdieu, *Sociology in Question* (London, Sage Publications, 1993); P Bourdieu, *Men hvem skabte skaberne?* (København, Akademisk Forlag, 1997).

[14] O Hammerslev and MR Madsen, 'The Return of Sociology in Danish Socio-Legal Studies: A Survey of Recent Trends' (2014) 10 *International Journal of Law in Context* 397–415; H Petersen, *Informel ret på kvindearbejdspladser* (København, Akademisk Forlag, 1991).

legal sciences and the general audience was from law.[15] This can be illustrated by Dalberg-Larsen's inquiries into the theoretical developments of the sociology of law. He published a number of books and papers on the concept of law against the background of, for example, post-modernism, legal pragmatism and pluralism.[16] While sociology of law at the law degree in Copenhagen was only a minor topic, with Dalberg-Larsen's textbook as mandatory reading,[17] the research on the topic was sporadic and the professor on the topic conducted research within criminology. At the Department of Sociology, University of Copenhagen, the topic was non-exciting except for Bertilsson's sporadic and mainly theoretical take on it.[18]

Upon transitioning from law to the Department of Sociology, my primary reading in the sociology of law was Dalberg-Larsen's textbook. Additionally, during a stay in London, I studied jurisprudence and the works of Giddens.[19] As a PhD student in sociology, I needed to read both sociological and socio-legal classics to, as my supervisor Bertilsson put it, 'demonstrate your sociological education ("Bildung" in German)'.

I was recruited to a project on the transformation of the legal profession and expert knowledge with then professor in sociology Margareta Bertilsson as principal investigator (PI), she was also my supervisor. Bertilsson had an interest in sociology of law and legal professions, which to a large degree was inspired by Weber,[20] the aforementioned Ross and Geiger debate, Vilhelm Aubert, Jürgen Habermas and Rick Abel and Philip Lewis' collection *Lawyers in Society*.[21] Compared to many legal scholars at the time, Bertilsson's profile was very

[15] J Dalberg-Larsen, 'Sociology of Law from a Legal Point of View' (2000) 23 *Retfærd.Nordic Legal Journal* 71–80; H Hydén, *Rättssociologi som rättsvetenskap* (Lund, Studentlitteratur, 2002).

[16] J Dalberg-Larsen, *Ret, tekst og kontekst* (København, Jurist- og Økonomforbundets Forlag, 1998); J Dalberg-Larsen, *The Unity of Law: An illusion?: On Legal Pluralism in Theory and Practice* (Berlin, Galda und Wilch Verlag, 2000); J Dalberg-Larsen, *Pragmatisk retsteori* (Jurist- og Økonomforbundet, 2001); J Dalberg-Larsen, *Ret, tekst & kontekst : postmodernisme og ret* (Jurist- og Økonomforbundet, 2007).

[17] Dalberg-Larsen (n 8).

[18] M Bertilsson, 'The Legal Profession and Law in the Welfare State' in AA Aarnia and T Kaarlo (eds) *Law, Morality, and Discursive Rationality* (Helsinki, Helsingin yliopisto, 1989); M Bertilsson (ed), *Rätten i Förvandling. Jurister mellan stat och marknad* (Stockholm, Nerenius & Santerus Förlag, 1995); M Bertilsson, 'An Ancient Science? On the Continuing Relevance of Law' in R Björk and K Molin (eds), *Societies Made Up of History* (Edsbruk, Akademitryck, 1996); M Bertilsson, 'On the Role of the Professions and Professional Knowledge in Global Development' in GEA Therborn and L.-L. Wallenius (eds), *Globalizations and modernities: experiences and perspectives of European and Latin America 99:5* (Stockholm, Forskningsrådsnämnden, 1999).

[19] A Giddens, *The Constitution of Society: Outline of the Theory of Structuration* (Cambridge, Polity Press, 1986); A Giddens, *Consequences of Modernity* (Cambridge, Polity Press, 1990); A Giddens, *New Rules of Sociological Method* (Cambridge, Polity Press, 1993).

[20] M Weber, *Economy and Society* (Berkeley, University of California Press, 1978).

[21] RL Abel and PSC Lewis (eds), *Lawyers in Society. The Civil Law World* (Berkeley, University of California Press, 1988); RL Abel and PSC Lewis (eds), *Lawyers in Society. The Common Law World* (Berkeley, University of California Press, 1988); RL Abel and PSC Lewis (eds), *Lawyers in Society. Comparative Theories* (Berkeley, University of California Press, 1989).

international. She came to Copenhagen from a position as lecturer in sociology at Lund University, had her master's degree and PhD from the University of California at Santa Barbara and had been on sabbatical abroad several times during her career. Moreover, she had been a member of the Independent Research Council Denmark and knew about the importance of attracting external funding in a time when it was not as important as today and definitely not as competitive. Soon after I started, Bertilsson introduced me to Aubert's influential article on the Norwegian legal profession and lent me her Abel and Lewis books as well as her own texts on the Swedish legal profession.[22] The project I joined aimed to examine the role of the legal profession in Denmark using data similar to Aubert's, to facilitate a comparison of the professions across Scandinavian countries. However, Aubert's studies, and the very few I found in Denmark on the Danish legal profession,[23] were embedded in functional theory. I realised, though, that Thomas Mathiesen had also studied the Norwegian legal profession, but with inspiration in Marxism.[24] I wanted to combine the perspectives and, at the same time, provide the expected data. Bertilsson lent me Pierre Bourdieu's *The State Nobility*,[25] which became an eye-opener and inspired me to combine the Scandinavian studies through a Bourdieusian framework. In my later studies, I was quite inspired by the Bourdieusian tools especially as they were used by Dezalay and Garth.[26]

III. THE 'STEPCHILD DEBATE'

Another important scholar for my career, who also introduced me to the latest international socio-legal discussions, was Reza Banakar. In 1997, Banakar moved to the Centre for Socio-Legal Studies in Oxford from the Sociology of Law Department in Lund, where he wrote and defended his PhD thesis.[27]

[22] V Aubert, 'The Changing Role of Law and Lawyers in Nineteenth- and Twentieth-Century Norwegian Society' in DN MacCormick (ed), *Lawyers in Their Social Setting* (Edinburgh, Green, 1976); Bertilsson (1989) (n 18); Bertilsson (1995) (n 18).

[23] BM Blegvad, *Juristernes rolle i samfundet* (Copenhagen, Nyt fra Samfundsvidenskaberne, 1973); BM Blegvad, 'De juridiske eksperter – tre professioner' in HEA Gullestrup (ed), *Eksperterne og magten: Professionelles rolle i organisationer og samfund* (København, Nyt Nordisk Forlag Arnold Busck, 1975). For an overview, see O Hammerslev, 'Convergence and Conflict Perspectives in Scandinavian Studies of the Legal Profession' (2010) 17 *International Journal of the Legal Profession* 135–52.

[24] T Mathiesen, *Ideologi og motstand* (Oslo, Pax Forlag, 1979).

[25] P Bourdieu, *The State Nobility. Elite Schools in the Field of Power* (Cambridge, Policy Press, 1996).

[26] Y Dezalay and BG Garth, *Dealing in Virtue. International Commercial Arbitration and the Construction of a Transnational Legal Order* (Chicago, University of Chicago Press, 1996); Y Dezalay and BG Garth, *The Internationalization of Palaces War: Lawyers, Economists, and the Contest to Transform Latin American States* (Chicago, University of Chicago Press, 2002).

[27] R Banakar, *Doorkeepers of the Law: A Socio-Legal Study of Ethnic Discrimination in Sweden* (Aldershot, Dartmouth/Ashgate, 1998).

Banakar had just published his stepchild article in the Nordic journal *Retfærd*.[28] In contrast to the majority of articles published in the journal, Banakar's was written in English. It argued that sociology of law was in a state of crisis. Banakar argued that for sociology of law to be recognized as a scientific field in its own right, it needed coherent theories and concepts that took both law and sociology seriously. Additionally, it had to be methodologically robust, meeting the scientific standards of its parent disciplines. The article sparked a debate among Nordic socio-legal scholars, all written in English, which was quite unusual.[29] In 2000, Banakar presented his article at a colloquium I organised in Copenhagen with participation of socio-legal scholars from all the Nordic countries. In many ways this debate invited self-reflection on the topic and not least on the methodological requirements for socio-legal studies. Thus, suddenly, the conceptualisation of sociology of law being an adjunct to law changed. It should be seen as a scientific field in its own right with specific methodological requirements. Banakar's article can also be seen as the beginning of a turn in Nordic sociology of law, pushing it towards international socio-legal agendas and methodologies.[30] Banakar insisted that sociology of law needed to live up to methodological standards and agendas that could be seen in sociology. Banakar's insistence that sociology of law had to take both law and sociology seriously also had an impact on my thesis, where I tried to examine judges' legal and social position.[31]

An illustration of the marginalization of sociology of law is that, due to the lack of a socio-legal environment, I, along with two PhD students from the law faculty, Rasmus Wandall and Christian Borch, who were researching the intersection of criminology and sociology of law, established a socio-legal study group. It included Hanne Petersen, Agnete Weis Bentzon, Torben Agersnap and others. We wanted not only to read the classics, but also to establish a forum that could discuss common research interests and projects. The forum did not receive the attention we had hoped, which illustrates the marginal position of sociology of law at the time, and it was dissolved around the time I submitted my PhD.

The first socio-legal conference I attended was – at the time – a bi-annual Nordic meeting with participants from all the Nordic countries with Scandinavian as main languages. The keynote speakers were – as far as I can recollect – the

[28] R Banakar, 'The Identity Crisis of a "Stepchild": Reflections on the Paradigmatic Deficiencies of Sociology of Law' (1998) 21 *Retfærd.Nordic Legal Journal* 3–21.

[29] H Hydén, 'Even a Stepchild Eventually Grows Up: On the Identity of Sociology of Law' (1999) 22 *Retfærd.Nordic Legal Journal* 71–80; T Mathiesen, 'Is It All That Bad to Be a Stepchild? Comments on the State of Sociology of Law' (1998) 21 *Retfærd.Nordic Legal Journal* 57–68; Dalberg-Larsen (n 15); IJ Sand, 'A Future or a Demise for the Theory of the Sociology of Law' (2000) 90 *Retfærd. Nordic Journal of Law and Justice* 55–73.

[30] Hammerslev and Madsen (n 14); O Hammerslev and MR Madsen, 'Reza Banakar and the Quest for a Sociology of Law' in H Håkan, C Roger, N David and S Ulrike (eds), *Combining the Legal and the Social in Sociology of Law: An Homage to Reza Banakar* (Oxford, Hart, 2023).

[31] O Hammerslev, *Danish Judges in the 20th Century: A Socio-Legal Study* (Copenhagen, DJØF Publishing, 2003).

male professors from the different countries. The PhD students, including me, presented our papers in smaller groups with senior scholars as commentators. At the time, we had no discussions about publication of the papers, and everyone wrote their thesis as a monograph – mostly in Scandinavian. However, I soon discovered the Law and Society Association and began to attend the meetings, with the annual meeting in Budapest (in 2001) as the first.

I visited Banakar as a student at the Centre for Socio-Legal Studies in Oxford in 2001 and remained in close contact with him until his passing. In the early 2000s, when no books on socio-legal methodology existed, Banakar generously invited me to two workshops he and Max Travers organized on the topic. The first workshop was held in Oxford in 2000, and the second took place at the International Institute for the Sociology of Law in Oñati, Spain, in 2003. These workshops led to their English-language collections, *An Introduction to Law and Social Theory* and *Theory and Method in Socio-Legal Research*.[32] Not only was my early involvement with icons Banakar and Travers crucial for my career, but it also provided me with exposure to English at a time when most of my colleagues, particularly in law and many in sociology, were still primarily publishing in Danish.

IV. EXTERNAL FUNDING AND INTERNATIONAL AGENDAS

At the time when I finished my PhD thesis, it was clear that there was an overproduction of PhD students at the Department of Sociology, and sociology of law was not a prioritised area of study. This meant that most of my PhD colleagues and I had to, if we wanted to stay in academia, find jobs at other departments or universities or find funding for a postdoc via, for example, the Independent Research Council Denmark – Social Sciences. In Denmark at the time, it was still possible to apply for an individual postdoc, which I did. But I did it without support from professional fundraisers or research support officers, which were not a visible part of Danish universities at the time. With a project concerning the production of assistance programmes and promotion of the rule of law in relation to the European Union enlargement towards Eastern Europe, I was lucky to get funding for two years. I applied from the Department of Sociology, knowing that it would be difficult pursuing a career at the department after my postdoc, as sociology of law was not a priority.

However, I heard that the law department at the University of Southern Denmark was about to establish a law degree. Following the international expansion of legal educational institutions,[33] the university, like the University of

[32] R Banakar and M Travers, M (eds), *An Introduction to Law and Social Theory* (Oxford, Hart Publishing, 2002); R Banakar and M Travers (eds), *Theory and Method in Socio-Legal Research* (Oxford, Hart Publishing, 2005).

[33] O Hammerslev, 'Globalisation and Education: Reconfigurations in Location, Scale, Form and Content' in RL Abel, H Sommerlad, O Hammerslev and U Schultz (eds), *Lawyers in 21st-Century Societies vol. 2: Comparisons and Theories* (Oxford, Hart Publishing, 2022).

Aalborg, recognized the importance of law due to estimates indicating sufficient potential students and an increasing demand for law graduates in regions outside Denmark's two largest cities. The Department of Law recruited legal scholars to take part in the establishment of the law degree, including – apparently – a socio-legal scholar. I contacted them and was overwhelmed by their enthusiasm, and I had no doubt of taking my funding with me to the University of Southern Denmark in 2004. Although it was not a tenure-track position, which did not really exist at the time, the department's leadership laid out a career plan for me. This was common in Danish legal departments at the time, given their expansion and sufficient funding. The department had its first intake of law students in 2004. This proved to be an opening for my career in terms of research, teaching, administration and dialogue with the surroundings – all aspects that would only become increasingly important over time.

The topic of my postdoc project opened new possibilities of relating to different scholars within different scholarly streams: Bourdieusian scholars examining different social aspects of society, state transformations, the European Union and Eastern Europe. Different opportunities opened up. First, in order to understand the Bourdieusian sociological tools better, I engaged in the Nordic Bourdieusian association, Hexis. Nordic Forum for Cultural and Social Sciences. In this we intensely read Bourdieu's books in study groups, such as *The State Nobility*,[34] *The Rules of Art*,[35] *The Social Structure of the Economy*,[36] *The Weight of the World*[37] and *Outline of a Theory of Practice*.[38] Second, I came into contact with Yves Dezalay and Bryant Garth, and not only did I join their 2004 Law and Society graduate workshop, but I was also invited to several sessions and meetings with them, including one in Chicago, which led to another chapter in an international collection.[39] Through this network, I also met and organised sessions at the Law and Society meetings with Mikael Rask Madsen, who had written his PhD with Dezalay as supervisor in Paris and had come back to the University of Copenhagen to study international courts, and a number of French scholars studying the construction of Europe, such as Antonin Cohen and Antoine Vauchez.[40] The Bourdieusian focus showed that there existed a gap

[34] Bourdieu (n 25).

[35] P Bourdieu, *The Rules of Art: Genesis and Structure of the Literary Field* (Cambridge, Polity Press, 1996).

[36] P Bourdieu, *The Social Structures of the Economy* (Cambridge, Polity Press, 2005).

[37] P Bourdieu, *The Weight of the World: Social Suffering in Contemporary Society* (Cambridge, Polity Press, 1999).

[38] P Bourdieu, *Outline of a Theory of Practice* (Cambridge, Cambridge University Press, 1977).

[39] O Hammerslev, 'The European Union and the United States in Eastern Europe: Two Ways of Exporting Law, Expertise and State Power' in Y Dezalay and BG Garth (eds), *Lawyers and the Rule of Law in an Era of Globalization* (New York, Routledge, 2011).

[40] A Cohen, 'Who Are the Masters of the Treaties? Law and Politics in the Birth of European Constitutionalism' [2007] *Praktiske Grunde.Tidsskrift for kultur- og samfundsvidenskab* 20–33; A Vauchez, 'Interstitial Power in Fields of Limited Statehood: Introducing a Weak Field Approach to the Study of Transnational Settings' (2011) 5 *International Political Sociology* 340–45.

in the literature on Bourdieu's engagement with the law, methodology, and then, Bourdieu's engagement with the state. This led to different publications both in English and Danish focusing on different aspects of Bourdieusian sociology, including a special issue of *Retfærd. Nordic Journal of Law and Justice* on Bourdieu on law,[41] Bourdieu and the state[42] and Bourdieu and methods.[43]

Moreover, the network also put me in contact with Bourdieusian scholars at the Educational and Cultural Sociology Group at Uppsala University where I was based as a visiting scholar through the period 2006–09. At the time, the department was led by Donald Broady who was one of the main figures in Scandinavia when it came to Bourdieusian scholarship. He had established a group of scholars examining various fields, such as the field of art and the field of education and developed different forms of geometric data analysis.[44] Compared to my home institution, the University of Southern Demark Department of Law, Uppsala University was very good at attracting external funding, and I realised how professionally they ran that part of their research practices.

V. LEGAL EDUCATION

In 2007, I got a permanent position as associate professor at the Department of Law, University of Southern Denmark. From 2009–13, I was the head of studies focusing on a number of new tasks coming to the university from the outside, such as accreditations, evaluations and collaboration with the surrounding society. In parallel, I took part in the *Menu for Justice* project between 2009–13. The project included scholars and legal practitioners from various disciplines and institutions from 30 European countries, and it was funded by the Life Long Learning Programme of the European Union. We explored different experiences of legal and judicial training. The final product was, in addition to two books,[45] recommendations for the European Union Commission on legal education and judicial training in Europe. Thus, legal education would be a sideline of my research and teaching practices, and it is closely linked to my interest in legal

[41] O Hammerslev and MR Madsen, 'Introduction: Pierre Bourdieu: From Law to Legal Field' (2006) 29 *Retfærd. Nordic Journal of Law and Justice* 1–5.

[42] J Arnholtz and O Hammerslev, 'Transcended Power of the State: The Role of Actors in Pierre Bourdieu's Sociology of the State' (2013) 14 *Distinktion: Scandinavian Journal of Social Theory* 42–64.

[43] O Hammerslev, J Arnholtz Hansen and I Willig, *Refleksiv sociologi i praksis: Empiriske undersøgelser inspireret af Pierre Bourdieu* (København, Hans Reitzels Forlag, 2009).

[44] D Broady, *Sociologi och Epistemologi: Om Pierre Bourdieus författarskap och den historiske epistemologin* (Stockholm, HLS Förlag, 1991); D Broady, 'French Prosopography. Definition and Suggested Readings' (2002) 30 *Poetics* 381; M Börjesson and D Broady, 'The Social Profile of Swedish Law Students: National Divisions and Transnational Strategies' (2006) 29 *Retfærd. Nordic Legal Journal* 80–107.

[45] D Piana, P Langbroek, T Berkmanas, O Hammerslev and OE Pacurari, *Legal and Judicial Training in Europe* (The Hague, Eleven International Publishing, 2013); P Policastro, (ed), *Towards Innovation in Legal Education* (The Hague, Eleven International Publishing, 2013).

professions and to classic Norwegian sociology of law about legal clinics (see below).[46]

Co-coordinating a Bachelor course in legal history, jurisprudence and sociology of law, I was frustrated with student evaluations of the existing literature in both jurisprudence – where we relied on too difficult English textbooks – and with Dalberg-Larsen's textbook in sociology of law.[47] Since the need for a book in jurisprudence was the most urgent, I asked Henrik Palmer Olsen, who is professor of jurisprudence at the University of Copenhagen, and my previous supervisor on my master's thesis on Ross and Dworkin,[48] if he wanted to co-edit a new book. At the University of Southern Denmark, we had used *Lloyd's Introduction to Jurisprudence*,[49] which both consisted of introductory texts and original extracts of key texts within jurisprudence (I knew the earlier version of the book from a course in jurisprudence I followed at the University College London in the middle of the 1990s). Instead of writing everything ourselves, we invited experts in Denmark to write the introductory texts and choose relevant original extracts. This resulted in a new book that is still used both in Copenhagen and at the University of Southern Denmark.[50]

After the publication of the book on jurisprudence, together with Mikael Rask Madsen, we invited Scandinavian socio-legal scholars to contribute similarly to an introduction in sociology of law. We wanted a book in Danish that did not have one theoretical or methodological paradigm but showed a range of approaches to the sociology of law. Moreover, we wanted it to cover a variety of empirical socio-legal topics, such as the legal profession, courts, law and politics and globalisation. To a certain extent, the focus of the first edition was shaped by the heritage from the existing Scandinavian textbooks in general and Dalberg-Larsen's in particular. While the first edition covered the history of Scandinavian sociology of law, these chapters had to be taken out in the second edition to get more space for more contemporary subjects.[51] The book is now used in Denmark, Norway and Sweden. An anecdote about the reception

[46] (Hammerslev (n 33); O Hammerslev, A Oleson and OH Rønning, 'Juss-Buss [Law Bus]: A Student-Run Legal Aid Clinic' in O Halvorsen, OH Rønning and O Hammerslev (eds), *Outsourcing Legal Aid in the Nordic Welfare States* (London, Palgrave, 2018).

[47] J Dalberg-Larsen, *Lovene og Livet: En retssociologisk grundbog* (København, Jurist- og Økonomforbundets Forlag, 2005).

[48] Published as my first academic article, see O Hammerslev, 'Myten om Herkules. Ronald Dworkins fortolkningsteori konfronteret med Alf Ross' (2000) *Retfærd. Nordisk Juridisk Tidsskrift* 3–15.

[49] MDA Freeman, *Lloyd's Introduction to Jurisprudence* (London, Sweet & Maxwell, 2008); H Genn, *Paths to Justice: What People Do and Think About Going to Law* (Oxford, Hart Publishing, 1999).

[50] O Hammerslev and H Palmer Olsen (eds), *Retsfilosofi. Centrale tekster og temaer* (København, Hans Reitzels Forlag, 2011); O Hammerslev and H Palmer Olsen (eds), *Retsfilosofi. Centrale tekster og temaer* (København, Hans Reitzels Forlag, 2019).

[51] O Hammerslev and MR Madsen, MR (eds), *Retssociologi: Klassiske og moderne perspektiver* (København, Hans Reitzels Forlag, 2013); O Hammerslev and MR Madsen (eds), *Retssociologi: Klassiske og moderne perspektiver* (København, Hans Reitzels Forlag, 2022).

of the first edition can illustrate how some of the dominating persons viewed textbooks. Mikael and I were invited to the Department of Criminology and Sociology of Law, University of Oslo, to present the book. At the presentation, we were criticized for opening sociology of law up for all sorts of theories and thus for not having a traditional textbook with a coherent paradigm. The tradition in Oslo had been that the professor in the topic wrote the textbook for students; first Aubert wrote his and later Mathiesen wrote his, both of which were also used at the Sociology of Law Department in Lund.[52]

VI. THE LAWYERS IN TWENTY-FIRST CENTURY SOCIETIES PROJECT

Being at a law department meant that I had funding to go to international conferences and meetings even without external funding. One meeting that came to set the direction for my work for the next eight years was the 15th meeting of the International Working Group on the Legal Professions under the Research Committee on the Sociology of Law in Frauenchiemsee, Germany, in 2014. The working group had met biannually since 1986 and was created against the backdrop of the comparative Lawyers in Society project led by Abel and Lewis.[53] I had just been promoted to full professor, in 2014, after having been professor with special responsibilities from 2011–14, and I considered how to engage more collaboratively with legal professions. The working group meeting was a great venue for such collaborations. I had an idea of revisiting the 1988/89 Abel and Lewis volumes in order to celebrate the work 30 years after the original publications. At the meeting, Hilary Sommerlad suggested a project along these lines when she, in one of the plenaries, presented the need to study the recent dramatic transformation of the geopolitical order promoted by and affecting the legal profession. Our two ideas were in alignment and a new project was born. Hilary and I asked Ulrike Schultz, contributor to the original project and then chair of the working group, to take part. We also asked Abel to join our editorial group. We held some brainstorming meetings about which countries we wanted to include and which kinds of chapters we wanted in a comparative volume. Since the original volumes from the 1980s, the world had opened up, and it was suddenly possible to include countries like Iran, Kenya, Burundi, Nigeria, Palestine, Serbia, Bosnia and Herzegovina and Myanmar,

[52] V Aubert, *Rettens sosiale funksjon* (Oslo, Universitetsforlaget, 1976); Aubert (n 9); T Mathiesen, *Retten i samfunnet: En innføring i rettssosiologi* (Oslo, Pax Forlag, 2005).

[53] Abel and Lewis, *Lawyers in Society. The Civil Law World* (n 21); Abel and Lewis, *Lawyers in Society. The Common Law World* (n 21); Abel and Lewis, *Lawyers in Society. Comparative Theories* (n 21); RL Abel and PSC Lewis (eds), *Lawyers in Society: An Overview* (Berkeley, University of California Press, 1995).

and scholars knowledgeable about these countries whom we knew through various projects, the LSA and/or the RCSL. Moreover, emails and Dropbox made it possible to share information and data just as we had online meetings through AdobeConnect (this was before the pandemic). This should be compared with the work on the original volumes where they used typewriters, made corrections with Wite-Out, rarely made the very expensive international phone calls and were limited to snail mail for communicating and transmitting drafts.[54] We managed to cover 46 jurisdictions (compared to 19 in the original volumes) written by 77 authors in volume one,[55] and volume two had 26 chapters written by 47 authors.[56]

The experiences and network following from the work with the Lawyers in Twenty-First Century Society opened new doors. First, Sara Dezalay and I decided to continue the project on lawyers as an International Research Collaboration under the Law & Society Association, focusing on the weakness of the category of profession. I knew Sara from the old Dezalay and Garth project, where we met in Chicago, and through the work with the Lawyers in Twenty-First Century Society project to which she contributed. We found that the category of the legal profession was not sufficient to describe developments of legal professionals, especially in regions hitherto left outside of the scope of the sociology of legal professions, for example the African South and the Middle East. We wanted to shed light on the inherent Western ethnocentrism of legal professional scholarship and the limitations of methodological nationalism.[57] Sara and I determined that one difficulty revolves around the understanding of the state as a coherent entity undergoing linear transformations from colonialism to independence, state-led economy to market economy and authoritarianism to democracy. Instead, we wanted to learn from decolonial literature and shift the focus from the category of legal professions towards a focus on historical and entangled processes of transformations of national fields of state power stressing lawyers' key role as intermediaries. Thus, in the International Research Collaboration, we wanted to trace the legacies of the past – imperialism and colonialism – in the politics of the present, while recognising the interconnectedness between lawyers and state trajectories across borders.

[54] RL Abel, H Sommerlad, O Hammerslev and U Schultz, 'Preface' in RL Abel, H Sommerlad, O Hammerslev, and U Schultz (eds), *Lawyers in 21st-Century Societies: vol. 2: Comparisons and Theories* (Oxford, Hart Publishing, 2022).

[55] RL Abel, O Hammerslev, H Sommerlad and U Schultz, *Lawyers in 21st-Century Societies vol 1: National Reports* (Oxford, Hart Publishing, 2020).

[56] RL Abel, H Sommerlad, O Hammerslev and U Schultz (eds), *Lawyers in 21st-Century Societies vol. 2: Comparisons and Theories* (Oxford, Hart Publishing, 2022).

[57] H Sommerlad and O Hammerslev, 'Studying Lawyers Comparatively in the 21st Century: Issues in Method and Methodology' in RL Abel, H Sommerlad, O Hammerslev and U Schultz (eds), *Lawyers in 21st-Century Societies vol 2: Comparisons and Theories* 1st edn (Oxford, Hart Publishing, 2022).

Another outcome is a project currently underway, with Scott Cummings, Tamara Butter and Sergio Anzola, which is concerned with the sociology of legal ethics, which taps into some of the world's great challenges and the United Nations' global goals; and at least in Scandinavia this is timely as the universities focus on these issues. For the project, which will end as a handbook with Elgar Publishing, we have gathered approximately 36 scholars to write about different aspects of the sociology of legal ethics.

VII. PRE-DISPUTE PHASE, LEGAL AID AND WELFARE STATE ENCOUNTERS

As head of studies, I was involved in establishing a master's degree in Cultural Sociology and Law at the University of Southern Denmark in a collaboration between the Department of Law and the Department of Sociology, Environmental and Business Economics. In addition to sociological courses, the master's programme needed three socio-legal courses taught jointly to our law students as elective courses. Moreover, I took part in establishing a new Bachelor degree in Market and Management Anthropology that would need a course in legal anthropology. Together with my colleague Annette Olesen, now lecturer at Aalborg University, I started to read intensively on legal anthropology and studies on legal encounters, legal consciousness and micro-sociological studies mainly from the law and society tradition – areas that hardly existed in Scandinavian textbooks at the time. Our work led to a strategic grant for a project on Legal Encounters from the Faculty of Social Sciences in the period 2016–18. I developed the project and the courses with Annette whom I had started to work with on several projects. Moreover, the Legal Encounter project employed a PhD student, Stine Piilgaard Porner Nielsen, who is now lecturer in sociology of law at Aalborg University. Stine and I came to work on different projects later.

In 2015, I was recruited to be part-time professor, Professor II, for three years at the Department of Criminology and Sociology of Law, University of Oslo. The department was undergoing a generational change and wanted an 'internal' professor to participate in the assessment process for upcoming vacancies and to fill the teaching gap. Scholars like Thomas Mathiesen, Kristian 'Kikki' Andenæs and Knut Papendorf had retired or were about to retire. Moreover, due to my experiences as member of The Danish Council for Independent Research – Social Sciences and the Swedish Research Council, I could assist the process of professionalising the department's funding strategy (however, the success of the strategy is due to the collective work at the department and not least Per Jørgen Ystehede's visionary work).

The Head of Department, Heidi Mork Lomell, invited Olaf Halvorsen Rønning and I to edit a book on legal aid which would be dedicated to Kristian

Andenæs instead of making a *festschrift*. The reason for the focus on legal aid was that Andenæs had been part of several legal aid projects throughout his career, including JussBuss (Law Bus) and street lawyers in Norway and Denmark.[58] With the help of Per Jørgen, we submitted a book proposal to Palgrave which was accepted, and we got funding for proofreading and open access. The latter was an important part of the new open science criteria. We wanted to make the first comparison of legal aid schemes in the Nordic countries, focus on specific renowned Nordic legal aid projects and situated the Nordic developments of legal aid within a broader field of legal aid. We invited experts from all the Nordic countries as well as other international scholars to write specific chapters.[59] This became a starting point in my legal aid focus and led me into different projects with different forms of funding and a close collaboration with a legal aid institution in a vulnerable living area in Odense, Denmark. To understand my interest in legal aid and clinical work and the important position of Norwegian sociology of law, it is important to know the history of the Norwegian legal aid clinic, JussBuss (Legal Bus), which was established in 1971. In the early 1970s, Oslo law students and young socio-legal pioneers like Thomas Mathiesen, Kristian 'Kikki' Andenæs and Jon T Johnsen were interested in questions concerning access to legal counselling. Inspired by American outreach legal aid, clinical legal education and sociology of law,[60] they wanted to combine scientific knowledge with the establishment of a legal aid clinic benefitting disadvantaged groups in Norwegian society.[61] JussBuss was established as a mobile legal aid clinic based on volunteer law students. Mathiesen argued that through this initiative, the critical legal scholar could not only help marginalised citizens with their legal problems, it was also possible to collect data about these persons' problems which, when systematised and analysed, could be used to raise the voice on behalf of citizens who were not otherwise heard. At the same time, it could help educate students and give them a critical perspective. In Mathiesen's version, sociology of law was closely related to showing flaws in the

[58] C Lied, *Gatejurister: Oppsøkende rettshjelp til folk med rusrelaterte problemer* (Oslo, Akademika forlag, 2013); SPP Nielsen and O Hammerslev, 'Gadejuristen [The street lawyers]: Offering Legal Aid to Socially Marginalized People' in O Hammerslev and OH Rønning (eds), *Outsourcing Legal Aid in the Nordic Welfare States* (London, Palgrave, 2017).

[59] O Hammerslev and OH Rønning, *Outsourcing Legal Aid in the Nordic Welfare States* (London, Palgrave, 2018).

[60] T Mathiesen, 'Juss-Buss 30 år' in Juss-Buss (ed), *Tvers igjennom lov til seir* (Oslo, Pax Forlag, 2001); GD Capua, 'Juss-Buss – Et rettshjelpstilbud for "vanlige folk"?' in A Eidesen, S Eskeland, and T Mathiesen (eds) *Rettshjelp og samfunnsstruktur* (Oslo, Pax, 1975); GD Capua, *Om å legge ut på dypet* (Oslo, Institutt for kriminologi og rettssosiologi, Avdeling for rettssosiologi, Universitetet i Oslo, 2001).

[61] O Hammerslev and T Mathiesen, 'Marxistisk retssociologi' in O Hammerslev and MR Madsen (eds), *Klassisk og moderne retssociologi. Centrale temaer og tekster* (København, Hans Reitzels Forlag, 2013); T Mathiesen, *Kritisk sosiologi – en invitasjon* (Oslo, Novus Forlag, 2011); S Eskeland and J Finne, *Rettshjelp: en analyse og empirisk undersøkelse av tradisjonell rettshjelps muligheter og begrensninger – særlig for folk som lever under vanskelige økonomiske eller sosiale kår* (Oslo, Pax, 1973).

welfare state and making a social impact through critical scholarship engaged in the public debate.[62] The employees were law students and young lawyers, while the then Institute of Sociology of Law, University of Oslo, created a post to help manage the initiative.[63]

In terms of research, I conducted different studies about legal aid infrastructures and barriers to justice together with my colleagues Annette Olesen and Stine Piilgaard Porner Nielsen. Annette and I took advantage of our readings of the law and society literature on the pre-dispute phase[64] and realised that one important aspect about peoples' possibilities to opt for legal aid was dependent on their ability to name, blame and claim their rights.[65] Moreover, with Stine, I studied barriers to justice among marginalised persons inspired by both Mathiesen's studies and Genn's classic study *Paths to Justice* as well as studies by Pleasence et al.[66] Our experiences from this research were translated into two legal aid projects. First, in collaboration with the legal aid institution in the marginalised living area in Odense, Retshjælpen Fyn, I established a legal clinical course modelled after the University of California, Los Angeles simulated legal clinical model. I had visited UCLA and Rick Abel and Scott Cummings a couple of times and attended some of UCLA's legal clinic classes to get an understanding of how they were designed. It became an elective course on the Bachelor level. It tapped very well into the accreditation institutions' focus on the role of the university for the surrounding society. The course was also a way to help the legal aid institution to get enough volunteer students, which it relied on due to the Danish legal aid scheme. Parallel with the course, we started to experiment with how we could reach different groups in the living area who did not seek legal aid, and at the same time we carefully monitored the results. Even though the projects, the legal clinical course and our experiments of reaching hard-to-reach groups were not tied fully together, it was heavily inspired by Mathiesen's understanding of JussBuss.[67]

[62] T Mathiesen, T (1975) 'Noen konklusjoner om rettshjelp, rettspolitikk og samfunnsstruktur' in A Eidesen, S Eskeland and T Mathiesen (eds), *Rettshjelp og samfunnsstruktur* (Oslo, Pax, 1975); Capua (1975) n 60; GD Capua and Juss-Buss, *Virksomheten i Juss-Buss i 1977* (Oslo, Universitetet i Oslo, Inst.for rettssosiologi, 1978).

[63] Hammerslev et al 2018 (n 46).

[64] With a starting point in WLF Felstiner, RL Abel and A Sarat, 'The Emergence and Transformation of Disputes: Naming, Blaming, Claiming' (1981) 15 *Law & Society Review* 631–54.

[65] A Olesen and O Hammerslev, 'Bourdieu's "The Force of Law": Interview with Richard Terdiman' (2021) 15 *Praktiske Grunde – Nordisk tidsskrift for kultur- og samfundsvidenskab* 5–14; A Olesen and O Hammerslev, 'Bringing Sociology of Law Back into Pierre Bourdieu's Sociology: Elements of Bourdieu's Sociology of Law and Dispute Transformation' (2023) 32 *Social & Legal Studies* 177–96.

[66] Genn (n 49); P Pleasence, A Buck, NJ Balmer, A O'Grady, H Genn and M Smith, *Causes of Action: Civil Law and Social Justice* (2004) (://www.researchgate.net/publication/32894969_Causes_of_Action_Civil_Law_and_Social_Justice, 12/6-2024); P Pleasence, H Genn, NJ Balmer, A Buck and A O'Grady, 'Causes of Action: First Findings of the LSRC Periodic Survey' (2003) 30 *Journal of Law and Society* 11–30.

[67] A Olesen and O Hammerslev, 'Reaching the Unreachable Through Action Research? Thomas Mathiesen and the Nordic Socio-Legal Tradition' (2024) 7 *Justice, Power and Resistance* 214–225.

In continuation of the project Legal Encounters, Stine and I got funding from the Independent Research Council Denmark for a project on the role of framework law on legal encounters between social workers and young people experiencing homelessness. Again, the project was inspired by classic Scandinavian sociology of law and its examination of the welfare state and its form of regulation characterised by framework law.[68] Framework law delegates authority from the regulators to the municipalities and relies on programmes and purposes rather than defined rules, which leaves great room for discretion for social workers. Theoretically, we wanted to combine Bourdieusian sociology with legal consciousness. We focused on how young people experiencing homelessness navigate welfare regulation as well as how social workers helping this group of people navigate law. The project related its research questions to greater welfare state reconfigurations where new and private organisations play an increasingly important role. The topic and theoretical framework linked us to my old as well as a new network of especially European legal consciousness scholars, like Marc Hertogh and Dave Cowan, scholars focusing on legal mobilisation, and Nordic and European scholars focusing on welfare state transformations.[69]

VIII. CONCLUSION

Focusing on my career in terms of positions, projects and readings, this chapter has outlined my position in the sociology of law field in Denmark seen (partly) in relation to the interlinked fields in Norway and Sweden. It has highlighted how the expansion of legal education has impacted my possibility of pursuing a career in academia and how, early in my career, I was guided towards internationalisation and external funding. This played a positive role later when the Scandinavian social science fields became internationalised with new forms of publication requirements and competitiveness in relation to external funding. Moreover, this chapter illustrates how my sociology of law readings have been formed by Scandinavian socio-legal literature, but also how it has expanded to, first European sociology of law and then to studies within the American law and society tradition. However, these lines are not entirely clear, as also, for example, Norwegian sociology of law scholars were heavily inspired by American sociology.[70] They do, however, give an indication of the reconfiguration of the fields.

[68] Aubert (n 22); J Dalberg-Larsen, *Retsstaten, velfærdsstaten og hvad så?* (København, Akademisk Forlag, 1984); N Christie, 'Konflikt som eiendom' (1977) *Tidsskrift for retsvæsen* 113.

[69] SPP Nielsen and O Hammerslev, *Transformations of European Welfare States and Social Rights* (London, Palgrave Macmillan, 2024).

[70] O Hammerslev, 'The Replacement of the Legal Profession: Vilhelm Aubert's Theory and Heritage in the Sociology of the Legal Profession' in D Newman (ed), *Leading Works on the Legal Profession* (London, Routledge, 2023); Olesen and Hammerslev (n 67).

A final note and illustration of the development of Scandinavian socio-legal fields is my move to the Sociology of Law Department in Lund (where I was visiting researcher in 2014, hosted by Banakar). Against the tragic background of the passing of Banakar, I was recruited (together with Anna Lundberg) as a one-year guest professor at the Sociology of Law Department, Lund University, in 2021. While being a guest professor, the department advertised one to two professor positions, which Anna and I were fortunate to be awarded in strong competition with internationally renowned scholars. The department was about to undergo a generational shift with the loss of Banakar, resignations and retirements. Håkan Hydén, who had been the long-time professor and who also attended the first Nordic socio-legal conference I attended, had retired, which opened the department up for new candidates. Since its establishment at the Faculty of Social Sciences in 1972, the department has always had a strong focus on the welfare state and welfare state law and is uniquely positioned with its degrees in sociology of law at bachelor, masters and PhD level.[71] In many ways, the trajectory of the department reflects the development of the social science field. Whereas it had been very Swedish with meetings in Swedish, PhD theses written as monographs in Swedish and funded internally, it has internationalised. Today the spoken language is mostly English, and it is a high priority to get external funding. Most of the PhD theses are in English written as compilations. However, while one focus is still on the development of the welfare state, technologies and welfare law, the department's research profile has expanded to also having strong foci on state transformations in post-communist countries, legal professions, legal mobilisation, migration and human rights. And recently, we have had hybrid seminars on decolonising sociology of law with participants from both the Global North and Global South.

[71] For the history of the department, see H Hydén, Ett ämne blir till soclaw.lu.se/sites/soclaw.lu.se/files/ett_amne_blir_till.pdf.

6

At the Crossroads of Sociology and Law: An Essay in Socio-Analysis

LIORA ISRAËL

'FROM WHICH STANDPOINT are you speaking?' is a question that resonates more with the critical political or psychoanalytical perspectives of the 1960s or 1970s than with the usual set of questions delivered in a book chapter today. However, a reflexive perspective on one's career in the world of socio-legal studies may well be fruitful to better comprehend the context of European academic institutions, especially regarding interdisciplinary socio-legal studies. Indeed, the field evolved enormously over the last decades, also on the international scale, as testified by the success of interdisciplinary events such as those organised by the Law and Society Association (several thousands of participants each year). Given the historical variations in the relations governing law and social sciences in different countries, and the social status of law and legal affairs in each society, socio-legal studies (or its equivalent) can be considered intrinsically singular in their positioning and in their history.

Regarding France, the landscape is indeed complex: despite several so-called founding fathers of sociology who produced significant concepts for, or insights into, the subfield of legal sociology (from Durkheim to Gurvitch), the current landscape is probably more influenced by the pull of the American-originated law and society tradition.[1] As Pierre Noreau and André-Jean Arnaud described it in a seminal article, 'The history of French legal sociology is not linear … French legal sociology has developed in discontinuous fashion … Legal sociology had to find its way without reference to any dominant paradigm whatsoever'.[2] As they clearly demonstrate, several tendencies emerged over the years, either

[1] L Israël, 'Legalise It! The Rising Place of Law in French Sociology' (2013) 9 *International Journal of Law in Context* 262–78.

[2] P Noreau and A-J Arnaud, 'The Sociology of Law in France: Trends and Paradigms' (1998) 25 *Journal of Law and Society* 257–58.

framed by practical issues, as in the legislative sociology praised by the famous law dean Jean Carbonnier or, contrarily, by perspectives originating from several social science traditions,[3] from Weber to Bourdieu. But despite the wide differences, the trends originating from law or from social sciences had in common the reference to sociology.

The term 'sociology of law' (*sociologie du droit*) is favoured by social scientists over 'legal sociology' (*sociologie juridique*), which is more often used by jurists. The term 'socio-legal' itself has had no real equivalent until today in French. If ever, it is used in reference to the American-centred law and society tradition. To quote Renaud Colson and Stewart Field in their comparative paper, one striking difference between France and the United Kingdom is the very absence of a body of knowledge explicitly conceptualised and characterised in terms of the label 'socio-legal'.[4] They stress the relative absence today of such interdisciplinary research in French law faculties, blaming the peculiar form of academic recruitment of full professors in law by a competitive exam (*agrégation du supérieur*), leading to reproduction of the same orthodoxy over change. By contrast, Field and Colson outline 'various fragments of the socio-legal in France',[5] to be found mostly outside the law faculties, namely in sociology (and more rarely political science) departments.

My own trajectory is undoubtedly related to this path, since my PhD adviser Jacques Commaille has been a central actor of the *renaissance* of French sociology of law in the 1980s. Several of his students have, what he recently described as, a 'French touch'.[6] My own contribution to this more general trend may have been a historical twist that can be thought of as the 'socio-' in 'socio-legal' being more inclusive of human and social sciences in general.

I. FROM CHANCE TO LUCK

In the following, I will share my trajectory as a student and then as an academic to contribute to the conversation of legal studies and legal theory across Europe. My story is by no means representative, even as I try to put it in perspective within the larger picture of French social sciences over the last 25 years.

Unsurprisingly, my story begins as a student. During my undergraduate and graduate studies in the 1990s, sociology of law – to refer to the most common term used to designate socio-legal studies in France – was almost never mentioned in classical training in sociology. While sociology of family, urban sociology, sociology of education, political sociology or even the study of (work) organisations

[3] J Carbonnier, *Flexible droit. Pour une sociologie du droit sans rigueur* (Paris, Librairie Générale de Droit et de Jurisprudence, 1969).

[4] S Field and R Colson, 'Socio-Legal Studies in France: Beyond the Law Faculty' (2016) 43 *Journal of Law and Society* 285–311.

[5] ibid 287.

[6] J Commaille, 'La *French Touch* de la recherche sur le droit' (2021) 107 *Droit et Société* 203–25.

were traditional domains of specialization, law and legal institutions were generally absent from the curriculum. Some of the founding fathers of the discipline that we learned to summarise in a few quotes sometimes mentioned law – the most famous being Emile Durkheim. His definition of solidarity (in *The Division of Labor in Society*, 1893) as organic versus mechanical, associated respectively to two forms of law and justice, restitutive versus repressive, clearly identified law as a crucial aspect in the structuration of society. But even if some other aspects of the Durkheimian thought also embraced law, such as *The Suicide*,[7] this dimension was barely mentioned and never really developed – as far as I can remember, at least.

My retrospective analysis on this near absence of the legal domain in my sociology training refers to the *summa divisio* between *Facultés de droit* (law faculties) and *Facultés de lettres* (where humanities are taught) in French universities. The absence did not vanish after the political and social turmoil related to May 1968 events.[8] On the contrary, the politicisation on the left of the *lettres* faculties as opposed to law faculties probably did increase the spontaneous reluctance to address legal questions in sociology or history departments (part of *Facultés de lettres*). Conversely, the relative isolation of law faculties and the demise of the French critical studies movement incurred by the majority in the legal academy reinforced the tacit reciprocal disinterest of law and social sciences, at least in the undergraduate curriculum.[9]

From a mainstream perspective in a sociology department back then, law was certainly more or less considered as being either purely technical (and thus tedious) or, in a more complex and Marxist-oriented vision, merely political (and thus not worthy of too much attention). In French Marxist ideology, law could be considered as a superstructure or an '*appareil idéologique d'État*' (ideological state apparatus, to quote Althusser) whose ideological function was to contribute to reproducing the power structure. Even more than 20 years after the heydays of May 1968, sociology departments in the 1990s were populated with professors whose training in politics, if not in sociology, had often been rooted in social movements. Nanterre University, where my sociology training partly originated, was especially well known as the epicentre of the events in 1968. As conspicuous evidence of the remaining divide between law and sociology students in the 1990s, I cannot remember having ever met law students – even though their building was adjacent to ours during my student years in sociology at that university.

During my education at Nanterre, I discovered, somewhat by chance, the sociology of law. I used to be a summer camp instructor as a student, and the year before graduating I happened to supervise children who were under the custody

[7] E Durkheim, *Le Suicide, étude de sociologie* (Paris, F Alcan, 1897).

[8] F Bourrillon, E Marantz, S Méchine and L Vadelorgue, *De l'Université de Paris aux universités d'Île-de-France* (Rennes, Presses universitaires de Rennes, 2016).

[9] X Dupré de Boulois and M Kaluszynski, *Le droit en révolution: regards sur la critique du droit des années 1970 à nos jours* (Paris, LGDJ-Lextenso, 2011).

of justice. My interest was awoken, also because it echoed a paper that I had greatly appreciated on juvenile delinquency – *La délinquance juvenile. Essai de construction d'objet*, by Jean-Claude Chamboredon.[10] Contrarily to law, delinquency and crime were beloved subjects in our training, most notably through the Chicago school of sociology, symbolic interactionism, or ethnomethodology. Howard Becker's *Outsiders* was a favourite book, the whiffs of marijuana adding interest to the content of the book itself.[11] It is thus on the basis of this influence that, in the following September, I set out to discuss a potential topic for a master's thesis with the professor likely to become my adviser, Isaac Joseph. Joseph, an urban sociologist, was notably famous for having introduced Erving Goffmann's sociology in France.[12] During one of our discussions, while I was trying to identify a research topic, he mentioned that the daughter of one of his best friends was a juvenile judge in a tribunal near Paris. He advised me to meet her, since I was interested in juvenile justice. I met the judge soon after, and what happened in this tribunal, the largest juvenile court in France, soon gripped me. It was the best known, given its location in the most deprived neighbourhood surrounding Paris, Seine-Saint-Denis. The judge, herself the daughter of a sociologist, was very keen to open the doors of the tribunal to a young social scientist. Today, I do not remember exactly how I initially framed my project, but I can reasonably assume that under Isaac Joseph's influence my line of inquiry revolved around an interactionist study of what happened in court, between the judge, the kids and their families. I began to spend at least one or two days per week in the tribunal, following the judge and soon other colleagues of hers, as well as educators, prosecutors, and other members of the tribunal. Among them, I quickly noticed some younger participants – they were future magistrates, working as apprentices in the courts. I shared with them my anxiety regarding my lack of legal knowledge, progressively circumscribed by the reading list that the judge that I was initially observing suggested (notably the training manual for juvenile judges that she used), and by their explanations shared during lunchtime to go over what I did not understand. In a way, my lack of legal training was not a big deal. I could raise questions about what was taken for granted in the tribunal and, in response, insightful justifications from the participants (judges, clerks, lawyers, educators and so on) were provided.

As my research evolved, I identified that the core aspect of the judicial process I was studying was related to the characterisation of the biography of the youth. This characterisation was produced at the intersection of two dimensions: the

[10] J-C Chamboredon, 'La délinquance juvénile, essai de construction d'objet' (1971) 12(3) *Revue française de sociologie* 335–77.

[11] H Becker, *Outsiders: Studies in the Sociology of Deviance* (London, Free Press of Glencoe, 1963).

[12] I Joseph, *Erving Goffman et la microsociologie* (Paris, Presses universitaires de France, 1998).

fact that the jurisdiction of the judge hinged on the address of the family, thus constant over the years; and the legal requirement to, at least try, to obtain the family's approval of the measure adopted. I focused on how the judge was pushed towards negotiating a label – in reference to 'labelling' theories – acceptable for the parents, notably regarding their parental deficiencies. Indeed, regarding civil matters the judge is supposed to seek the parents' consent. This difficult process was shared with other participants, who were eventually producing competing labels over the youth's situation (educators, instructors, psychologists, psychiatrists, and for criminal matters police members or prosecutors etc).

This first encounter with the world of justice and legal matters was exciting. However, back then, I never framed it in terms of sociology of law or socio-legal studies. I rather referred to classical sociologists, such as Goffman (regarding the staging of social life) and Bourdieu (in relation to the power relations involved). It is only for the defence of my master dissertation, when Isaac Joseph invited Jacques Commaille – then research professor in Grenoble for his last year – because no one in Nanterre University was an expert, that I really discovered the field.

II. CROSSING DISCIPLINARY, NATIONAL AND LINGUISTIC BOUNDARIES

Jacques Commaille was encouraging and gave me the opportunity to publish my first paper, in *Droit et Société*, on the basis of my master's thesis.[13] He then pushed me to explore further the study of legal questions from a sociological standpoint. One year later, in 1998, for my master's programme second year (compulsory before engaging in a PhD in France), I chose to return to Ecole Normale Supérieure (ENS) in Cachan[14] where the graduate programme in social science benefited from the teaching of several researchers and professors interested in socio-legal matters. The faculty included, amongst others, Jacques Commaille, recently hired as a professor, other socio-legal pioneers in the field such as Pierre Lascoumes and Francine Soubiran-Paillet,[15] Anne Boigeol and Alain Bancaud – heirs of Bourdieu in the study of legal professions and members of the same research centre in history[16] – and Claude Didry, Evelyne Serverin and

[13] L Israël, 'Les mises en scène d'une justice quotidienne' (1999) 42(1) *Droit et Société* 393–419.

[14] I had been admitted there as an 'elève normalienne' in 1995, and followed parallel tracks at Nanterre University between 1995 and 1998. It was nevertheless not compulsory to stay in Cachan for the master's or doctoral programme. It is probably not by chance that this interdisciplinary network of scholars was hosted by a 'grande école' (competitive graduate school) and not by a university, the latter being more rigidly organised around departments related to disciplines.

[15] P Lascoumes, 'Changer le droit, changer la société : le moment d'un retournement' (2009) 77 *Genèses* 110–23; F Soubiran-Paillet, 'Défense des travailleurs immigrés et pratique de la sociologie au milieu des années 1970' (2009) 77(4) *Genèses* 124–36.

[16] Institut d'Histoire du Temps Présent, IHTP.

Alessandro Stanziani who then worked on labour- or economic-related topics in a research centre focusing on economic issues. This concentration of researchers in Cachan at the time, working on law-related topics from sociological, historical and economic perspectives, was quite unique, and it did not last long (mostly due to interpersonal and institutional reasons). But I was lucky enough to benefit from this ecosystem during my master's and PhD years. Moreover, the PhD was taking place in a timeframe where the relations between law and social science had improved and developed, even if it was probably not yet sufficiently explicit from the perspective of undergraduate students.[17]

It is now clear, in retrospect, that this concentration of talents was not only extraordinary but also without precedent. In contrast with the lack of interdisciplinarity between law and social science in the academy, the Centre National de la Recherche Scientifique (CNRS) had been developing an interest for the sociology of law since the 1980s. Jacques Commaille drove that process. All the people named above had joined the CNRS as full-time researchers, some (then in their 50s) after having worked in the research departments of the ministry of justice under the influence of Jean Carbonnier[18] regarding civil affairs (ie Jacques Commaille, Anne Boigeol), or on criminal-law related studies under the influence of Philippe Robert, a judge and researcher (ie Pierre Lascoumes).

As a master's student initiating her research, I knew that my interest lay with a law-related topic of inquiry, but I did not know what I wanted to investigate. I began to ask several researchers for insights: Anne Boigeol advised me to study the election of the first woman at the head of the Paris Bar. It seemed to be interesting, but I was not totally convinced – Anne Boigeol did conduct the research and wrote on the subject, brilliantly, a few years later.[19] In the process, I met the historian Henry Rousso who was giving a course together with Jacques Commaille on the history and sociology of justice. Henry Rousso, a specialist of World War II and the Vichy Regime,[20] had just undergone the experience of the Papon trial, where a former prefect under the Vichy regime had been condemned for his role in the deportation of Jews from Bordeaux. During the trial, Rousso had met one of the lawyers of the victims, Joë Nordmann, already an old man. Nordmann had told him of his role in the French Resistance and possessed some documentation regarding these years – he lent a piece of archive regarding the post-war purges among magistrates to Henry Rousso, who was working with Alain Bancaud on the subject.[21] Rousso told me that lawyers in

[17] Noreau and Arnaud (n 2).

[18] This famous jurist has called for a sociology of law aimed at informing the drafting of new legislation, especially regarding family.

[19] A Boigeol, 'Le genre comme ressource dans l'accès des femmes au "gouvernement du barreau": l'exemple du barreau de Paris' (2007) 67(2) *Genèses* 66–88.

[20] H Rousso, *Le Syndrome de Vichy: 1944–1948* (Paris, Éd. du Seuil, 1987).

[21] A Bancaud and H Rousso, 'L'épuration des magistrats à la Libération (1944–1945)', in Association française pour l'histoire de la justice *L'Épuration de la magistrature de la Révolution à la Libération: 150 ans d'histoire judiciaire, Histoire de la Justice*, 1993, n° 6, 117–44.

the resistance during World War II could be a compelling subject, even though he was not sure that it would be suitable for a sociologist. Moreover, he warned me that he had never read anything on the subject and feared that the subject might be too small to even offer me enough material for a master's dissertation. I met Joë Nordmann, and quickly discovered that there was a treasure trove there. He had just written his memoirs where his experience as an underground member during the war was described.[22] He also possessed 'some' archives. I quickly understood that his roomy apartment on the banks of the Seine was filled with boxes of archives, especially in the false ceilings above the window overlooking the river. In the boxes, as I soon found out, numerous documents piled up about the underground movements he had created and participated in during the war. Boxes and boxes brimmed with clandestine reports, secret messages and drafts of the underground press or flyers written to convince the public of the legitimacy of resistance against the Vichy regime. Of course, this incredible discovery filled me with excitement and interest. However, a critical question was emerging: I was no historian, how could I deal with archives – especially regarding a period such as World War II? Even if it was thrilling, I engaged on this path most notably because I had access to the Institut d'Histoire du Temps Présent (Institute for History of Present Times) directed by Henry Rousso, then the most famous research centre regarding World War II, including its library. But if I could manage the novelty of archival research, this did not mean that I could address the topic sociologically. Under the influence of the then flourishing Weberian sociology of law, in the wake of the first translation of his sociology of law and several articles – notably one by Lascoumes and Serverin[23] – praising the Weberian approach on law, I initially framed my research question as follows: How are we to account for legal professionals choosing to join movements grounded in disobedience?[24] I imagined that from a Weberian perspective, it would be possible to solve the conundrum by contrasting their disrespect of positive law with their faith in natural law,[25] and more precisely with their respect of legal and moral principles disregarded by the Nazi authorities and their French allies.

It would take too much space to explain how I discovered that it was far more complicated than I thought. Several theories helped me to figure out what occurred, especially the sociology of professions, theories of collective action and socio-legal studies (originated in the United States). Anne Boigeol, whose help was crucial during these formative years, advised me during a short research stay in Chicago to meet her colleague and friend Bryant Garth. I had no idea who he was, but beginning to study resistant lawyers in France I was confronted

[22] J Nordmann, *Aux vents de l'histoire: mémoires* (Arles, Actes Sud, 1996).

[23] P Lascoumes and E Serverin, 'Le droit comme activité sociale : pour une approche wébérienne des activités juridiques' (1988) 9(1) *Droit et Société* 165–87.

[24] M Weber, *Sociologie du droit* (Paris, Presses universitaires de France, 2007).

[25] M Coutu, *Max Weber et les rationalités du droit* (Paris Québec, LGDJ les Presses de l'Université Laval, 1995).

with a lack of resources regarding activist lawyers, and especially Communists. The sociologist in France who was an expert on lawyers, Lucien Karpik, had just published his masterpiece, published in English under the title *French Lawyers: A Study in Collective Action*,[26] where the profession was defined by its political moderation. It was very different from what I was observing in the archives and the documentation regarding the formative years of Joë Nordmann and fellow Communist lawyers in the 1930s. Unfortunately, Bryant Garth was not in Chicago during the summer 1999 (as far as I can remember). However, when I asked him if he had ideas regarding the sociology of radical legal professionals, he answered back: 'You're working on cause lawyering?' I had no idea what 'cause lawyering' meant, but I quickly checked it on the computer of the University of Chicago library. Two book references emerged from the machine: one was the first cause lawyering volume by Sarat and Scheingold,[27] and the second, *Rights at Work*, by Michael McCann.[28] I could not imagine how important these two books would prove to be for me, and a few years later I would have the privilege to have exchanges with their authors. But so far, thanks to these books, I had stepped into a fascinating new research field which opened very different perspectives on law and legal professionals.

Later, thanks to Anne Boigeol (she was well integrated in international networks, as was her friend and colleague Yves Dezalay), I applied to participate in the graduate workshop of the annual meeting of the Law and Society Association in Budapest (2001). It was my first international conference, and the graduate workshop gave me the opportunity to not only meet graduate students from all over the world in socio-legal studies (some of them would become close friends and future colleagues), but also to be in discussions with some of the leading socio-legal scholars of that time. Our professors and mentors for the workshop were Michael McCann, Kitty Calavitta, Austin Sarat and Lauren Edelman, to name but a few. I also became acquainted with Sarat and Scheingold, as I presented a paper in the conference in the cause lawyering network (CRN) they chaired. I thus had the opportunity to refine my 'transplant' of the cause lawyering framework to the study of French Communist and underground lawyers from the 1930–1940s.[29] In the work of scholars focusing on cause lawyering, I was particularly interested by the transferability of concepts from one society or one period to another. In my chapter in the cause lawyering

[26] L Karpik, *French Lawyers. A Study in Collective Action, 1274–1994* (Oxford, Oxford University Press, 1999).

[27] A Sarat and S Scheingold (eds), *Cause Lawyering: Political Commitments and Professional Responsibilities* (Oxford, Oxford University Press, 1998).

[28] M McCann, *Rights at Work: Pay Equity Reform and the Politics of Legal Mobilization* (Chicago, University of Chicago Press, 1994).

[29] To be published later as L Israël, 'From Cause Lawyering to Resistance. French Communist Lawyers in the Shadow of History, 1929–1945' in A Sarat and S Scheingold S (eds), *The Worlds Cause Lawyers Make. Structure and Agency in the Legal Practice* (Stanford, Stanford University Press, 2005).

volume *The Worlds Cause Lawyers Make*,[30] I tried to focus on the transformation that cause lawyering produced within an authoritarian context where political opinions could not be expressed freely, in line with other scholars such as Mara Loveman in her study of high-risk collective action.[31] This reflection over the circulation of concepts and categories was also nurtured by the need to translate notions to mobilize them in French. This question led me, for example, to dedicate a seminar for a whole year to the translation of a single chapter of *The Common Place of Law* by Susan Silbey and Patricia Ewick.[32] This translation, realised collectively with a group of colleagues and students,[33] made us think through questions such as the notion of law itself, between *loi et droit* in French; peculiar epistemological options, such as the use of narratives, in the book; or the contrast in the secular notion of property between France and the United States. (The latter could be implied from the cover of the book figuring a chair standing in the snow as a symbol of territorial appropriation.) Translation in social sciences raises a peculiar issue regarding the social characteristics associated with notions and concepts, and it also raises critical questions to bear in mind in the perspective of 'transplanting' them into other contexts, especially when it comes to the legal domain.[34] Paying attention to translation issues and thus to national idiosyncrasies is important, but should never justify to renounce to comparison or concept imports – the risk being to construct national differentiation instead of demonstrating it.

Beside my research on judicial resistance, my growing knowledge in law and society scholarship quickly raised interest, as I was able to see by the attention paid to a review of the first volumes of the Texte cause lawyering series that I wrote for *Droit et société*.[35] According to Google Scholar, it is until this day my most cited research article. (I certainly owe a lot to my quite involuntary role of a smuggler between American and French socio-legal scholarship, as I proposed this review to *Droit et société* to obtain these expensive volumes for free, a powerful incentive for a graduate student.) I continued to work on the translation and discussion of law and society scholarship in France, notably in *Droit et Société*, where I edited later a special issue around the translation of Mark Galanter's 'Why the Haves Come Out Ahead?'.[36] At the same time, I navigated back and

[30] Israël, ibid.

[31] M Loveman, 'High-Risk Collective Action: Defending Human Rights in Chile, Uruguay, and Argentina' (1998) 104 *American Journal of Sociology* 477–525.

[32] P Ewick and S Silbey, *The Common Place of Law: Stories from Everyday Life. Language and Legal Discourse* (Chicago, University of Chicago Press, 1998).

[33] P Ewick and S Silbey, 'La construction sociale de la légalité' (translation by Cassan, G, Didier, D, Gardella, E, Israël, L, Lutaud, R, Ollivier, C, Pélisse, J, Pujuguet, M, Souloumiac, J, Trespeuch, M, Truc, G, Williams, B) (2004) 6 *Terrains & travaux* 112–38.

[34] L Israël and J Pélisse, 'Quelques éléments sur les conditions d'une "importation" (Note liminaire à la traduction du texte de S Silbey et P Ewick) (2004) 6(1) *Terrains & travaux* 101–11.

[35] L Israël, 'Usages militants du droit dans l'arène judiciaire : le cause lawyering' (2001) 49(3) *Droit et société* 793–824.

[36] L Israël, 'Les joueurs répétés ont-ils plus de chance de gagner ? Débats sur le sens de la justice. Présentation du dossier' (2013) 85(3) *Droit et société* 543–57.

forth between participating with enthusiasm in the Law and Society Association community (sometimes complaining of seeing that working on a non-United States country prompted my contribution almost immediately to be categorised as the 'French case' in a series), and relative frustration about the attention paid in France to the import export trafficking that I was organising, maybe at the price of less attention paid to the content of my research itself. Nevertheless, I was lucky enough to be recruited as an associate professor at Ecole des Hautes Etudes en Sciences Sociales, School for Advanced Studies in Social Sciences (EHESS) in Paris two years after my PhD. This unique institution in the French context gave me the rare opportunity not only to continue my interdisciplinary navigation in an institution that defines itself as the space where social sciences entertain in-depth discussions (in contrast to French universities), but also to strengthen my international networks by providing resources and incentives.

III. COMING TO TERMS WITH LAW AS A DISCIPLINE

As I was advancing in my career and became more familiar with international settings, I could observe a striking difference between France and other countries. While in France I was clearly considered as a sociologist (or sometimes mistakenly as an historian given the period I studied for my PhD), international invitations almost always were issued from law schools or law faculties, either in the United States, in Canada, in Belgium or in Italy, for example. I was often confronted with the fact that despite the growing interest for law and justice in the social sciences in France, it was certainly not from the law faculties that either the impulse or the interest came from. The main exception was from law faculties where the political dimension of law was more clearly addressed, most notably Nanterre. Its renowned human rights lawyers could in many ways be considered as cause lawyers, most notably Danièle Lochak, the former President of the GISTI,[37] an activist group who developed litigation for immigrant rights.[38]

The relation to law as a discipline in France can be manifold from the perspective of sociology of law. In a way, I considered French lawyers – including academic lawyers – mostly as informants and as subjects of inquiry. As for sociology of law, their publications were mostly considered as a resource to understand what to 'think as a lawyer' means, to quote Elizabeth Mertz' title.[39] Legal academics even became the subjects of my inquiry in a research project

[37] Groupe d'information et de Soutien des Immigrés (Immigrants' Information and Support Group).

[38] D Lochak, 'Quarante ans de combats pour défendre la cause des étrangers: l'arme du droit à travers le cas du GISTI' (2017) 170(4) *Migrations Société* 109–17.

[39] E Mertz, *The Language of Law School: Learning to 'Think Like a Lawyer'* (Oxford, Oxford University Press, 2007).

I conducted on elite legal education with Rachel Vanneuville (2008–12).[40] In this framework, I conducted an ethnography of legal classes delivered at the then newly created School of Law at Sciences Po Paris. For the first time in my life, I attended law classes, specifically a contract law course. It was, at the same time, fascinating and puzzling to do this ethnography, behaving at the same time as a student (in class, having to learn everything on the subject), as an ethnographer (trying to decipher the behind-the-scene stakes of the teaching), and as a fellow professor from a neighbouring institution to Sciences Po, observing the work of a colleague (who was aware of my presence, of course). I must confess that my colleague did not appreciate the parts of the research where I endeavoured to describe and analyse his role in class – most notably regarding how his tall stature played a role in his pedagogic performance.[41] He later asked me: 'Would you have pointed that out if I were a small woman?' My answer was: 'Yes, of course, it would have induced a totally different presence in the classroom!'

This anecdote might be relevant if one considers the status of empirical data in the legal academy in France today. It still appears to be irrelevant to mobilise empirical data in a PhD dissertation in law, as doctrinal analysis and jurisprudence is still at the core of legal research. And among various methodological options, ethnography is certainly one of the least considered by legal scholars. Nevertheless, the field seems to be moving. Interest in empirical legal methods is growing on the basis of two (related) trends – first, the appeal of international scholarship, and second, the demands of national or international research calls (such as European Research Council (ERC) Grants) which require empirical datasets and do not consider black-letter law[42] analysis as sufficient. Over the last few years, I have often been confronted by colleagues in law faculties asking for 'advice regarding methodology' or wondering if I could help them with their interview grid. Even if one may consider this trend as a sign of growing interdisciplinarity, nothing is certain. The pull of the policy audience, to quote Sarat and Silbey,[43] tends to equate the production of empirical data with social sciences. This 'empirical turn' often misses the epistemological reflection on the underlying theories for each type of analysis, or insufficient attention is paid to the necessity of framing research questions carefully to be able to produce relevant interpretations and to situate them in the social science literature. This trend can be identified in the United States, in the 'empirical legal studies' movement, which is far more sophisticated methodologically than anything

[40] Research Project Elidroit, 'La formation au droit des élites du public et du privé depuis 1958. Quels savoirs juridiques pour quels modes de gouvernement?', funded by the Agence Nationale de la Recherche (ANR), research grant ANR-08-GOUV-065.

[41] E Biland and L Israël, 'A l'école du droit. Les apports de la méthode ethnographique à l'analyse de l'enseignement du droit' (2011) 52 *Les cahiers de droit* 619–58.

[42] 'Black-letter law' refers, in common law systems, to the known and accepted principles of law set down and established, either in legislation or case law, and ascertainable from printed sources. The established, uncontested body of law. (black-letter law. *Oxford Reference*, at www.oxfordreference.com/view/10.1093/oi/authority.20110803095510675).

[43] A Sarat and S Silbey, 'The Pull of the Policy Audience' (1988) 10(2–3) *Law & Policy* 97–166.

existing in France in law departments. In contrast to law and society scholarship, empirical legal studies most often lack critical perspective and assume a positivist attitude towards data within a policy-oriented vision of law often echoing the law and economics perspective.

Today, in the French context, despite a few exceptions, interdisciplinary research between lawyers and sociologists of law does not appear to be that productive. In a way, both perspectives may be too instrumental towards each other, given the historical context in which each discipline developed. It does not mean that lawyers and sociologists (or other social scientists) should despise or avoid each other; on the contrary, one should advocate frankly considering different perspectives, notably on law and legal institutions, from each side. I recently undertook an experiment while teaching a class for three years with a colleague, a lawyer specialising in jurisprudence, Olivier Cayla. Instead of trying to situate ourselves 'in the middle ground' between law and sociology, the choice we made was to contrast various ways of addressing the same objects from our respective disciplines, in this case, by studying supreme court and adjudication.

In doing so, I also moved to a more ambitious perspective on law and legal subjects. I moved from a standpoint where I considered that a sociological perspective was more realistic regarding law, adding flesh and blood to our knowledge of socio-legal phenomenon, to the ambition of producing an alternate vision of a classical legal object.[44] For example, my ongoing research is dealing with a small profession, *Avocats au conseil d'État et à la Cour de cassation* (French Supreme Courts lawyers). In their scholarship, French (and other) academic lawyers tend to focus on the decisions of the highest courts to identify the meaningful precedents and strive to explain them, without considering the social process whereby cases have acquired this singular status. The traditional doctrinal approach in French legal studies is based on the search of analytical insights, built on the study of black letter law, that is, doctrinal analysis is still at the basis of legal understanding. The decision is interpreted as a solution to a legal problem with 'the' judge being an abstract entity through which justice is done. (The expression in French is that judges are 'the mouths of law'.) In this context, how legal subjects access law (and its various levels), and the role of legal auxiliaries such as lawyers – almost always compulsory at this level – are barely, if ever, mentioned. The question is dealt with as mere 'procedure', namely the practical aspects of the judicial process and deference to legal formalism is considered as the guarantee of fair trial. To shed light on how French supreme courts are actually working, it is worth considering how cases are transformed into causes brought before the highest jurisdictions.[45] It

[44] L Israël, 'A Realist Perspective on Legal Strategy in (the) Practice' in S Talesh, E Mertz and H Klug (eds), *Research Handbook on Modern Legal Realism* (Cheltenham, Elgar Publishing, 2021).

[45] C Durand and L Israël, 'Porter la cause devant les Hautes Cours. Justiciables et auxiliaires du droit entre politisation et technicisation' (2022) 139(3) *Politix* 117–43.

is thus worthy of interest to bring into light a little-known but crucial actor: the *avocats aux conseils*, French supreme courts' lawyers. This distinct profession has enjoyed a monopoly on defence before the French high courts (Cour de cassation and Conseil d'Etat) for several centuries, since the Ancien Régime. (Before the French Revolution of 1789, their title was 'King's counsels'). Unknown to most citizens, these highly specialised lawyers are limited in number (131 at present, for 70 offices) but are nevertheless compulsory intermediaries to bring one's case before these highest-rank jurisdictions. Moreover, they play a role before other jurisdictions where they do not benefit from a monopoly, such as the Constitutional Court (Conseil constitutionnel), where they operate in approximatively 50 per cent of cases, or at the level of European jurisdictions. The hypothesis developed in the research project devoted to this profession[46] is that it is not reasonable to consider that this abstraction named 'the judge' is producing a decision as if the role of lawyers was negligible, especially in the matters brought before the supreme courts that require the most sophisticated expertise. Empirically, to fully understand adjudication means paying attention to legal auxiliaries such as lawyers in their relation to the judges, including their mutual social and historical relations. More theoretically, it implies that adjudication should be understood as a collective and social process, far from the disincarnated and analytically informed vision of the creation of precedents.

IV. CONCLUSION

'Socio-legal studies' does not translate easily into French. In relation to traditional boundaries in the national academic world, the sociology of law has been the closest field of research to such an interdisciplinary approach. However, sociology 'of' law indicates a direction, from sociology to law, the latter being the subject of inquiry of the former. This relation, prevailing as it is in France, or maybe this subjection alone, makes a difference compared to 'socio-legal studies' as it has been developed most notably in the United States. Building on legal realism,[47] it has given birth to an interdisciplinary perspective on law based on social sciences, but mainly located in law faculties and tailored to enhance legal knowledge, notably for reform purposes.[48] As this chapter elaborated, the American perspective has progressively attracted scholars from abroad, helping to launch an interdisciplinary and international dialog on various phenomena

[46] Collective project 'Avoconseils: Accès à la justice et défense devant les hautes cours. Le rôle des avocats aux conseils', funded by the French National Research Council (ANR), research grant ANR-21-CE41-0020. Members are Claire Lemercier (CNRS), Laure Blévis (U Nanterre), Mélanie Sargeac (post-doc), Ana-Maria Falconi (data analyst) and Liora Israël (EHESS) – PI.

[47] B Garth and J Sterling, 'From Legal Realism to Law and Society: Reshaping Law for the Last Stages of the Social Activist State' (1998) 32 *Law & Society Review* 409–72.

[48] A Vauchez, 'Entre droit et sciences sociales. Retour sur l'histoire du mouvement' *Law and Society*' (2001) 45(4) *Genèses* 134–49.

related to law. The consequences are certainly manifold, but two of them could be of interest for a general reflection. First, if new fruitful concepts have emerged (eg cause lawyering) or have been reframed (eg legal consciousness) in the law and society scholarship, their mobilisation in other national and historical concepts ought to take account of the cultural, national and institutional variations intrinsically related to law and legal institutions. Second, the pull of the policy audience is triggering new incentives to develop empirical approaches to legal phenomena. Nevertheless, the call for interdisciplinarity should not entail neglect of epistemological and reflexive analyses, which remain necessary to assess critically the powers of law in contemporary societies.[49]

[49] M García-Villegas, *The Powers of Law: A Comparative Analysis of Sociopolitical Legal Studies* (Cambridge, Cambridge University Press, 2018).

7

Interdisciplinary Labour Law Studies: From Critical Legal Studies to the Sociology of Law and Back Again

EVA KOCHER

SINCE 2009, I have held the 'Chair for Civil Law, European and German Labour Law as well as Civil Procedure' at my university. In 2018, I renamed the unit 'Center for Interdisciplinary Labour Law Studies' (C*LLaS), marketing my socio-legal approach to labour lawyers internationally.[1] The term 'interdisciplinary labour law studies' is meant to represent my intellectual and professional development between labour law and socio-legal studies, and that's why this autoethnographic chapter[2] will be built around the ideas and concepts behind it. There is rather little research on the relationship between the two areas,[3] so part of the following report comes from anecdotal evidence of my own professional career.

I. GERMAN SOCIOLOGY OF LAW VERSUS CRITICAL LEGAL STUDIES

In 1980, the German *Journal of the Sociology of Law* (*Zeitschrift für Rechtssoziologie*, *ZfRSoz*) came out with its first issue.[4] Establishing an academic journal is an event that marks institutionalisation. The first issue can therefore

[1] See the self-description of C*LLaS on the German socio-legal blog (Eva Kocher, 'Kartographie rechtssoziologischer Forschung: C*LLaS in Frankfurt (Oder), 29 September 2021, https://barblog.hypotheses.org/4068).

[2] H Chang, *Autoethnography as Method* (London, Routledge, 2008).

[3] Exceptions are mentioned below in the section 'Labour Law's Contribution to Socio-Legal Studies, and Vice Versa'.

[4] cf S Machura, 'Milestones and Directions: Socio-Legal Studies in Germany and the United Kingdom' (2020) 21(7) *German Law Journal* 1318; predecessor (1977–79) was *Informationsbrief für Rechtssoziologie.*

be regarded as a positioning statement, not only for the editors, but also for the academic community they intend to represent.

The editors'[5] Preface[6] positions the discipline in tension with the legal profession and mainstream legal academia: 'Sociology of law has always been of particular appeal to the legal profession, but it has also been the object of particularly fierce opposition' ('Die Rechtssoziologie ist für die juristische Profession stets von besonderem Reiz, aber auch Gegenstand besonders heftiger Abwehr gewesen'). In addition, however, they situate the journal also in opposition to an important school of legal-academic thought, namely Critical Legal Studies. Issue one of *ZfRSoz* in 1980 contains a chapter with texts by German socio-legal scholars Ekkehard Klausa, Klaus F Röhl, Ralf Rogowski and Hubert Rottleuthner (three of them editors of the journal), who together wrote an omnibus review of several publications that founding members of Critical Legal Studies (CLS) had indicated to them as important texts representing what CLS in the United States was up to. On 40 out of the 140 pages of *ZfRSoz*' first issue, Klausa and others show how the CLS movement started off as a counter-movement to the Law and Society Association's sociology of law. In their view, CLS's political goals were at best 'romantic communal thinking and de-formalisation of the law'; they saw a certain 'cloudiness', 'hard on the edge of a guru system'.[7]

This strong distancing of German sociology of law from CLS is remarkable but no surprise if one considers the history of the sociology of law in the first half of the twentieth century. It shows that searching for the origins of the German socio-legal tradition in that period can be misleading. In fact, German socio-legal studies in the 1950s and 1960s could not look back on a continuous history of intellectual development and academic institutionalisation. With the murder and the emigration of many socio-legal scholars with socialist and/or Jewish backgrounds, German legal academia was cut off from the Weimar tradition after the Second World War. Some of the emigrés were later instrumental in building a socio-legal tradition in the United Kingdom.[8]

The story of how, in the Federal Republic of Germany, sociology of law restarted in the 1960s, in close connection with the debate about legal education, has been told before.[9] After all, socio-legal studies and the sociology of

[5] The journal was founded by Erhard Blankenburg, Volkmar Gessner, Wolfgang Kaupen, Ekkehard Klausa, Rüdiger Lautmann, Niklas Luhmann, Klaus Röhl, Hubert Rottleuthner and Manfred Weiss.

[6] Zeitschrift für Rechtssoziologie (editorial board), 'Zum ersten Heft der Zeitschrift für Rechtssoziologie' (1980) 1 *Zeitschrift für Rechtssoziologie* 1, 1–3.

[7] E Klausa, 'On Duncan Kennedy: Form and Substance in Private Law Adjudication' 92–97 in E Klausa et al, 'Rezension eines Denkansatzes: Die Conference on Critical Legal Studies' (1980) 1 *Zeitschrift für Rechtssoziologie* 85–126.

[8] On Kahn-Freund, see, for example, M Freedland, 'Otto Kahn-Freund (1900–1979)' in J Beatson and R Zimmermann (eds), *Jurists Uprooted. German-Speaking Émigré Lawyers in Twentieth-Century Britain* (Oxford, OUP, 2004); R Lewis, 'Kahn-Freund and Labour Law: An Outline Critique' (1979) 8 *Industrial Law Journal* 202. More below in Section III.A.

[9] M Wrase, 'Rechtssoziologie und Law and Society – Die deutsche Rechtssoziologie zwischen Krise und Neuaufbruch' (2006) 27(2) *Zeitschrift für Rechtssoziologie* 289; E Kocher,

law were reinvented more or less from scratch with the student revolution in the 1960s (and its predecessors, such as Wolfgang Kaupen).[10] The radical thinking of the 1960s and 1970s, that is, the political movements and their translation into policy by social democrats, had their part in shaping the development of German sociology of law.

As a consequence, when the window of opportunity for profound reforms of legal education and for institutional experiments was starting to close by the 1980s, it also did so for the attempts to embed socio-legal interdisciplinary thinking in German law faculties.[11] The movement had not succeeded in sustainably institutionalising a renewal in legal education, and the pilot projects of one-phased interdisciplinary education that had hosted most of the socio-legal scholars of the time now started to come to their end. When the term for these experiments – undertaken, for example, in Bremen, Hamburg, Hannover or Konstanz – expired in 1985,[12] it became obvious that little space for socio-legal studies would be left. Faculty nomination policies again looked for doctrinal scholars that would prepare students for state exams, which until today mainly ask for doctrinal thinking and writing.[13]

This was the situation in which the founders of *ZfRSoz* felt the need to distance themselves from Critical Legal Studies and position themselves on the side of socio-legal studies as represented by the Law and Society Association in the US. The debates about a reorientation of German law faculties and German legal education were at the time strongly charged as a political rather than an academic topic, and this worked against the socio-legal reformers. The distancing from CLS in *ZfRSoz* 1/1980 can be interpreted as part of the struggle to frame the discipline as a mainly academic exercise.

II. MY OWN ACADEMIC TRAJECTORY

A. A Critical Legal Scholar, at the Fringes of Academia

Since the beginning of my academic career, I have been involved at the other side of that opposition, that is, on the side of critical legal studies. Since 2001,

'Rechtssoziologie': Das Recht der Gesellschaft und die Gesellschaft des Rechts' (2017) 2 *Zeitschrift für rechtswissenschaftliche Forschung* 153; Machura (n 4).

[10] This is also how the editorial board describes it in issue 1: Zeitschrift für Rechtssoziologie (editorial board), 'Zum ersten Heft' (n 6) 2.

[11] On the links between these developments, see Wrase 'Rechtssoziologie' (n 9); E Kocher, 'Gelegenheitsstrukturen interdisziplinären Arbeitens – damals und heute' (2022) 5 *Mittelweg 36* 55–56, following the approach of C Morrill et al, 'Conversations in Law and Society. Oral Histories of the Emergence and Transformation of the Movement' (2020) 16(1) *Annual Review of Law and Social Science* 97–116.

[12] This happened with a revision of s 5d of the German Judiciary Act (*Deutsches Richtergesetz*, DRiG) which regulates legal education.

[13] The state of institutionalisation is summarised, for example, by H Uebach and S Leuschner, 'Zum Stand der rechtssoziologischen Lehre und Forschung im deutschsprachigen Raum' (2010) 31(2) *Zeitschrift für Rechtssoziologie* 303–09.

I have been one of the editors of the journal *Kritische Justiz* (KJ), the first issue of which appeared in 1968. This date tells you most of what you need to know about KJ.[14] It is no coincidence that it was a text on gender and the state that got me involved with *Kritische Justiz*, a text that can be seen as an attempt to find my place in legal academia as the feminist I considered myself to be.[15]

As a researcher, I have grown rather at the fringes of legal academia. I had not been set on an academic career for a long time. The reason I was interested in a PhD at all in 1990 was my experience as a moderator/facilitator (we were called *Teamer*) in courses for Works Council members organised by the German Trade Union Association (DGB, *Deutscher Gewerkschaftsbund*). Some of these courses focused on corporate restructuring, and there was a specific doctrinal question that we routinely worked around. I became interested in exploring how this doctrinal question could be addressed in a juridical/technical way. That's why I took some time after my first state exam to write a dissertation.[16]

The PhD was funded by Hans-Böckler-Stiftung, an academic foundation which German journals tend to characterise as *gewerkschaftsnah* (close to trade unions). During my PhD, I did not really make contact with academia as a community. After my second state exam, I planned to work as a practising lawyer. It was Professor Dr Heide Pfarr who changed my course in a one-hour talk. She suggested to me that – contrary to what I had been feeling – a 'professor' is not a different kind of human being, but a professional career one could aspire to. And while I did not feel like entering a German law faculty, things worked out when I was offered a job as an assistant (*Wissenschaftliche Assistentin C1*) at what was then the Hochschule für Wirtschaft and Politik in Hamburg, later renamed Hamburger Universität für Wirtschaft und Politik (HWP, Hamburg University for Economics and Politics). The HWP is – or rather was[17] – an institution with a very special and different academic tradition. It was founded as a trade-union academy, particularly addressing students without formal university entrance qualification, with project-oriented forms of teaching and learning, interdisciplinary design, departmental structures, almost no formal hierarchy amongst academics and a strong tradition in labour and consumer law.

HWP and KJ both were great places for me. I very much doubt that I would have been able to develop my own thinking and writing in a traditional legal academic environment. Nevertheless, these were the wrong places to learn something about academic habitus and the workings of German law faculties.

[14] On the intellectual development of *Kritische Justiz* cf S Buckel, A Fischer-Lescano and F Haschmann 'Die Geburt der Kritischen Justiz aus der Praxis des Widerständigen' (2008) 3 *Kritische Justiz* 235–42; T Hitzel-Cassagnes, 'Ein halbes Jahrhundert!?' (2018) 51(4) *Kritische Justiz* 394–95.

[15] E Kocher, 'Geschlechterdifferenz und Staat' (1999) 32(2) *Kritische Justiz* 182.

[16] E Kocher, 'Neue Sozialplaninhalte bei EDV-Einführung, insbesondere: Die Regelung von Arbeitsinhalten sowie von Versetzungsansprüchen in einem Sozialplan nach § 112 Abs. 4 BetrVG 1972' (Dissertation 1994).

[17] See U Reifner, *Sozialökonomie in Hamburg. Abschied (von) der HWP* (2012) (https://fsr-sozialoekonomie.de/wp-content/uploads/2018/12/Abschiedsvorlesung_komplett.pdf).

Only when I started to apply for professor positions at German law faculties did I become aware of how far off the mainstream I was perceived. My applications were so unsuccessful that I finally, in 2008, gave up trying and took a job as the director of Akademie der Arbeit in Frankfurt/Main, a trade-union academy.[18] It was pure luck that after all I suddenly did get a belated offer for a professorship, in Frankfurt (Oder), on the third spot of a list of three for the least attractive professorship possible (W2). That's where you still find me today, having meanwhile moved up to a chair (W3).

B. On Not Becoming a Socio-Legal Scholar

European University Viadrina proved to be the perfect place for me. The rather marginal and specially profiled university at the German-Polish border close to Berlin provided the space to pursue my own ideas, projects and approaches. And these have always been interdisciplinary. My PhD thesis, for example, argued against the *herrschende Meinung* (prevailing opinion) stating that social plans (Sec. 112 (5) Works Constitution Act (*Betriebsverfassungsgesetz*, BetrVG)) could provide more than financial compensation and also establish displacement rights for employees.[19] The main argument came from organisational studies and confronted the traditional legal view of how decision-making processes in firms are empirically organised and constructed.

My PhD thesis would probably not have been considered socio-legal at the time it was written. In 1993, sociology of law was still considered a discipline and not an adjective that could be applied to cross-sectional exercises such as these. My habilitation thesis (postdoctoral thesis to qualify as a university professor), however, could easily have been considered as sociology of law, and it is interesting to think about the reasons why I did not frame it this way, and why it has not been noticed by sociologists of the law. My habilitation thesis was concerned with the functions of jurisdiction in the resolution of social conflicts.[20] It compares German and English civil procedure with a functional approach to comparative law. For me, this meant thinking about the possible societal functions of jurisdiction in theoretical terms using Luhmannian and Habermasian approaches. While I learned a lot in the process, the work has hardly been read. I published it in a book series on comparative law and with a traditional editor (Mohr Siebeck) because I myself had not realised or understood that this was in fact a socio-legal book that could have been addressed to sociologists of law. Well, it may have been lost to these as well, hermetic as I had constructed it.

[18] It has since been renamed as Europäische Akademie der Arbeit.

[19] Kocher (n 16).

[20] E Kocher, *Funktionen der Rechtsprechung: Konfliktlösung im deutschen und englischen Verbraucherprozessrecht* (Tübingen, Mohr Siebeck, 2007).

III. THE SOCIO-LEGAL TRADITION OF LABOUR LAW

However, more or less right from the start of my academic career, there was an epistemic community that was taking note of what I was doing, and that has ultimately defined my career for many years: I have been considered a labour lawyer. The reason why this has been a good fit has probably something to do with the traditions of the epistemic communities of labour law.

A. A 'Sociological Method'? Labour Law in the Weimar Republic and After

German sociology of law developed from law and not from sociology.[21] Many of the socio-legal scholars of the Weimar Republic were labour lawyers or at least invested in labour law. Hugo Sinzheimer and Otto Kahn-Freund were practical lawyers from the field of labour law. Weimar social democratic lawyers created the concept of 'social law',[22] which found its expression in Hugo Sinzheimer's formula: 'Social law grasps man not as a person but as a social being' ('*Das soziale Recht erfasst den Menschen nicht als Person, sondern als soziales Wesen*').[23] Social law claims to look at the social power relations behind the formal equality of legal subjects and thus the human being in its social embedding. This is what Hugo Sinzheimer's 'sociological method' was mostly about.[24]

An influential example is the way Sinzheimer developed the law of collective bargaining out of the social practices he found of collective bargaining. He proposed regulating it according to what was needed to endorse collective agreements as acts of social self-determination, that is, a process of the formation of law out of society.[25] Another example is the stimulatingly titled text *Das soziale Ideal des Reichsarbeitsgerichts* (*The Social Ideal of the Reich's Federal Labour Court*) by Kahn-Freund of 1931. The text confronts the jurisdiction of that court with its effects in social life.[26] When the author later distanced himself from the text's bold assumptions about judges' subjective positions implicit in the text,

[21] S Machura, 'Zum kritischen Potential der Rechtssoziologie' in H Hof and PG von Olenhusen (eds), *Rechtsgestaltung – Rechtskritik – Konkurrenz von Rechtsordnungen. Neue Akzente für die Juristenausbildung* (Baden-Baden, Nomos, 2012) 220–31.

[22] A Seifert, '"Von der Person zum Menschen im Recht": Zum Begriff des sozialen Rechts bei Hugo Sinzheimer' (2011) 1(2) *Soziales Recht* 62; E Eichenhofer, 'Soziales Recht: Bemerkungen zur Begriffsgeschichte' (2012) 2(2) *Soziales Recht* 76; S Blanke, *Soziales Recht oder kollektive Privatautonomie?: Hugo Sinzheimer im Kontext nach 1900* (Tübingen, Mohr Siebeck, 2005); U Zachert, 'Hugo Sinzheimer: Praktischer Wissenschaftler und Pionier des modernen Arbeitsrechts' (2001) 54(2) *Recht der Arbeit* 104.

[23] H Sinzheimer, *Ein Arbeitstarifgesetz. Die Idee der sozialen Selbstbestimmung im Recht* (Berlin and Leipzig, Duncker & Humblot, 1916).

[24] Seifert (n 22) 65–66; Blanke (n 22) 101 seq.

[25] Sinzheimer (n 24) in particular at 186.

[26] O Kahn-Freund, *Das soziale Ideal des Reichsarbeitsgerichts: Eine kritische Untersuchung zur Rechtsprechung des Reichsarbeitsgerichts* (Bensheimer, Verlag, 1931).

he still endorsed the methodology of – as one might call it today – sociology of judicial decision-making.[27]

This proximity of labour law, social law and sociology of law is not a coincidence. After all, labour law is mostly built upon empirical assumptions such as the imbalance of power,[28] which is at the heart of labour law's very raison d'être.[29] Labour law is all about protecting the employee by compensating for this imbalance. For collective labour law, one of the most famous formula of the German Federal Labour Court (*Bundesarbeitsgericht*, BAG) justifies why the right of strike needs a stronger legal protection than the employers' right to lock out: Without the right to strike collective bargaining for trade unions would be nothing else than 'collective begging' ('*kollektives Betteln*').[30] This undoubtedly socio-legal formula, first used in 1980,[31] has been repeated time and time again in German labour law, most recently by the German Federal Constitutional Court (*Bundesverfassungsgericht*, BVerfG).[32]

B. Labour Law in the Federal Republic of Germany: The Development of an Epistemic Community

However, German labour law has travelled a long way from Sinzheimer to the 1980 formula. As in the legal system more generally,[33] labour law in the Federal Republic of Germany restarted after 1945 with mostly those lawyers and jurists who had more or less supported national socialism – the

[27] O Kahn-Freund and W Luthard, 'Autobiographische Erinnerungen an die Weimarer Republik: Interview mit Wolfgang Luthard' (1981) 14(2) *Kritische Justiz* 183, 193–94. On Kahn-Freund as socio-legal and multidisciplinary thinker, see Freedland (n 8); Lewis (n 8).

[28] On the socio-legal figure of 'structural imbalance' – a figure from the Federal Constitutional Court that always had socio-legal scholars as judges, such as Jutta Limbach, Brun-Otto Bryde, Grimm, Hassemer, Hoffmann-Riem, Di Fabio, Lübbe-Wolf and, most recently, Susanne Baer – see K Röhl, *Rechtssoziologie – die Zukunftsdisziplin der Jurisprudenz. Aus der Abschiedsvorlesung ‚Auflösung des Rechts' von Prof. Röhl am 31. Juli 2003 in Bochum* (2003), www.ruhr-uni-bochum.de/rsozinfo/pdf/Zukunftsdisziplin.pdf.

[29] H Collins, G Lester and V Mantouvalou (eds), *Philosophical Foundations of Labour Law* (Oxford, OUP, 2018); E Kocher, *Digital Work Platforms at the Interface of Labour Law: Regulating Market Organisers* (London, Bloomsbury Publishing, 2022). This concept/approach was dubbed '*Kryptosoziologie*' (crypto sociology) by T Ramm, 'Zur Bedeutung der Rechtssoziologie für das Arbeitsrecht' (1970) 3 *Kritische Justiz* 175–84, 177.

[30] BAG 10 June 1980 (1 AZR 168/79), marg. 22.

[31] The court used a term apparently coined by Blanpain (who was mentioned in name in the judgment). Unfortunately, the pun (bargaining/begging) gets lost in translation (M Franzen, 'Kampfverbote für einzelne Tarifinhalte?' in V Rieble (ed), *Zukunft des Arbeitskampfs* (München, ZAAR Verlag, 2005) 141–67 (fn 2); on the origin with Blanpain see G Thüsing, *ZIP 2003*, 693 (701 (there fn. 69)).

[32] BVerfG 9 July 2020 (1 BvR 719/19), marg. 14, following BAG 12 Sept 1984 (1 AZR 342/83), marg. 14); updated in substance in BVerfG 19 June 2020 (1 BvR 842/17), margs. 27–32.

[33] The German Democratic Republic (DDR, *Deutsche Demokratische Republik*) is a wholly different story, one that was cut off in 1989/90. As German law of today mostly follows in the footsteps of BRD, I will leave DDR history aside in this text.

socialists/social democrats having emigrated or been killed under national socialism. The history and biographies, for example, of the judges of the Federal Labour Court in the 1950s and 1960s, with the ambivalent figure Hans-Carl Nipperdey at its head,[34] remains to be researched.[35] As for the representation of academic labour lawyers on the court, Britta Rehder shows the continuities on the conservative part of the labour law community who nevertheless then tended to take on Sinzheimer's ideas on industrial democracy.[36]

Against that background, it was an important step when the trade unions in the Federal Republic of Germany developed their own approach to the law. After having started, in the second half of the 1950s, with a rather intuitive critique of legalisation of political processes,[37] they subsequently developed approaches that would analyse how the law could be put to good use for trade unions. An important occasion in this development was the legal dispute after the strike in the Schleswig-Holstein metal industry, in 1956/57. This strike was the longest labour dispute in the history of the Federal Republic of Germany, lasting 16 weeks and involving a total of 34,000 people. The event was regarded as outstanding already by contemporaries. Michael Kittner who went on to be in-house legal counsel at industrial metalworkers' trade union IG Metall from 1972 on for almost 25 years, identified this as the event with which IG Metall entered into the history of the Federal Republic as a significant player.[38] While at the beginning of the 1970s 'there were hardly a dozen serious lawyers in Germany who were qualified in labour law in the trade union camp', this changed rapidly.[39]

For politically minded students after the 1968 movement, labour law became (next to criminal law) one of the fields which provided room for activism. With the growth of legislation and legalisation of social policy, corporate lawyers also entered the field. Legal and doctrinal (including academic) literature in German law is now mostly shaped by journals that primarily serve the huge and lucrative

[34] On Nipperdeys influence: B Rehder, *Rechtsprechung als Politik: Der Beitrag des Bundesarbeitsgerichts zur Entwicklung der Arbeitsbeziehungen in Deutschland* (Frankfurt Main Campus, Verlag, 2011) 239; T Tschenker, *Politischer Streik. Rechtsgeschichte und Dogmatik des Tarifbezugs und des Verbots des politischen Streiks* (Berlin, Duncker&Humblot, 2023) on Nipperdey's thinking.

[35] For a first attempt, see M Borowsky, 'Die NS-Belastung des Bundesarbeitsgerichts: Vorläufige Bilanz zur personellen Kontinuität' (2022) 55(4) *Kritische Justiz* 399; Research project 'Geschichte des Bundesarbeitsgerichts' (History of the Federal Labour Court) started in 2022 (press release 28/21 of 29/09/2021, www.bundesarbeitsgericht.de/presse/forschungsvorhaben-geschichte-des-bundesarbeitsgerichts/).

[36] Rehder (n 34) 178.

[37] For this discussion cf E Kocher, 'Solidarität und Menschenrechte – Zwei verschiedene Welten?' in H Lindemann et al (eds), *Erzählungen vom Konstitutionalismus: Festschrift für Günter Frankenberg* (Baden-Baden, Nomos, 2012); Kocher (n 28).

[38] M Kittner, *50 Urteile: Arbeitsgerichte schreiben Rechtsgeschichte* 3rd edn (Frankfurt/Main, Bund-Verlag, 2023) 287.

[39] M Kittner, '"Der Zeitzeuge" und die Toten' (2009) *Kritische Vierteljahresschrift für Gesetzgebung und Rechtswissenschaft* 427, 429 (who also links this development to 'post-1968' (his fn 11)).

market of commercial law firms.[40] For the years from 1965 on, Britta Rehder, who studied the epistemic community of German labour law with a focus on the intellectual development of the judges of the Federal Labour Court, found that with the effect of the growth, disintegration creeped into the epistemic community of labour law.[41]

C. Labour Law's Contribution to Socio-Legal Studies, and Vice Versa

Interest in a sociology of law in Germany reappeared at around the same time that actors such as trade unions and corporations entered the field of labour law. Both developments started being shaped by the opportunity structures the 1968 movements created. With Manfred Weiss, the *ZfRSoz* had a labour lawyer on its editorial board from the start. And at least those (academic) labour lawyers who were close to trade unions[42] or were part of the 1968 movement[43] took up labour law's Weimarian socio-legal tradition. In 1976, for example, the IG Metall's science foundation *Otto-Brenner-Stiftung* had Otto Kahn-Freund and Thilo Ramm edit a collection of Hugo Sinzheimer's texts and speeches.[44] In 1975, editors of *Kritische Justiz* put together a reading book with source texts on the history of labour law in Germany since 1840, also covering texts on economic development, political-social conflicts and legal changes with the intent of showing the social conditions of the law.[45] Kahn-Freund's cue was taken up by Wolfgang Däubler's *Das soziale Ideal des Bundesarbeitsgerichts* (*The Social Ideal of the Federal Labour Court*) in 1975, who found that, based on a Marxist analysis of objective interests, the Federal Labour Court was consistently prioritising companies' interests.[46,47]

[40] On issues of academic quality assurance, cf Kritische Justiz (Editorial board), 'Editorial. Ist die KJ peer reviewed? Wie wir Redaktionsverantwortung verstehen' (2021) 1 *Kritische Justiz* 126–30. cf the discussion around a racist contribution in the labour law journal *Neue Zeitschrift für Arbeitsrecht*, see M Jacobs and JM Schubert, 'Man wird doch wohl noch sagen dürfen … – Nein!' (2021) 4 *Neue Zeitschrift für Arbeitsrecht* 233–34.

[41] Rehder (n 34) 243 seq.

[42] Such as Wolfgang Däubler, Heide Pfarr, Otto Ernst Kempen and Ulrich Zachert.

[43] Such as Thomas Blanke, Rainer Erd and Ulrich Mückenberger (all long-time editors of *Kritische Justiz*).

[44] H Sinzheimer, *Arbeitsrecht und Rechtssoziologie: Gesammelte Aufsätze und Reden* ed by T Ramm and O Kahn-Freund (Frankfurt Main, Europäische Verlagsanstalt, 1976); cf Kittner (n 39) 429.

[45] T Blanke et al (eds), *Kollektives Arbeitsrecht. Quellentexte zur Geschichte des Arbeitsrechts in Deutschland 1840–1933* (Reinbek, Rowohlt, 1975); the labour law journal of the DGB (*Deutscher Gewerkschaftsbund*, German Trade Union Association) published a rather critical review by a historian (F Tennstedt (1977) 25 *Arbeit und Recht*, 24–25).

[46] W Däubler, *Das soziale Ideal des Bundesarbeitsgerichts* (Frankfurt Main, Europäische Verlagsanstalt, 1975) 22 seq on the concept.

[47] In 2010 Ulrike Wendeling-Schröder again used the title ('*Das soziale Ideal*') in her critique of the ECJ's decisions in Viking, Laval and Rüffert (U Wendeling-Schröder, 'Das soziale Ideal des Europäischen Gerichtshofs: Eine kritische Untersuchung der aktuellen Rechtsprechung des EuGH zum Arbeitskampf- und Tarifrecht' in T Dieterich et al (eds), *Individuelle und kollektive Freiheit*

Against the backdrop of an ongoing employment crisis beginning 1974/75, the end of the 1970s brought two large empirical projects, one on the mobilisation of dismissal protection by employees, and another more general one on procedures before the labour courts. After a sharp increase in the number of actions for protection against unfair dismissal brought before the labour courts, dismissal protection became a contested political topic. The Federal Ministry of Labour and Social Affairs funded an empirical research project from 1978 to 1980,[48] conducted by the *Sozialwissenschaftliche Forschungsgruppe* (Social Science Research Group) that had already been established in 1975 at the Max Planck Institute for Foreign Private Law and Private International Law in Hamburg. Its purpose was initiating interdisciplinary and comparative research in the socio-legal field.[49] A second study at the Freie Universität Berlin[50] was coordinated by Hubert Rottleuthner.[51] The projects also reflected and expressed a renewed general interest in research about judiciaries and judging. The book *Arbeitsgerichtsprotokolle* (*Labour Court Records*) documents an interesting aspect: it collects a large report from a group of labour judges who collectively reflected on their experiences and the social fabric they saw in their cases.[52]

The two research projects on dismissal protection and labour courts had a majority of lawyers on the teams some of whom doubled as sociologists or legal philosophers. They were prolific in their contribution to the German socio-legal field. Although the research group at the Max Planck Institute

im Arbeitsrecht: Gedächtnisschrift für Ulrich Zachert (Baden-Baden, Nomos, 2010)). The decisions discussed here are at the centre of a long (and ongoing) debate on the role of social policy in the context of the (neo)liberal economic policies of the EEC and the ECJ; see, for example, R Blanpain and AM Świątkowski (eds), *The Laval and Viking Cases: Freedom of Services and Establishment v. Industrial Conflict in the European Economic Area and Russia* (Alphen aan den Rijn, Wolter Kluwers, 2009); M Freedland and J Prassl (eds), *Viking, Laval and Beyond* (London, Hart Publishing, 2016).

[48] Results published here: J Falke et al, *Kündigungspraxis und Kündigungsschutz in der Bundesrepublik Deutschland: Bd. 1 und 2* (Bonn, BMAS, 1981).

[49] D Martiny, 'Entstehung, Tätigkeit und Perspektiven der Sozialwissenschaftlichen Forschungsgruppe' in K Plett and K Ziegert (eds), *Empirische Rechtsforschung zwischen Wissenschaft und Politik – Zur Problemlage rechtssoziologischer Auftragsforschung* (Tübingen, Mohr Siebeck, 1984) 19–26. From April 1977 to 1982, the research group had also received funding by *Volkswagen Stiftung*.

[50] Results published here: R Ellermann-Witt, H Rottleuthner and H Russig, 'Einleitung der Herausgeber' in R Ellermann-Witt, H Rottleuthner and H Russig (eds), *Kündigungspraxis, Kündigungsschutz und Probleme der Arbeitsgerichtsbarkeit: Beiträge zur Regelung und Praxis in der Bundesrepublik Deutschland, in Großbritannien und den USA* (Opladen, Westdeutscher Verlag, 1983); H Rottleuthner (ed), *Rechtssoziologische Studien zur Arbeitsgerichtsbarkeit* (Baden-Baden, Nomos, 1984) (reviewed by KJ Bieback (1985) *Arbeit und Recht* 256–57).

[51] These researchers shared and confronted their empirical results with the UK Social Science Research Council's 'Industrial Relations Research Unit' at the University of Warwick that at the same time did a survey among the parties of dismissal protection proceedings in British employment tribunals. Cf Ellermann-Witt, Rottleuthner and Russig (n 49) on the one side and L Dickens et al, *Dismissed: A Study of Unfair Dismissal and the Industrial Tribunal System* (Oxford, Basil Blackwell, 1985) on the other side.

[52] K Feser et al, 'Arbeitsgerichtsprotokolle' in K Feser et al (eds), *Arbeitsgerichtsprotokolle* 2nd edn (Neuwied, Darmstadt, Luchterhand, 1982).

was not established permanently within the institute after Konrad Zweigert retired as director,[53] efforts to find funding succeeded with Land Bremen funding the *Zentrum für Europäische Rechtspolitik* (ZERP, Centre for European Legal Policy) that concentrated on law in Europe and the law of the European Economic Community.[54] While ZERP itself (which still exists) did not become a fixed institutional presence of sociology of law or socio-legal studies, Josef Falke and Armin Höland continued their socio-legal work at that centre. Each served for quite some time as editors of *Zeitschrift für Rechtssoziologie*.

Armin Höland as well as Hubert Rottleuthner also came to be professors at German law faculties. Their careers indicate how the epistemic communities of labour law and sociology of law intersect as well as diverge, and how research interests and projects had to be balanced between the fields. Armin Höland, professor for labour law at Martin-Luther-University Halle (Saale) from 1999 to 2014, continued to cross borders by providing empirical data on important developments in labour law, as well as reflecting on socio-legal theory.[55] Together with Wolfhard Kohte (who is still on the advisory board of *ZfRSoz*), he established a focus of (what I would now call) interdisciplinary labour law studies at the law faculty in Halle (Saale).

Hubert Rottleuthner, on the other hand, had always been more of a sociologist of law and even published a textbook for students on the field.[56] He invested in labour law due to his interest in research on the judiciary. Having written his PhD under the supervision of Jürgen Habermas,[57] he was also no stranger to *Kritische Theorie* (*Critical Theory*) and had published some theoretical considerations on judges' practices in *Kritische Justiz*[58] at around the same time his book *Rechtswissenschaft als Sozialwissenschaft* (*Law as a Social Science*)[59] became the reference for those interested in an interdisciplinary reform of legal studies in Germany. Rottleuthner was one of the first editors of *ZfRSoz* (and took part in the exercise of evaluating critical legal studies for the first issue of the journal). He held the chair for sociology of law at the law faculty at Freie Universität Berlin from 1975 to 2012.

[53] cf protest note by both German associations for the sociology of law, as documented and commented by E Klausa, 'Der Fall Hamburg: Aufstieg und Demontage einer Forschungsgruppe und etwas Überlebenshoffnung' (1980) 1 *Zeitschrift für Rechtssoziologie* 135–37.

[54] Martiny (n 49).

[55] For example, A Höland, U Reim and H Brecht, *Flächentarifvertrag und Günstigkeitsprinzip. Empirische Beobachtungen und rechtliche Betrachtungen der Anwendung von Flächentarifverträgen in den Betrieben* (Baden-Baden, Nomos, 2000); A Höland et al, *The Roles, Resources and Competencies of Employee Lay Judges. A Cross-National Study of Germany, France and Great Britain* (Düsseldorf, Working Paper Forschungsförderung, 2017).

[56] H Rottleuthner, *Einführung in die Rechtssoziologie* (Darmstadt, Wissenschaftliche Buchgesellschaft, 1987).

[57] H Rottleuthner, *Richterliches Handeln: Zur Kritik der juristischen Dogmatik* (Frankfurt Main, Athenäum, 1973).

[58] H Rottleuthner, 'Zur Soziologie richterlichen Handelns I' (1970) 3(3) *Kritische Justiz* 283; H Rottleuthner, 'Zur Soziologie richterlichen Handelns II' (1971) 4(1) *Kritische Justiz* 60.

[59] H Rottleuthner, *Rechtswissenschaft als Sozialwissenschaft* (Frankfurt Main, Fischer, 1973).

In labour law, the tradition of large empirical studies was resumed in 2001 when Heide Pfarr was director of the (trade-union-funded) Institute of Economic and Social Research (*Wirtschafts- und Sozialwissenschaftliches Institut*, WSI) at Hans-Böckler-Stiftung. At a time when dismissal protection had once again become a contested political topic, she initiated empirical studies and surveys on dismissal practices and protection against dismissal (designed explicitly in the tradition of the MPI-studies of the 1980s),[60] on labour market regulation[61] and on the use of labour law by human resources departments in companies.[62] First results were presented at the 64th German Jurists Forum (*Deutscher Juristentag*)[63] in Bonn 2004 where Heide Pfarr gave one of the presentations. The voting in the final resolution may give an impression of how polarised the field has been, and how strongly empirical work as such has been considered trade union activism. On the question of how to relieve burdens on small and medium-sized enterprises, the Labour Law Section of the Forum, with 55 votes against 15 (15 abstaining), rejected that the conference 'acknowledge the sociological representative studies on the establishment and termination of employment relationships, … carried out especially last year, as a significant contribution to ensuring a rational legal policy discussion'.[64] Interdisciplinary labour law studies seem to have ended up just as torn in politics as sociology of law had been in the 1970s.[65]

IV. SOCIO-LEGAL STUDIES AS INTERDISCIPLINARY LEGAL STUDIES

For me as an academic scholar, labour law and its interdisciplinary currents were, for a long time, a better fit than sociology of law and socio-legal studies.

[60] A Höland, U Kahl and N Zeibig, *Kündigungspraxis und Kündigungsschutz im Arbeitsverhältnis: Eine empirische Praxisuntersuchung aus Sicht des arbeitsgerichtlichen Verfahrens* (Baden-Baden, Nomos, 2007); see also J Falke and A Höland, *Die Rechtspraxis der Beendigung von Arbeitsverhältnissen. Vorüberlegungen zu einem neuen Forschungsprojekt* (Bremen, ZERP, 1997).

[61] H Pfarr et al, *Der Kündigungsschutz zwischen Wahrnehmung und Wirklichkeit: Betriebliche Erfahrungen mit der Beendigung von Arbeitsverhältnissen* (Augsburg Rainer Hampp, Verlag, 2005), with an update of 2007/2008: M Gensicke, H Pfarr, N Tschersich, K Ullmann and N Zeibig, 'Rechtstatsachen zum Kündigungsschutz: Neue Erkenntnisse über die Beendigung von Arbeitsverhältnissen in der Praxis' (2008) 56(12) *Arbeit und Recht* 431–38.

[62] F Schramm and U Zachert (eds), *Arbeitsrecht in der betrieblichen Anwendung. Mythen und Realität* (Augsburg Rainer Hampp, Verlag, 2005).

[63] Information on the association can be found in English on https://djt.de/djt-e-v/der-verein/english/.

[64] Deutscher Juristentag, 'Die Beschlüsse des 65. Deutschen Juristentags Bonn 2004' (2004) *Neue Juristische Wochenschrift* 3242–44.

[65] The highly polarised voting with participation of corporate lawyers present at the forum but not at the section, leading to a majorisation by employers' interests between 1978 and 2004, led to a suspension of voting in 2006 and again in 2014 (cf M Weiss, 'Arbeitsrecht als Gegenstand der Beratungen des Deutschen Juristentags' in Ständige Deputation des Deutschen Juristentages and F Busse (eds), *Festschrift 150 Jahre Deutscher Juristentag 1860–2010* (München, Beck, 2010) 371–410).

After all, what has most characterised my academic work is interdisciplinary and empirical work at the interfaces of disciplines and in interdisciplinary cooperation[66] similarly to how Armin Höland, Wolfhard Kohte, Felix Welti (a social security and rehabilitation law lawyer) and others have been working.

It took me around 20 years to start thinking about myself as a socio-legal scholar and position my work in the context of the sociology of law. I had learned a lot about the pitfalls of interdisciplinarity and about the need to develop methodologies for interdisciplinary work. In my experience, many social scientists underestimate how much legal knowledge structures any empirical field, but overestimate the law's regulative effects and neglect the socio-political dynamics working inside 'the law'. Analysing these experiences led me to theoretical reflections on transdisciplinarity and interdisciplinarity.[67]

At the same time, the German academic community of the sociology of law came to meet me halfway by, for example, the German Association for the Sociology of Law renaming itself *Vereinigung für Recht und Gesellschaft* (German Association for Law and Society) in 2010. Considering that German sociology of law had hibernated quite successfully with systems theory,[68] this reinvention (or rather opening) of the field has with good reason been perceived as a sign of weakness of the socio-legal community.[69] The fact that since 2018, it is me who is the president of the *Vereinigung* can be seen as just another expression of such weakness – considering that my work has been considered as rather off the mainstream, and that the socio-legal community still finds it hard to accept the marginalisation critical legal studies tends to provoke.[70]

[66] The results have been published, for example, in E Kocher et al, *Das Recht auf eine selbstbestimmte Erwerbsbiographie: Arbeits- und sozialrechtliche Regulierung für Übergänge im Lebenslauf. Ein Beitrag zu einem Sozialen Recht der Arbeit* (Baden-Baden, Nomos, 2013); E Kocher, 'Codes of Conduct and Framework Agreements an Social Minimum Standards – Private Regulation?' in O Dilling, M Herberg and G Winter (eds), *Responsible Business* (London, Hart Publishing 2008); I Hensel et al (eds), *Selbstständige Unselbstständigkeit: Crowdworking zwischen Autonomie und Kontrolle* (Baden-Baden, Nomos, 2019); D Schönefeld et al, *Jobs für die Crowds: Werkstattbericht zu einem neuen Forschungsfeld* (Frankfurt (Oder) Arbeit|Grenze|Fluss vol. 1, 2017); M Ivanova et al, *The App as a Boss?: Control and Autonomy in Application-Based Management* (Frankfurt (Oder) Arbeit|Grenze|Fluss vol. 2, 2018); B Emunds et al, 'Gute Arbeit für Live-In-Care: Gestaltungsoptionen für Praxis und Politik' (Frankfurt Main, NBI-Positionen 2, 2021).

[67] In particular: E Kocher, 'Die transdisziplinäre Rechtsforschung braucht die Rechtssoziologie – und umgekehrt' (2016) 36(2) *Zeitschrift für Rechtssoziologie* 245–54.

[68] eg, Gunther Teubner (Frankfurt/Main) had established a rather influential school of socio-legal thought; at University Bielefeld, in particular with Alfons Bora, the Luhmannian socio-legal tradition in sociology is being continued (see, eg A Bora, 'Responsive Rechtssoziologie' (2016) 36(2) *Zeitschrift für Rechtssoziologie* 261–72).

[69] cf on the one side Wrase (n 9); on the other side K Röhl, '§ 13.II. Von Law-and-Something zu Law-and-Society', *Rechtssoziologie-online* (2012) https://rechtssoziologie-online.de/kapitel-2/%C2%A7-13die-rechtssoziologie-gegenwart/.

[70] See, eg M Wrase (2000) 4 *Zeitschrift für Didaktik der Rechtswissenschaft* 247–48.

Nevertheless, interest in the discipline has grown almost exponentially. Socio-legal conferences have been overrun by early-career researchers, even in Germany and the German-speaking community. This could be the result of intersecting developments. Societal opportunity structures for socio-legal studies[71] are more favourable today than they were in the 1990s and 2000s, partly thanks to an accumulation of crises. Mainstream legal education as well as methods are stuck in a dead end and are looking for stimuli from outside.[72] New social movements and socio-political debates – today often organised as social media campaigns such as #MeToo or Black Lives Matter (BLM) – offer opportunities for the formation of academic communities in critical and in interdisciplinary legal research.

As of today, much of the interest in socio-legal studies is fostered by theoretical critiques of the law[73] and focusses on intersectional questions of gender, race and class. The collective review in issue one of *ZfRSoz* shows the height of the case that has arisen. The same theorists that the German legal sociologists then called 'the woolly darkies from the camp of the French structuralists'[74] have come to dominate the field. German legal academia is grappling with what American Thomas Heller had already explained back then in 1980: Critical Legal Studies was and still is about 'a new agenda for cultural politics'. Ultimately, empiricism may 'do no more than report the ideological reproductions of an individualistic culture which appears at the level of an actor's consciousness'.[75] Feminist legal studies, critical race theory, postcolonial legal criticism or queer legal theory question the symbolic structures of law and the legal system and look at forms of social power and hegemony that had previously only played a marginal role in the sociology of law.[76]

In spite of this renewed interest, there is a lack of institutional academic infrastructures for socio-legal studies and sociology of law in Germany that

[71] For this approach: Morrill et al (n 11); Kocher, 'Gelegenheitsstrukturen' (n 11).

[72] E Hilgendorf and H Schulze-Fielitz (eds), *Selbstreflexion der Rechtswissenschaft* 2nd edn (Tübingen, Mohr Siebeck, 2021); J Jestaedt and O Lepsius (eds), *Rechtswissenschaftstheorie* (Mohr Siebeck, Tübingen, 2008); E Engel and W Schön (eds), *Das Proprium der Rechtswissenschaft* (Mohr Siebeck, Tübingen, 2007). See also Wissenschaftsrat (ed), *Perspektiven der Rechtswissenschaft in Deutschland. Situation, Analysen, Empfehlungen* (Hamburg, Wissenschaftsrat, 2012).

[73] On the different dimensions of 'critical' cf Machura (n 21); M Valverde, *Chronotopes of Law. Jurisdiction, Scale and Governance* (New York, Routledge, 2015) 31.

[74] H Rottleuthner, 'On Isaac Balbus, Commodity Form and Legal Form: An Essay on the "Relative Autonomy" of the Law' in Klausa et al 'Rezension' (n 7) at 109–14.

[75] T Heller, 'A Brief Rejoinder to the Discussion of the CCLS' in Klausa et al, 'Rezension' (n 7) at 129.

[76] Kocher (n 9); see, eg C Barskanmaz, 'Rassismus, Postkolonialismus und Recht – Zu einer deutschen Critical Race Theory?' (2008) 41(3) *Kritische Justiz* 296; D Liebscher, *Rasse im Recht – Recht gegen Rassismus: Genealogie einer ambivalenten rechtlichen Kategorie* (Frankfurt Main, Suhrkamp, 2021); S Baer, 'Komplizierte Subjekte zwischen Recht und Geschlecht. Eine Einführung in feministische Ansätze in der Rechtswissenschaft' in C Kreuzer (ed), *Frauen im Recht – Entwicklung und Perspektiven* (Baden-Baden, Nomos, 2001) 9–25; P Dann, I Feichtner and J von Bernstorff (eds), *(Post)Koloniale Rechtswissenschaft: Geschichte und Gegenwart des Kolonialismus in der deutschen Rechtswissenschaft* (Tübingen, Mohr Siebeck, 2022).

could absorb and foster this interest. First, treating socio-legal and interdisciplinary as the adjectives they are, means that there are academic communities around that define fields and separate socio-legal scholars from one another. It is one thing to address all socio-legal scholars in name; it is another thing to gather socio-legal researchers on family law matters, economic justice or labour law, and expect that they have common issues to talk about. What the intersections come down to are often general questions of research on judges and judging or intersectional inequalities. Interest in interdisciplinary labour law research still remains restricted to labour lawyers.

At the same time, general theoretical thinking on the sociology of law does still not have an adequate space in a community framed as socio-legal.[77] The same is true for methodological thinking on how to do interdisciplinary and, in particular, empirical legal studies – beyond postmodern cultural studies and the economists' tradition of quantitative *Empirische Rechtswissenschaft* (Empirical Jurisprudence).[78] Questions that remain to be asked as well as answered: How can we study the effects of a certain law when legal concepts themselves are necessarily indeterminate and disputed?[79] How can we avoid treating the empirical results of social science research as the 'ultimate subsumption or even super-revision authority'?[80] How can the 'effects' of a private-law claim be studied if the law itself is aimed at nothing more than establishing bargaining positions? How do you do discourse analysis when it comes to legal discourses? How does the knowledge contained in the law relate to its normativities?[81] Where do we look to find the knowledge of 'the law'? How do we answer for our own social positionality, as academics, but also for practical lawyers and judges?[82] This is where interdisciplinary experiences such as mine could contribute.

[77] Cf Bora (n 68); T Gutmann, 'Intra- oder Interdisziplinarität. Chance oder Störfaktor' in Hilgendorf and Schulze-Fielitz (n 72) 93–118; H Rottleuthner, 'Methodologie und Organisation der Rechtswissenschaft' in Hilgendorf and Schulze-Fielitz, *Selbstreflexion* (n 72) 241–58.

[78] A Engert, 'Empirische Rechtswissenschaft – Vorstellung einer Forschungsrichtung' (2022) 1 *Berliner Rechtszeitschrift* 3–13.

[79] H Rottleuthner and M Mahlmann, *Diskriminierung in Deutschland: Vermutungen und Fakten* (Baden-Baden, Nomos, 2011) 447, who answer that question by calling the legal definition of discrimination insufficient for the social science perspective, and pay the price of no longer being able to claim to say something about the effects of the law; see A Klose, 'Wie wirkt Antidiskriminierungsrecht?' in M Cottier, J Estermann and M Wrase (eds), *Wie wirkt Recht? Ausgewählte Beiträge zum Ersten Gemeinsamen Kongress der Deutschsprachigen Rechtssoziologie-Vereinigungen* (Baden-Baden, Nomos, 2010) 347–67.

[80] Rottleuthner and Mahlmann (n 79) 38. More examples: Kocher (n 67).

[81] D Schweitzer, 'Diskursanalyse, Wahrheit und Recht: Methodologische Probleme einer Diskursanalyse des Rechts' (2015) 35(2) *Zeitschrift für Rechtssoziologie* 201.

[82] E Kocher, 'Objektivität und gesellschaftliche Positionalität' (2021) 54(3) *Kritische Justiz* 268–83; S González Hauck, 'Weiße Deutungshoheit statt Objektivität: Der "objektive Dritte" und die systematische Abwertung rassismuserfahrener Perspektiven' (2022) 42(2) *Zeitschrift für Rechtssoziologie* 153–75.

V. C*LLaS

In a way, I may have been overtaken. Now that gender and diversity in the law has become an issue for mainstream editors,[83] yet I still find myself on the margins. Even in the feminist legal community, the margins may not always be attractive for young lawyers who might rather choose working at a renowned university with a male colleague who has his contacts in Harvard. And if you want to make the case for your own research as a younger socio-legal scholar, it may seem useful to stress how novel your thinking is – a practice that can end up overlooking existing but hitherto marginalised research.

On the other side: Once you have been lucky – as I have – and been appointed as a university professor, you no longer depend on acceptance by the mainstream. You can do whatever you like, including critical legal studies, and even interdisciplinary labour law studies. My approaches, contributions and ideas were often at odds with the knowledge created in mainstream academia – not because I came to different results, but because I developed arguments that started at different ends and were hard to connect to the prevailing argumentation. But there are sometimes colleagues curious enough to search for alternative models and precedents, and some of my texts seem to have been reread.

Also, I finally found out that my approaches and positions are not so exotic once you leave Germany. For example, the Labour Law Research Network (LLRN) regularly gathers lawyers and sociologists, and so do other international conferences on labour and social law or regulation. My founding the 'Center for Interdisciplinary Labour Law Studies' and publishing a book with an interdisciplinary approach in the English language,[84] seems to have resonated in this international labour law community.

After all, a lack of habitus and integration in mainstream academia can even help one along. I am still convinced that the editorial practices that KJ developed, where peer review is not separated from editorial work, where the editors themselves spend time on reading, commenting and conversing with authors,[85] produces higher quality and more interesting academic work. In this same vein, I hope the Center for Interdisciplinary Labour Law Studies will continue making its way as a hub for interdisciplinary work on labour law issues, where advanced and early-career scholars build community, with open feedback mechanisms, and methodological approaches for interdisciplinary work, in cooperation and with open minds.

[83] Siehe z.B. M Grünberger et al, *Diversität in Rechtswissenschaft und Rechtspraxis: Ein Essay* (Baden-Baden, Nomos, 2021).

[84] Kocher (n 29).

[85] Editorial board of Kritische Justiz, 'Editorial. Ist die KJ peer reviewed? Wie wir Redaktionsverantwortung verstehen' (2021) 1 *Kritische Justiz* 127–30.

8

On the Matter of the Law and Socio-Legal Identifications

REVITAL MADAR

THE FOLLOWING CHAPTER questions the prerequisites of socio-legal identifications. This question is addressed through three vignettes: a short autobiographical reflection about my trajectory and research, an examination of the limits of socio-legal identifications and a discussion of the emergence of socio-legal studies in Israel. Throughout these sections, I reflect on how the presence of the law, as a matter, may determine disciplinary belongings. I claim that, unlike other matters, concepts and theories that travel between disciplines without necessarily restricting disciplinary identities, law – regardless of the approach one adopts towards it – tends to be more imposing. At a time when the law is no longer the sole domain of legal scholars or law departments, it still claims its authority and resists interdisciplinary and anti-disciplinary work.

I. INTRODUCTION

> I am suspicious of the very idea of policy. Policy implies the existence of an elite group – government officials, typically – that gets to decide on something ('a policy') that they then arrange to be imposed on everybody else. There's a little mental trick we often play on ourselves when discussing such matters. We say, for instance, 'What are we going to do about the problem of X?' as if 'we' were society as a whole, somehow acting on ourselves. But, in fact, unless we happen to be part of that roughly three per cent to five per cent of the population whose views actually do affect policy makers, this is all a game of make-believe. We are identifying with our rulers when, in fact, we're the ones being ruled.[1]

I share Graber's suspicion of policy recommendations. Beyond the limits these mechanisms impose on our political imagination (e.g. can we imagine a world

[1] D Graber, *Bullshit Jobs A Theory* (New York, Penguin Books, 2019) 270.

without policy elites and politicians?), I find policy recommendations to be an epistemic obstacle, a means to divert us from the core issue that sets the terms of the problem we are confronting.

I still remember the sense of relief I felt when two authors, writing about the sexual harassment Palestinian women experience when visiting relatives in Israeli prisons, stated that 'the clearest way to address the sexual violence occurring in Israeli prisons and jails is … ending the 47-year occupation of Palestine for nationhood'.[2] For once, a policy recommendation did not feel like a cosmetic solution designed by what global governance considers feasible and realistic. It pinpointed the origin of the problem rather than attempting to render an unbearable situation more bearable.

Graber's claim that there is a game we are playing when a politician or an expert announces a policy, a game in which we imagine ourselves to be part of the ruling class and not the ruled class. It implies that the possibility of crafting a policy recommendation, of thinking in terms of policy recommendations, is also conditioned by one's belonging. It can be a matter of class or a personal experience of marginalisation of another kind. However, it may also signify and require a certain belief and confidence in the institutions that design and execute policies. On the policy makers' side, there should also be apparent confidence arising from their understanding, if not internalisation, of the limits of what policies can offer and what they can't and with which language.

In contrast to the confidence with which policies are delivered, the writing of this chapter lacks the confidence of an expert. If it weren't for the material conditions in which this text is published, the term 'essay' would be a more appropriate description of the words composing this chapter. To somewhat overcome the sense of estrangement accompanying the writing process, I follow Philippopoulos-Mihalopoulos's advice about (legal) writing.[3] It includes the importance of approaching essays as a trial while foregoing the requirement of producing a 'well-formed section-arranged consistency' article with a clear resolution. This chapter, which is more of an essay, is a trial of contributing to socio-legal studies undertaken by an early-career scholar who is not a legal scholar nor a sociologist but whose matter is the law. Consequently, she, as in I, is often identified as a socio-legal scholar despite obtaining a PhD from the cultural studies program at the Hebrew University of Jerusalem and being trained mainly in philosophy.

Although trials lack a clear resolution, they do not lack a direction. This chapter is a response to the editors' invitation to reflect on my socio-legal

[2] FA-R Al Issa and E Beck, 'Sexual Violence as a War Weapon in Conflict Zones: Palestinian Women's Experience Visiting Loved Ones in Prisons and Jails' (2021) 36(2) *Affilia* 167–81, 178.

[3] A Philippopoulos-Mihalopoulos, 'Writing beyond Distinctions' in N Creutzfeldt, M Mason and K McConnachie (eds), *Routledge Handbook of Socio-Legal Theory and Methods* (London, Routledge, 2020) 74.

trajectory as an Israeli scholar who works on law from Europe.[4] As such, and despite the difficulty in defining Europe and considering myself part of it, what follows is a fragmented discussion that addresses at large how I came to be identified as a socio-legal scholar and, more particularly, what this identification unveils concerning the law's capacity to colour other aspects of one's work. In that respect, I hope to shed light on the paradoxical nature of the law as a matter that resists interdisciplinarily and even anti-disciplinarily. In other words, I am interested in how attempts to challenge the law, incorporate context into it and sully it with questions and issues that harm its claim for purity, further emphasise the law's authority from a disciplinary perspective.

In the context of socio-legal studies, a sub-discipline that can be characterised, among others, as an ongoing attempt to overcome the law's claim for authority, it is possible that the attempt to follow how I came to be identified as a socio-legal scholar may provide insight on the paradoxical nature of the law. Especially if we consider how the emergence of socio-legal studies accompanied the displacement of the political into the legal sphere and how scholarly attempts to write about law beyond legal institutions led to the discovery that the law can be traced everywhere and may perhaps be designated as (almost) everything.[5]

In what follows, instead of examining this paradox on a normative level, I will first offer a short discussion of my positionality and work. This part stresses how the law's presence, even if only as a matter, may overshadow other aspects of interdisciplinary research. In the second part, I discuss the limits of my identification as a socio-legal scholar and the implications I identify in these limits for socio-legal studies. Lastly, I tackle my encounter with socio-legal studies, the emergence of socio-legal studies in Israel, and the affinity between socio-legal studies and the golden age of critical theory in Israel. This section allows pinpointing a relationship and influence that is less pronounced in the socio component of socio-legal studies, that is, the humanities, and challenges the socio-legal studies distinction between the theoretical and the empirical. In the concluding section, I suggest that overcoming the centrality of this distinction for socio-legal studies may enable interdisciplinary scholars whose work is situated between faculties, and not only disciplines, to be more at home within socio-legal studies and consequently own their identification as part of this sub-field.

[4] It is always a struggle to identify as an Israeli. The incorporation of a hyphen and the word 'Jewish' following the adjective Israeli may clarify my situatedness in the Israeli colony. Yet, instead of solving this problem, it may further blur the settler-colonial nature of this state whose main goal is to erase Palestinian identity and being. Instead of emphasizing ethnic identity alone, or in addition to it, Israelis should position themselves in relation to their political affiliation with their state's overarching Zionist regime. Although it has been the case since 1948, the ongoing Israeli genocide on Gaza underscores the increasing necessity of this political positionality.

[5] see, eg M Constable, L Volpp and B Wagner, *Looking for the Law in All the Wrong Places: Justice Beyond and Between* (New York, Fordham University Press, 2019).

II. A NET OF UNPOSITIONALITIES

As someone trained in continental and contemporary philosophy, it is hard to pinpoint when I encountered law, since beyond legal procedures and institutions, the law, at least as a rule and a norm, is always present in philosophy, implicitly or explicitly. Beyond scholarly work, growing up in Tel Aviv in a rather anti-institutional Jewish family of Tunisian origin meant that law in everyday life never appeared in the form of a remedy. Rather, it was a threat that, most of the time, resulted in injustice towards my working-class Mizrahi family, other disadvantaged groups, and mostly, Palestinians living under Israeli control.[6] I could not trust the law and am still incapable of doing so. That has also limited my capacity to orient my energy and activities toward legal reforms. That may explain why, in my work, I approach the matter of the law and its performances as a channel, not as an object of research.

Being an active member of women's associations in Israel and leading different campaigns on sexual violence against women, I was fascinated by the resemblance, if not identical nature, of denials expressed by male predators. I always found the content of the denial to be very telling, from statements that sought to slander the victim, to claims over her consent to the act or total denial of any encounter with her. Whether the denial is literal, interpretive or implicatory,[7] the patterns of denial provide essential markers. The form that denial takes and the content of that denial can indicate inter alia what is regarded as normal, acceptable and legitimate.

In the same vein, I looked for moments in which the state repudiates violence as the outcome of its own doing yet does not deny its occurrence or illegality. However, I wasn't interested in formal denials but rather in moments when the state has less control over the 'discursive explosion' that takes place.[8] As the state investigates itself, a crucial cacophony emerges. It unveils the realities that legal processes conceal and exposes the truths and narratives they produce.

To address these questions, I looked at trials of Israeli soldiers who were prosecuted by the Israeli state for crimes committed against the bodies and lives of Palestinians. I consider these trials as moments in which the state's obligation to claim the illegality of the soldier's act and the defendant's need to claim the act was indeed legal, a vital lens to understand better how the old sovereign right to kill legalises violence. In the case of Israel, first and foremost, violence against Palestinians.

The lens of soldiers' trials, which in my current project was broadened to trials of state security agents, proved fruitful in unearthing how the emphasis

[6] Mizrahi in Hebrew is a general term that refers to Jews whose families immigrated to Israel from Africa and Asia. The literal meaning of the word is eastern.

[7] S Cohen, *States of Denial: Knowing about Atrocities and Suffering* (Cambridge, Polity, 2001).

[8] M Foucault, *The History of Sexuality: vol 1: An Introduction* (New York, Pantheon Books, 1978) 17.

of Judge Benjamin Halevy on the equal status of the Palestinian citizens of Israel allowed, de facto to shove aside a far more challenging question, that of Palestinian refugees.[9] Questions arise of how scholars' adoption of wartime rape in the context of Israel-Palestine silenced Israeli sexual state violence against Palestinians.[10] Further, questions arise of how Israeli rules of engagement strip Palestinian death of both its singularity and political meaning.[11] I will elaborate on the broader implications of this study in the last section. For now, I want to discuss how the framework of trials of Israeli soldiers, or rather, simply that of trials, affected my trajectory thus far.

As a first-generation student, my knowledge of academia was acquired gradually. When I entered Tel Aviv University, I did not know there was such a thing as a master's degree, let alone a PhD. I only knew from my parents that I needed to go to university to have a better job than the ones they had. I probably did not have the slightest understanding of how my professors came to be professors. What directed me was my interest and the pleasure I found in studying philosophy and later in doing research. Consequently, I never stopped to think about how, for example, my decision to work with a legal scholar and a criminologist while being affiliated with the cultural studies programme would be understood by those who would, later on, decide whether I am entitled to a fellowship and/or should be hired by them. Research shows this is often true for first-generation students.[12]

As for the university, my department celebrated my project as the first collaboration between the law department and the cultural studies programme, and around me, everyone cheered for interdisciplinarity. As I applied for visiting fellowships, it became clear that despite not studying law formally, it was easier to communicate what I do to law departments. It seems as though the mere presence of the law in my research overshadowed other aspects, such as my interest in state violence, sovereignty and legitimacy. At the same time, when it came to grant proposals and choosing the committee that would review my application, I was repeatedly advised to refrain from law committees, as they would probably consider my project unfavourably. So I was told. Discussions at the inaugural conference of the Swiss Network for Law and Society (September 2022, Lausanne University) affirmed this concern. Participants expressed difficulties

[9] R Madar, '"Do You Know What's an Arab Bystander?": The Kafr Qasim Trial as a Case Study for a Sovereign Failure' in A Jamal (ed), *The Conflict – Sociological, Historical and Geographical Aspects* (Walter Lebach Institute for Jewish-Arab Coexistence through Education, Tel Aviv University, 2019), 25–48 [in Hebrew].

[10] R Madar, 'Beyond Male Israeli Soldiers, Palestinian Women, Rape, and War: Israeli State Sexual Violence Against Palestinians' (2023) 9(1) *Conflict and Society* 72–88.

[11] R Madar, 'The Construction of Palestinian Death as an Exceptional Repetition in Israel' (2023) 31(3) *Identities* 333–50 https://doi.org/10.1080/1070289X.2023.2259218.

[12] E Ben Shoshan Gazit, 'What Are We Talking About When We Speak about "First Generation Students" (and What We Are Not Talking about)?' conference paper *First Generation: Critical Perspectives, 18 April 2021* (Tel Aviv University, Minerva Centre for Humanities, Academia for Equality, 2021).

in obtaining funding when classifying their work under legal studies. Currently, the disciplines one can choose from when applying for funding from the Swiss National Science Foundation do not include sub-disciplines and socio-legal scholars. Interdisciplinary researchers working on law need to decipher which committee might understand their methodological and theoretical choices and not consider them as bad scientific practice.

Interdisciplinarity could be 'instrumental' and function as a code word that easily fits the corporate logic of a neo-liberal university. It can also be 'conceptual' and challenge institutional knowledge arrangements.[13] The latter may serve as an ongoing reminder of the conflict of disciplines at the heart of the university.[14] It may destabilise the current structure of knowledge production and perhaps even challenge the idea of 'making a contribution' to a discipline. Theory (especially when not conceived in opposition to the empirical) is critical here because theories travel between disciplines.[15] At the same time, in my short experience, the structure of the university and how journals define their aims and review manuscripts often limits what interdisciplinarity can be. The idea of a 'contribution' is by itself problematic as it often requires reading within a discipline and, if not, at least defining the contribution in such terms. The situation in sub-disciplines, which are often inherently interdisciplinary, is especially interesting because it allows examining which disciplines and approaches come together, and which are considered foreign objects. That also has to do with distinctions between context and matter and the theoretical versus the empirical, which are almost required to make sense of sub-disciplines that challenge existing structures of knowledge production.[16]

As someone trained in philosophy, I always found the distinction between the theoretical and the empirical odd. This distinction was at centre stage in the Swiss Network for Law and Society conference mentioned above. Legal work was often considered theoretical and juxtaposed with sociology and anthropology as empirical. This distinction also limited the disciplines considered natural within the social component of law and society research. This led me to question my place within socio-legal studies. What leads people to identify my work as socio-legal, considering I am neither a legal scholar nor a sociologist? What does engagement (another term saturated with corporate logic) mean? Does the affiliation of those I read and quote determine one's disciplinary belonging? Or rather, is it what is identified as the research matter? How do disciplines function as gatekeepers in a world that advocates for interdisciplinarity, and how do sub-disciplines follow the same steps?

[13] L Salter and A Hearn, *Outside the Lines: Issues in Interdisciplinary Research* (Montreal, McGill-Queen's Press, 1996).

[14] A Hearn, 'Interdisciplinarity/Extradisciplinarity: On the University and the Active Pursuit of Community' (2003) 3 *History of Intellectual Culture* 1, 1–13.

[15] M Davies, 'Doing Critical-Socio-Legal Theory' in N Creutzfeldt, M Mason and K McConnachie (eds), *Routledge Handbook of Socio-Legal Theory and Methods* (London, Routledge, 2019).

[16] Philippopoulos-Mihalopoulos (n 3).

To the set of partial disciplinary belongings is added the complex positionality of Israel as a case study. Much of interdisciplinary work can be traced to area studies. However, beyond the arbitrariness and colonial heritage of boundaries, as well as problems arising from such divisions, Israel's regional belonging is hard to decipher. Geographically, it is situated in what came to be known as the Middle East. However, as a colonial project that has enjoyed the political and economic support of the United States and is occupying Palestinian territories, it is also seen as a foreign entity in the region. Consequently, some scholars refuse to include it under the umbrella of the Middle East. The state's official language of Hebrew and the fact that Arabic in Israel is spoken today by Jews mainly for military objectives increase the foreignness of Israel in circles of scholars who work on the Middle East.[17] Israel's cultural affiliations with Europe, such as its membership in the Union of European Football Associations and Israel's participation in Eurovision, further problematise Israel's regional belonging. Academically, while in the early years of the Israeli state, European states such as Britain, France, and Germany had a significant influence on Israeli academia, currently, Israeli universities are influenced by North American academia.[18] That is especially the case concerning Israeli law and legal education.[19] It is also evident in the language of Israeli academia, which today is English, when in the statehood years, it was German and French.[20] In the fourth section, I will elaborate on these influences concerning the emergence of socio-legal studies in Israel.

Between disciplinary, thematic and regional belongings that are tailored into my biography, the discussion above showcases, not necessarily in this order: (1) the gap between cheering for interdisciplinarity and the reality of conducting interdisciplinary research; (2) the specific difficulties that arise from researching Israel; and (3) how the presence of the matter of the law in interdisciplinary research may overshadow other aspects, even when the approach adopted seeks to overcome the law's claim for authority. The coupling of these points was meant to set the ground for the question of what impacts the identification of a researcher as a socio-legal scholar. This is clearly a passive description of the order of things (I stress how I am identified, not necessarily how I identify). In that sense, this identification, and mostly its limits, implies a search for a community and, in some sense, the success of finding one. However, as discussed in the next section, this identification has its limits. As such, it is also a reminder that no community can absorb its members wholesomely.

[17] Y Mendel, 'Arabic Language in Israel' (2015) 9 *Mafte'akh: Lexical Review of Political Thought* 31–52 [in Hebrew].

[18] S Guri-Rosenblit, 'Changing Boundaries in Israeli Higher Education' (1999) 4(2) *Mediterranean Journal of Educational Studies* 91–114.

[19] P Lahav, 'American Moment[s]: When, How, and Why Did Israeli Law Faculties Come to Resemble Elite U.S. Law Schools?' (2009) 10(2) *Theoretical Inquiries in Law* 653–97.

[20] Guri-Rosenblit (n 18); GN Kheimets and DA Epstein, 'Languages of Higher Education in Contemporary Israel' (2005) 37(1) *Journal of Educational Administration and History* 55–70.

III. WHERE MY IDENTIFICATION REACHES ITS LIMITS: ON LAW AS A THREAT

As noted above, I do not trust the law. I acknowledge its societal role and the need to be assisted by it, but I mostly, and first and foremost, consider it a threat. Among other reasons, because court orders authorised people to knock on my family's doors when I was young to take some valuable belongings and, later, through court proceedings, we had to live with the threat of having our home taken away from us (it wasn't, eventually). It is also court orders that authorise and legalise the evictions of Mizrahis and Palestinians from their homes, the demolition of Palestinian homes, the imprisonment of Palestinians in administrative detention and the limitation of Palestinians' movement in Israel and the occupied Palestinian territories. In this state of affairs, suggesting a cosmetic reform or a procedural change to assist the victims of these legal atrocities requires disregarding the conditions that created and have maintained these crimes. Even if these suggestions are made in the name of a lesser evil. Yet, recommendations of this kind are more likely to be discussed, if not accepted, than policy reforms that tackle the core of the crimes listed above. Policy recommendations, in this sense, not only require disregarding the conditions of possibility, they also render other recommendations like abolishing private property and ending Israel's colonisation of Palestine 'less serious'.

In the same vein, I doubt the law's capacity to be an imperfect saviour that, with some minor adjustments, can stop posing a threat to the less fortunate. Can it be less harmful? No question about that. Yet, I cannot be invested in it. If anything, I can commit to wrestling with its epistemic colonisation of our political imaginations. That is why I cannot but approach it as a matter in my work.

This combination of my approach to law (as a threat) and its presence in my work as a matter creates a paradoxical situation when examined on the backdrop of socio-legal itineraries and belongings. As much as the presence of the law as a matter in my work often leads to my consideration as a socio-legal scholar, this aspect also marks the point where this identification reaches its limits. In other words, rarely do I find in socio-legal scholarship not only suspicion of the law but also a wholesale disregard and rejection of its terms, rules, and epistemic and metaphysical boundaries. These works exist but are often classified under critical criminology, legal anthropology and philosophy.

We should ask ourselves why this is the case, and if it can be otherwise. Can socio-legal studies make room for these approaches? However, prior to these questions, a different debt has to be settled regarding the meaning of approaching the law as nothing more than a matter. I will try to explain that through my work on trials of repudiated violence.[21]

Four elements render a trial into a repudiated one: (1) the identity of the perpetrator (an agent of state security forces); (2) the victim (a member of a

[21] R Madar, *Repudiated Violence and Sovereign Power: The Case of Israel* (Thesis (PhD) The Hebrew University of Jerusalem, 2021).

group the state considers its enemy); (3) the type of violence employed (physical); and (4) the state's decision to prosecute the agent. In a political reality saturated with police brutality and state violence worldwide, framing trials of repudiated violence in this manner sets aside the question of the sentence or a state's rule of law. It rejects the premise that the solution lies at the feet of the legal system. In too many places, for too many people, the lethal violence inflicted in the name of global and national security is a brutal expression of the rule of law. To understand this violence, it is necessary to move beyond the terms that settle it in established legal grooves and their attendant normative justifications. Privileging trials of repudiated violence as an analytical framework over the established legal alternatives enables us to do just that if we understand the judicial documentary trail left by such acts as a relatively open archive of state violence.

I will not try to convince you here of the particularity and importance of these trials. Instead, within the context of socio-legal itineraries and the use of the law as a matter, I'd like to discuss the implications of defining some trials in this manner. The framing of repudiated violence in the manner described above rethinks what a legal taxonomy can be and, more importantly, who and what legal taxonomies can serve if we are willing to taxonomies law beyond the law. In that sense, it is a step in Hutchinson and Cohen's direction.[22] According to them, as vital as it might be to better situate cases and to challenge the law's presuppositions and classifications, it is not enough. I would add it is especially not enough if we are interested in exploiting law as a means to an end. That is, the legal taxonomy we are offering is not meant to serve the legal system but, instead, to be of service to scholars from other disciplines and to political activists and movements. It is only in this way that work on the law can slow down the displacement of the political into the legal.

As a legal taxonomy, trials of repudiated violence do just that. They leech off the law but don't approach it as a remedy. The legal taxonomy of repudiated violence entails the creation of a legal family that is based on categories that lack any official legal meaning: the occupation of the perpetrator, the social/political/national belonging of the victim, the impersonal relation of enmity between the perpetrator and the victim, the violence employed, and the identity of the prosecuting body and its relation to the perpetrator. Together, these elements sully the law with the political and lay the groundwork for a legal taxonomy of state violence that is not bound to existing legal categories.

In the context of socio-legal studies, trials of repudiated violence also allow bypassing the distinction, if not division, between the empirical and the theoretical. Because this paradigm and analytical tool is not bound to a legal epistemology, nor to the mere categories which arrange crimes in a certain way and name violence in a legally legible manner, the analysis of the documentary

[22] A Hutchinson and D Cohen, 'Of Persons and Property: The Politics of Legal Taxonomy' (1990) 13 *Dalhousie Law Journal* 20–54.

trail of these trials does not attempt to convince law scholars that empirical work is necessary to unpack the law and advance it. Instead, it shows that the division between the theoretical and the empirical is misleading because by employing an ethnographic sensitivity,[23] we can render some readings of some documents just as empirical. In other words, the empirical is found in more than just the field. It is part and parcel of how we approach the law. By approaching it as a matter, we bring in materiality.

This entails a different positionality and motivation all together. Existing limitations over what can be considered part of the socio in socio-legal studies are telling in this respect. Although there are ongoing attempts to include more disciplines and approaches under this socio component, the majority of work done in socio-legal studies take its cues from sociology and sociological and anthropological methodologies. Consequently, the empirical does not come to the front from the mere decision to read the law beyond its own terms, but rather, to incorporate ethnography, interviews, and other social-sciences methods into the reading and analysis of the law. There is little space left here for works that do not incorporate the empirical in this sense.

What's more, there is a sense of foreignness scholars can sense (similar to the one described above in the context of the conference of the Swiss Network of Law and Society) if they do not incorporate these methodologies into their work, yet also are not a black letter law scholar. This is particularly so if the motivations of these scholars are not making law better, and the findings of works of this nature cannot be translated to clear policies that can be implemented easily. Considering the established place socio-legal studies have in the present, it may be time to do away with this distinction, knowing that those who consider the law an autonomous discipline and field of knowledge would always consider every work that sullies the law as misleading. Instead, this may be the time to open up the gates of this sub-discipline by doing away with the distinction between the empirical and the theoretical, inviting in works that consider the two to be intertwined.

I opened this section with my distrust of the law. This distrust and perception of the law as a threat align with Graber's unease regarding policy makers and policies. Yet, here, I approached this unease through my relation to the law and how it shapes my approach to it. Discussing the paradigm of repudiated violence, I explained what it means to approach the law as a matter and connected it to a distinction that is central to socio-legal studies and which I offer to do away with. This has also allowed visiting the limits of my identification as a socio-legal scholar.

[23] E Schatz, 'Introduction: Ethnographic Immersion and the Study of Politics' in E Schatz (ed), *Political Ethnography: What Immersion Contributes to the Study of Power* (Chicago, University of Chicago Press, 2009).

The implications to socio-legal studies are twofold: (1) the interaction with the law should allow approaching it as a matter and sullying it with terms that lack any legal meaning, similarly to how criminologists of the state have approached it;[24] and (2) the division of labour between the theoretical and the empirical has to be advanced to acknowledge the empirical also in those works that do not rely on ethnographies, interviews and surveys. Both implications entail making more room for the theoretical while at least partially renouncing the law's authority and the capacity of (at least some) socio-legal studies to be legible for legal scholars and practitioners.

IV. BEYOND THE SOCIO-LEGAL DISTINCTION BETWEEN THE EMPIRICAL AND THE THEORETICAL

I was first identified as a socio-legal scholar shortly before submitting my PhD thesis. I discussed the conclusion with a friend when she said, 'clearly, you are doing socio-legal work. That's where your contribution should be'. Lost among disciplines as I am, and shortly before entering a job market that is better in claiming it seeks to advance interdisciplinary/multidisciplinary work but de facto is still more assured when encountering candidates that have a clear discipline (and capacity to teach the department's core courses), I began exploring this sub-discipline. I found out I am engaging with socio-legal scholars. Yet, I differ from them. Most of the socio-legal scholars I engaged with were trained in law or sociology and published in either law or sociology journals. What is more, whereas on a thematic level, there were apparent affinities between my work and that of the socio-legal scholars I read, the questions differed and did not share the same objectives.

What characterises the socio-legal scholarship on Israel I engaged with was a critique of Israel and, at times, the overall Zionist project. What drew me to this literature was the approach to law, precisely the necessity to sully law by exposing and discussing how colonialism has determined legal decisions, limited the outcomes of trials and directed Israeli legislation. So, beyond – or rather alongside – the over-imposition of the trials as a legal matter that overshadowed other aspects, it seems that my rejection of a positivist approach to law in the context of Israel could not but lead me to critical socio-legal work.

However, is that enough to consider one's work as socio-legal? Beyond publications and institutional affiliations, what kind of affinity, proximity, and

[24] A Korn, 'Criminalization of Political Conflict: Crime Within the Israeli Arab Population in the Fifties' (1999) 8 *Plilim – Israeli Journal of Criminal Law* 157–91; JP Green, and T Ward, 'State Crime, Human Rights, And the Limits of Criminology' (2000) 27 *Social Justice* 1, 79, 101–15; S Razack, 'The Space of Difference in Law: Inquests into Aboriginal Deaths in Custody' (2011) 1 *Somatechnics* 87–123; N Shalhoub-Kevorkian, 'The Occupation of the Senses: The Prosthetic and Aesthetic of State Terror' (2017) 57(6) *The British Journal of Criminology* 1279–300; N Shalhoub-Kevorkian, 'Necropenology: Conquering New Bodies, Psychics, and Territories of Death in East Jerusalem' (2020) 27(3) *Identities* 285–301.

relation are prerequisites to being identified as a socio-legal scholar? Is it the theme of the law or other derivative and closely related objects of inquiry that render the inclusion within the pool of socio-legal scholars a pre-determined result, or rather, the scholars whose work we quote? And what are the conditions in the Israeli context? Can specific politics coupled with an approach to state violence that tackles the state's epistemic origins, alongside the presence of some legal matter, determine one's identity as a socio-legal scholar? The following discussion attempts to address these questions through the history of socio-legal work in and about Israel.

Whereas Barzilai identifies the inception of law and society research in Israel in the 1950s,[25] Sebba considers the late 1980s as the moment in which socio-legal work in Israel began to flourish.[26] Considering that the first national meeting of the Israeli Law and Society Association was held in November 1990, it is probable that the emergence of law and society research in and about Israel can be traced more adequately to the late 1980s. Further, the close affinity between critical theory and law and society scholarship in Israel strengthens the claim that law and society scholarship in Israel emerged in the late 1980s. The 1990s were the golden years of Israeli critical theory. Although the questions raised by critical theory scholars from a variety of disciplines did not translate into an institutional shift, it was during these years that we saw a tsunami of publications that questioned central Israeli myths, such as its moral superiority, the justification of its wars, policy towards Palestinians and the occupied territories and claims over the unification of its Jewish citizens.

A critical platform for these publications was *Theory and Critique*, established in 1990. Although this is not a legal journal, many of the original research articles published in it were written by prominent Israeli law and society scholars, such as Kedar and Yiftachel, Mautner, Shamir and Ziv (with Shamir).[27] In addition, this journal published Hebrew translations of philosophers such as Balibar, Foucault, De Certeau, Deleuze and Guattari and Derrida and Nancy,[28] whose work informed law and society scholars. When concluding a decade as the journal's editor, Shenhav noted that although the journal was dedicated

[25] G Barzilai, 'Analysis of Israelis [Jews and Arab–Palestinians]: Exploring Law in Society and Society in Law' (2015) 11(3) *International Journal of Law in Context* 361–78.

[26] L Sebba, 'Law and Society in Israel: An Emerging Agenda' (2001) 17(1) *Israel Studies Forum* 83–110.

[27] O Yiftachel and AS Kedar, 'Landed Power: The Making of the Israeli Land Regime' (2000) 16 *Theory and Criticism* 67–100 [in Hebrew]; M Mautner, 'The Reasonability of Politics' (1994) 5 *Theory and Criticism* 25–53 [in Hebrew]; R Shamir, 'The Politics of Reasonableness' (1994) 5 *Theory and Criticism* 7–23 [in Hebrew]; N Ziv and R Shamir, '"Politics" and "Sub-Politics" in the Struggle against Land Discrimination' (2000) 16 *Theory and Criticism* 45–66 [in Hebrew].

[28] É Balibar, 'Is there a "New Racism"?' (2004) 24 *Theory and Criticism* 73–83 [in Hebrew]; M de Certeau, 'The Invention of Everyday Life' (1997) 10 *Theory and Criticism* 15–24 [in Hebrew]; G Deleuze and F Guattari, 'A Thousand Plateaus Clause XIV: An Axiomatic System and the Current Situation' (2000) 17 *Theory and Criticism* 132–44 [in Hebrew]; J Derrida and J-L Nancy, 'Eating Well, or the Calculation of the Subject: An Interview with Jacques Derrida' (2019) 51 *Theory and Criticism* 189–213 [in Hebrew].

to critical theory, works published in it were characterised by two discourses about sovereignty: a legal discourse and a political one.[29] Overall, it seems that as much as critical socio-legal scholars needed critical theory to decipher Israeli law beyond legal rationale, critical theory scholars who explored Israel's colonial origins, population management and violence could not avoid incorporating Israeli law into their analysis.

To the best of my knowledge, no work has been conducted thus far on the close affinity between the evolution of law and society and critical theory in Israel. This kind of project can contribute to our understanding of how these theories, many of which are philosophical works, informed critical approaches to the law. Further, considering the relative absence of philosophy – compared with other disciplines – from what is understood and included within the socio component of a socio-legal scholarship, this line of inquiry can shed light on the philosophical works that informed empirical and critical approaches to the law. It may also broaden the socio-component of socio-legal studies and open it to the humanities, thus blurring the old distinction between the humanities and the social sciences. A distinction that echoes the tension between the empirical and the theoretical.

Although this line of inquiry is beyond the scope of this chapter, considering Barzilai's (2015) decision to focus on Israeli socio-legal works that are occupied with the question of the Israeli nation-state,[30] then the temporal affinity between Israeli law and society research and critical theory can be explained beyond American influences on Israeli academia and law departments.[31] Instead, this temporal affinity can be explained through the combination of (1) a specific theme (the Israeli nation-state); (2) a critical approach to Israel's constitutive myths; and (3) the matter of the law, which within colonial and settler-colonial contexts is always already constitutive to the state's project. It matters less if these scholars identify Israel as a settler colony or acknowledge its colonial origins and the nature of its rule. It is less about the use of these terms but rather what these frameworks entail: a gaze backwards that allows identifying the origins and conditions of possibility that define the political in Israel, and that render positivistic approaches, and even liberal critiques, insufficient, if not altogether inadequate.

Both Sebba's (2001) and Barzilai's (2015) mapping of socio-legal studies in Israel considers Israel's relation to its Palestinian citizens and the question of the Israeli occupation of Palestinian territories a central domain addressed by socio-legal scholars working on Israel. Within this group, Barzilai differentiates

[29] Y Shenhav, 'What is the Colour of Critical Theory? Thoughts about a Post-Westphalian Sovereignty' in G Eyal (ed), *Four Lectures on Critical Theory* (Tel Aviv, The Van Leer Jerusalem Institute / Hakibbutz Hameuchad, 2012).

[30] Barzilai (n 25).

[31] Kheimets and Epstein (n 20); Lahav (n 19).

between critical legal scholars[32] and liberal socio-legal scholars.[33] Whereas Barzilai draws the line between critical and liberal approaches with respect to Palestinians' individual and collective rights,[34] an additional differentiation can be made around these scholars' analysis of Israel in colonial, postcolonial and settler colonial terms. This framework renders the liberal approach manifestly limited in addressing the nature of the Zionist project and its capacity to reach the democratic liberal values these scholars aspire to. This framework also requires challenging the 'critical' in Barzilai's definition of Israeli critical socio-legal scholars because his definition is still more legal than political.

Jabareen makes two substantial claims in this regard.[35] He criticises the examination of Israel as a Westphalian state, arguing that this framework disregards Israel's colonial settings.[36] Further, he shows how legal education and scholarship in Israel are based on a geographical differentiation that addresses 'internal' legal issues (within the green line) through constitutional law, and 'exterior' legal issues (in the West Bank and Gaza) through the lens of international law.[37] Consequently, even critical Israeli legal scholars fail to address what Jabareen terms the essence of Israeli law: the political, in the Schmittian sense, that differentiates between friend and foe. Shenhav makes a similar claim about Israeli sociology.[38]

The need I identify in further stressing and challenging the critical in critical socio-legal scholarship on Israel is closely related to the paradox of the law I discussed above and, more specifically, to the working of the law in colonial and settler colonial contexts. Israel's control over Palestinians, at least until October 8th 2024, is maintained through the employment of vanquished and not explicit violence.[39] This violence is characterised by

[32] A Kedar, 'Majority Time, Minority Time: Land, Nation, and the Law of Adverse Possession in Israel' (1998) 21(3) *Eyunei Mishpat [Tel Aviv University Law Review]* 665–746; H Jabareen, 'Hobbesian Citizenship: How the Palestinians Became a Minority in Israel' in W Kymlicka and E Pföstl (eds), *Multiculturalism and Minority Rights in the Arab World* (Oxford, Oxford University Press, 2014); H Jabareen, 'Epilogue: Criticism of the Study of the Law in Israel' (2020) 43 *Iyunei Mishpat (Tel-Aviv University Law Review)* 505–27; I Saban and M Amara, 'The Status of Arabic in Israel: Reflections on the Power of Law to Produce Social Change' (2002) 36(2) *Israel Law Review* 5–39; R Shamir, '"Landmark Cases" and the Reproduction of Legitimacy: The Case of Israel's High Court of Justice' (1990) 24(3) *Law & Society Review* 781–805; R Shamir, 'Suspended in Space: Bedouins under the Law of Israel' (1996) 30(2) *Law & Society Review* 231–57; Yiftachel and Kedar (n 27).

[33] R Gavison and D Hacker, *The Arab-Israeli Rift – A Reader* (Jerusalem, Israel Democratic Institute, 2000); S Smooha, 'Ethnic Democracy: Israel as an Archetype' (1997) 2(2) *Israel Studies* 198–241.

[34] Barzilai (n 25).

[35] Jabareen (2014) (n 32); Jabareen (2020) (n 32).

[36] Jabareen (2014) (n 32).

[37] Jabareen (2020) (n 32).

[38] Shenhav (n 28).

[39] Azoulay, A and Ophir, A (2007) 'Separation, Subordination, and Violence' (2007) 31 *Theory and Criticism* Winter 155–172 [in Hebrew]. Revisions to this chapter are made more than a year into Israel's genocidal attack on Gaza. The claim about the nature of Israeli violence towards Palestinians does not take into consideration this attack, which is still ongoing. To incorporate it into Israel's overall control of Palestinians and its use of violence, some distance is required. A distance that is still unavailable at the time of writing this chapter.

hyperlegality[40] and, as a colonial system, is made of a patchwork of legal tools.[41] It is not a space of lawlessness, but rather, a space saturated with colonial legality, that is, an exceptionalist and racially based legality of 'lawfare'.[42]

The implications of the entanglement between vanquished violence and hyperlegality for scholars who work on Israeli violence against Palestinians is that the legal – regardless of disciplinary affiliations and the questions addressed – is already present as a problem and a mechanism that cannot be resolved through local reforms and policy recommendations. The latter entails the acceptance of the structural terms. Thus, alongside the mere presence of the law as a matter overshadowing other disciplinary aspects (even when it is approached critically), in the Israeli case (and in other colonial and settler-colonial realities), the paradox of the law as a matter of research is intensified. Consequently, it is possible that in the Israeli context, a critical approach to the Israeli nation-state functions as the prerequisite that may render almost every scholar whose matter is, or includes the law, a potential socio-legal scholar.

I have refuted, thus far, offering any definition of socio-legal studies. At the same time, I have insinuated that what may validate my identification by others as a socio-legal scholar can be attributed to the fact that my approach to law sullies it with a historical context and political interpretations of the juridical process. This approach can also be characterised by a disregard for legal justifications and my attempt to read the trials while disregarding two hyper-legal pronouncements that further the displacement of the political to the legal sphere: verdicts and sentencings. I also considered, implicitly, that my engagement with socio-legal scholarship may further validate claims that I am, at least also, a socio-legal scholar. As Israël's review of socio-legal scholarship in France shows, that is not a prerequisite.[43] Despite not engaging with socio-legal literature and discussions, some scholarly works are considered part of socio-legal scholarship.[44] Suppose we are willing to hold on to the thin yet broad definition of socio-legal studies as any work that sullies the law and refuses its authority and claims for objectivity. In that case, we may add Dorlin and Thénault to Israël's list.[45]

[40] N Hussain, *The Jurisprudence of Emergency: Colonialism and the Rule of Law* (Ann Arbor, University of Michigan Press, 2006).

[41] E Kolsky, 'The Colonial Rule of Law and the Legal Regime of Exception: Frontier "Fanaticism" and State Violence in British India' (2015) 120(4) *American Historical Review* 1218–46.

[42] LJ Comaroff, 'Symposium Introduction: Colonialism, Culture, and the Law: A Foreword' (2001) 26(2) *Law & Social Inquiry* 306.

[43] L Israël, L (2013) 'Legalise It! The Rising Place of Law in French Sociology' (2013) 9(2) *International Journal of Law in Context* 262–78.

[44] For example, B Latour, *The Making of Law. An Ethnography of the Conseil d'État* (Cambridge, Polity Press, 2010); L Boltanski and L Thévenot, *On Justification: Economic of Worth* (Princeton, Princeton University Press, 2006).

[45] E Dorlin, *Self-Defense: A Philosophy of Violence* (London, Verso, 2022); S Thénault, *Une Drôle de Justice: Les Magistrats Dans La Guerre d'Algérie* (Paris, La Découverte, 2001).

V. CONCLUSION

Throughout this chapter, I have tried to understand how I came to be identified as a socio-legal scholar. Following my itinerary and different positionalities, I found that one explanation can be the mere presence of the law, as a matter, in my work. Unlike other matters, concepts and theories that travel between disciplines without necessarily firmly restricting the disciplinary identities of those who work on them, law – regardless of the approach one adopts towards it – tends to be more imposing. At a time when the law is no longer the sole domain of legal scholars or law departments, it still claims (and tends to receive) its authority.

Addressing this question from within the Israeli context, I found that alongside the presence of the law as a matter, there is an additional layer at work – that of colonialism and settler colonialism – two realities that require further precision regarding the critical in critical socio-legal studies. The saturation of these realities with 'lawfare'[46] and 'hyperlegality'[47] means that it is pretty challenging to refute the presence of the law when addressing colonial and settler-colonial states' control and oppression mechanisms. What's more, it renders it impossible to take law – even if in a challenging and culturally and socially informed manner – on its terms. When the levels of impunity are so high, the law needs to be reduced to a matter.

The need to sully law is key here. It functions as a thin yet broad definition of what can be termed socio-legal scholarship. In that sense, beyond what falls under the socio in socio-legal studies, the hyphen of this sub-discipline represents the presence of the political, historical and epistemic conditions that, from a narrow legal perspective, are considered as tainting law. This saturated hyphen does not mean that my identification as a socio-legal scholar does not reach its limits at some point. Paradoxically, the presence of the law as a matter in my work both allows me to be included in socio-legal studies and limits this sense of belonging. In this regard, I suggest making more room for treatments of the law as a matter whose empiric nature does not necessarily originate from a limited set of methodologies. But rather, from a particular approach to it.

[46] Comaroff (n 42).
[47] Hussain (n 40).

9

A Eurolatin Career in Comparative Public Law: From Analytic Legal Theory to Sociology of Law

FRANCISCA POU GIMÉNEZ*

BEING AN ACADEMIC lawyer, the attempt to write a piece that explicitly brings together personal trajectories with analysis of law-related issues seems an imposing task. Yet the promise attached to the possibility of identifying epistemic communities that certainly exist, and that have nurtured me and my work, while putting important intellectual and academic developments under a new light, is certainly attractive. It habilitates the possibility of forecasting some of the social, institutional and personal underpinnings of views that we have learned to aseptically portray as 'fields', 'currents', 'schools' or even 'theories'; it provides the chance of rescuing some of these fields and currents from invisibility; and it invites discussion on their nature and contours – all of them worthy, mobilising endeavours.

The journey of my career as a public lawyer is a journey across different geographies, academic cultures, methodologies and asymmetric power sites. At one level, it is a journey through Southern Europe, Anglo North America, Latin America and back to a flexibly defined space that brings together those three areas – a journey advanced in Catalan, several modalities of Spanish and global academic English. It is also the portrait of a methodological transit that starts with the heirs of Wittgenstein (the transnational *latin* network that educated me in Barcelona) struggling to build an innovative approach to the understanding of law; it continues with normative constructivism, moral reading and neo-constitutional doctrine; and it ultimately lands on the embrace of

* Institute for Legal Research, National Autonomous University of Mexico (UNAM). I thank the convenors of the Workshop on Socio-Legal Trajectories in Europe in Comparative Perspective, who made most valuable comments and helped structure a productive collective conversation in a mostly uncharted terrain. I also thank Roberto Lara Chagoyán, Juan Jesús Garza Onofre, Rodolfo Vázquez, Marcelo Ferrante and Pablo Ariel Rapetti for helpful feedback and comments on a previous draft.

an inter-disciplinary understanding of legal knowledge and action where the socio-legal becomes the core.

My successive absorption of different theoretical approaches illustrates how professional scenarios favour the internalisation of certain methodologies and the setting aside of others, and how power contexts progressively nourish professional interests, attitudes and accents. The line of coherence that links the various stages of my career is probably the adoption of a critical but internal or 'engaged' approach to existing law. During my formative years in Spain, analytic approaches were the path to being critical and separate from previous, politically conditioned approaches to public law. During my first years in Latin America, when I clerked in the Mexican Supreme Court and got to know the constitutional dynamics in other Latin American countries, the moral reading and normative constitutionalism provided a way of taking distance from traditional formalism and advancing towards the effective constitutionalisation of the legal system. In my current stage as a constitutional scholar with a full-time academic dedication, the embrace of socio-legal approaches is indispensable to simultaneously participate and problematise existing structures and methodologies of academic knowledge.

In my view, the methodological transits I portray in this chapter are not only personal but evocative of patterns that are common among the public law scholars of my generation. During our formative years, the analytic tradition enjoyed a centrality in leading-edge scholarly work on constitutional law that has currently diminished its relative weight. Later on, when so many countries in Southern and Eastern Europe and Latin America underwent transitions to democracy, varieties of moral-reading constitutionalism and the kind of constitutional scholarship it nurtured became central. At the moment, having expounded with the necessary thoroughness what constitutional normativity means, how it unfolds *de iure*, and how its principles and mandates can be made operative, an emphasis on efficacy, change, interactions, social consequences, actual operation and evaluation takes centre stage.

It is clear, in any case, that we will be simply glancing at the interaction among disciplines and academic communities that exist independently and beyond their share of influence in the domain of public law, and that should be the object of a more holistic reconstruction. In the context of a collective project bent on exploring socio-legal trajectories in Europe in comparative perspective, it will be especially necessary to more thoroughly reconstruct what the contemporary 'socio-legal turn' in constitutional studies does imply in places – Spain, Latin America – where sociology of law was traditionally alien to law school curricula.

The narrative in the chapter will be also instrumental in placing unto the socio-legal map something that would make this map inaccurate if missing: the fact that some of the legal-academic communities of southern Europe are actually communities that bring together Europe and Latin America indistinguishably, at the impulse of the common use of Spanish. The contribution of this chapter, in other words, does not necessarily take the project beyond Europe, but indicates and portrays how Europe contains, among other things, a transnational *latin* academic community – or, more properly, how Southern Europe falls within the scope of this transnational community. This is a phenomenon different, and to a great extent independent, from the increasing globalisation of academic interchanges that we have witnessed over the last decades, which is responsible for the turn towards 'context' that is increasingly impacting the work of critical comparative public scholarship advanced from the Global South – mine included.

Finally, I should add that there are other subscripts intertwined in the narrative of the chapter that invite analysis from additional perspectives but will not be explored on this occasion. The role of gender and class in the individual and collective journeys I will portray is surely one of the elements to be further examined – both if we ground the analysis in my experience as a preliminarily un-adjectivised person who is progressively drawn to (partially) self-identify as a female, white and/or *latina*, or on the institutional and sociopolitical preconditions of the collective developments I will delve into.

The structure of the chapter will follow a temporal line. In the first section, I will focus on the early 1990s, when I started my studies of law, and on previous transformations that had occurred timidly in Spanish university structures. In that context we will find space to speak about the analytic tradition in legal theory and its influence in constitutional law. In the second section, our attention will advance up to the late 1990s and the decade of the 2000s, when I moved to the United States and later to Latin America, to embrace communities focused on the theoretical building of substantive constitutional norms. Finally, we will move to the decades of the 2010s and 2020s to account for the spaces, communities, methodologies and dynamics that influence my current work as a comparative constitutional scholar. A few closing remarks will follow.

I. A EUROPEAN LEGAL EDUCATION IN THE 1990s: CONSTITUTIONAL LAW AND LEGAL THEORY

Back in the day, Spain was a country that had just left behind almost four decades of fascist dictatorship and was starting a new chapter of history within the frame of the 1978 Constitution.[1] The costs of the negotiated Spanish transition – initially cheered as exemplary – would transpire only decades later. The country enjoyed a long period of stability, cultural and social liberalisation, progressive politics under the lead of the Socialist Party, and experienced a

[1] For general reference on the Spanish transition, see, for instance, Rafael Queirosa-Cheyrouze Muñoz, *Historia de la transición en España. Los inicios del proceso democratizador* (Biblioteca Nueva, 2007).

general wave of 'modernisation', substantially bolstered by the intense process of European integration then under way.[2]

The Spain of the 1990s was also the country of the infinite middle class. As everybody else around me, I was part of it. After an unpretentious but good education in my hometown in Mallorca and passing the Selectivity Exams applied to all students in the country, I could enjoy a high-quality public university education at a small cost. Because my parents had saved money to support a few years of housing outside Mallorca, I had the additional chance of attending a newly created public institution: Pompeu Fabra University (UPF) in Barcelona. I knew about UPF only by chance because my beloved professor of Greek, Joana Bonet, mentioned it to our small group of classic language devotees at our high school in Felanitx. (The idea of studying law had emerged, in part, as a result of another of the touches of luck I received at age 17 as an anonymous member of the infinite middle class: a scholarship to participate in 'Aventura '92' and make a life-changing educational boat trip to Latin America.)

Entering the UPF in 1991 made me a witness of one of the most ambitious efforts at educational renovation underway in the country at the time. The Law Degree programme at Pompeu Fabra had been launched in 1990, the year the university was founded.[3] The curriculum was designed under parameters different from those that were common in the necessarily grey university landscape left by 40 years of dictatorship. Law students at UPF would take two mandatory courses of Economics, students of Economics would take two courses of Introduction to Law, and all of us would enjoy a number of 'free configuration' credits that could be chosen from any of the programmes offered at the university. (I chose most of mine from courses offered in the Humanities degree.) The teaching was organised in trimesters, and the Law Degree was obtained in four years instead of the traditional five. We could use and write in Catalan as we wished – a great achievement after decades of repression and great efforts to recover the public use of the language in formal spheres.

Some of the professors had a rigorous but more traditional outlook and would expose us to what in our tradition is called 'legal dogmatics' – the effort at rationally and systematically reconstructing the contents of positive law. Some were cultivating a space between legal dogmatics and high theory, as occurred with the criminal lawyers. Others, as Pau Salvador Coderch at the department of 'civil law' (covering personality, contracts, property, torts, inheritance and family law), would teach us torts (*dret de danys*) in the United States' style, with a law and economics twist, at a great distance from the parameters that had

[2] See Francisco Villar Ortiz de Urbina, *La transición exterior de España. Del aislamiento a la influencia, 1976–1996* (Madrid, Marcial Pons, 2016); Carlos Sanz Díaz y Antonio Moreno Juste, 'El relato europeo de Felipe González en la transición a la democracia: un estudio de narrativa digital', *Amnis* 3 (2021), 4 October 2021; Juan Díez Medrano, *Framing Europe. Attitudes to European Integration in Germany, Spain and the United Kingdom* (Princeton, Princeton University Press, 2003) 159–78.

[3] See a brief recount at the institutional website: www.upf.edu/web/universitat/historia-de-la-upf.

traditionally presided over the understanding of extra-contractual civil responsibility in the continental tradition. As regards philosophy of law, in Introduction to Law – the course that was taken also by the Economics students – we would use Carlos Nino's books and a bit of Manuel Atienza, while the advanced course was entirely dedicated to deepening into HLA Hart's *The Concept of Law*.[4] Both of my teachers in the legal philosophy courses were Argentinians: Jorge Malem and Riccardo Caracciolo. (The other group had Albert Calsamilgia Blancafort, one of the founders of the UPF and a central figure among the theoretical innovators of the time, who died way too young in 2000.[5])

Incidentally, sociology of law was nowhere in view at law schools at that moment. Although even the briefest reconstruction of the emergence and place of sociology as a discipline or a methodology in Spain could not be attempted here, I would only say that during my time at law school, socio-legal was definitely associated with mostly newly founded Political and Social Science schools, or with Sociology and Anthropology ones.[6] There was a traditional opening to the socio-legal in criminology, integrated into Criminal Law departments, and a few hints at international relations in International Law ones. By and large, in any case, it was alien to what legal methodology was understood to be at the time.

Pompeu Fabra was not the only university providing drops of novelty in a still uneven intellectual landscape. A few developments which had occurred 15 years before at the University of Oviedo would turn out to be consequential. They revolve around the figure of Elías Díaz, who had studied in Italy with political theorist Norberto Bobbio and legal sociologist Renato Treves, and was key in taking philosophy of law away from natural law, which was what the discipline had been largely reduced to in the Spain of Franco.[7] Elías Díaz advised one of his disciples at Oviedo, Manuel Atienza, not to dedicate still another doctoral thesis to HLA Hart (the scholar the renovators in Spain were studying at the time) but to the work of a group of philosophers that he (barely) knew existed in Buenos Aires.[8] Atienza ended up travelling to Buenos Aires in 1975 and, as he has recounted, returned absolutely amazed by the richness of what

[4] HLA Hart, *The Concept of Law* 3rd edn (Oxford, Clarendon Press, 2012 (1st edn, 1961)).

[5] For a brief account of his life and legacy, see www.upf.edu/web/lphi/history-of-the-group.

[6] For a classic, most interesting reconstruction of the genesis of sociology in Spain and its evolution as a still small and weak discipline until the mid-twentieth century, see Enrique Gómez Arboleya, 'Sociología en España' (1958) 98 *Revista de Estudios Políticos* 47–83. For a reconstruction of the contemporary landscape, see Manuel Fernández Esquinas and Màrius Domínguez Amorós (eds), *La sociología en España: diagnóstico y perspectivas de futuro* (Madrid, Marcial Pons, 2021), especially the chapter by José Beltrán Llevador and Miguel Ángel García Calavia, 'Titulaciones y planes de estudio. Marcos de interpretación de la presencia de la sociología en las universidades españolas', 205–34.

[7] Rafael Buzón and Juan José Garza Onofre, *La escuela de Alicante de Filosofía del Derecho. Argumentación jurídica y postpositivismo* (Valencia, Tirant lo Blanch, 2022) 20–30.

[8] Manuel Atienza, 'Una nueva visita a la filosofía del derecho argentina' (2009) 7(14) *Academia. Revista sobre la enseñanza del derecho* 9–10.

he found there. He met Genaro Carrió, Enrique Marí, Eugenio Bulygin, Carlos Alchourrón, Roberto Vernengo and Eduardo Rabossi, who were following the lead of Carlos Cossio and Ambrosio Lucas Gioja.[9] Later on, he would meet two additional individuals who were to be immensely influential at several levels: Ernesto Garzón Valdés and Carlos Santiago Nino.

The intensity, breath and rigour of the philosophical discussion in Buenos Aires– which would occur at the University of Buenos Aires or under the umbrella of the SADAF (*Sociedad Argentina de Análisis Filosófico*), Argentine Society of Philosophic Analysis – left a profound imprint on Atienza.[10] The Argentinians discussed American and Scandinavian realism, Kelsen (the second edition of the *Reine Rechtslehre* was translated into Spanish by Roberto Vernengo) and the Anglo-analytic work done by Russell, Wittgenstein, Carnap and others in the Vienna Circle. George Henrik Von Wright's famous 1951 article, 'Deontic Logic', would ignite many new developments.[11] In 1971, Carlos Alchourrón and Eugenio Bulygin had published *Normative Systems*, a book that inspired, in its turn, the work of several generations of scholars who would do legal theory and ethics within the analytical tradition in the form it adopted after the 'linguistic turn'.[12]

Meanwhile in Spain, Elías Díaz and Manuel Atienza had moved away from Oviedo, as they struggled to find a permanent position in post-authoritarian Spain. Díaz would eventually settle at Universidad Autónoma de Madrid, an institution which, together with Carlos III University later on, would be the hotspot of renovation at the centre of the country. Atienza ended up landing at the University of Alicante where he would meet Juan Ruiz Manero and welcome Josep Aguiló, whom he had encountered during his brief stay at the University of the Balearic Islands.[13] Atienza, Ruiz Manero and Aguiló are the triumvirate around which the 'legal argumentation approach' in legal theory would develop in the following decades.[14]

At their turn, many of the Argentinian philosophers had to go into exile after the coup that installed a terrible military dictatorship in their country between 1976 and 1983. Many of them travelled to Europe or other countries

[9] ibid, 10.

[10] ibid, 10–11.

[11] George H von Wright, 'Deontic Logic' (1951) 60(237) *Mind* 1–15.

[12] Carlos Alchourrón and Eugenio Bulygin, *Normative Systems* (Berlin, Springer-Verlag, 1971). For an overview of these developments, see Pablo Navarro, 'Deontic Logic and Legal Philosophy'; Diana I Pérez and Gustavo Ortiz Millán, 'Analytic Philosophy'; Eduardo Rivera López 'Contemporary Ethics and Political Philosophy'; all of them in Susana Nuccetelli, Ofelia Schutte and Otávio Bueno (eds), *A Companion to Latin American Philosophy* (Oxford, Wiley-Blackwell, 2010).

[13] Buzón and Garza Onofre (n 7) 35.

[14] Manuel Atienza, *El derecho como argumentación* (Barcelona, Ariel, 2006) (comprehensively developing earlier work); Manuel Atienza and Juan Ruiz Manero, *Las piezas del derecho* (Barcelona, Ariel, 2002); Manuel Atienza, *Curso de argumentación jurídica* (Madrid, Trotta, 2013). About the 'triumvirate', see also Rodolfo Vázquez, 'Elogio de la amistad. A Manuel Atienza y el grupo de Alicante', in Buzón and Garza Onofre (n 7) 17.

of Latin America. Ernesto Garzón Valdés moved to Mainz in Germany and Carlos Nino had stays in several countries. An unending flux of visiting scholars and professors sharing a common approach to the study and understanding of law would start to develop and move around Barcelona, Girona, Genoa, Mainz, Tampere, Mexico City, Alicante and, after the return of democracy in Argentina, Córdoba and Buenos Aires. The Imperia seminar, the Genoa and the Alicante master's programmes and the García Máynez seminar in Mexico, were the spaces articulating the legal philosophy groups in Italy, Spain and Latin America. *Doxa*, *Isonomía* or *Analisi e Diritto* were the journals where their debates would develop.[15]

It was in the midst of these developments (and fully ignorant of them) that I had started my law studies at Pompeu Fabra. I was lucky to breath the oxygen of the founding moment and be taught by the leading professors in each department. Several in my class decided to enter the doctoral programme at UPF and joined one or another department as *becarios/as* (graduate scholarship holders). It was relatively easy to enter at the time, us being the second generation of UPF law graduates, but it would be extraordinarily difficult to get a decent mid-level position, and almost impossible to get a senior one. In pretty much all of Spain, at least in what concerns the newly created Constitutional Law departments (replacing the Political Law departments), the senior positions had been recently occupied by our teachers' generation, who would hold them until retirement – just starting to occur now. During the doctorate courses that we took in the way to writing the *tesina* (thesis) that would award us the 'research certification' necessary to start the doctoral thesis, we would take classes but, above all, we would read for long hours in the shared offices of the fourth floor, and we would train ourselves in writing and intellectual discussion.

The relations between the department of Constitutional Law and the department of Philosophy of Law were the closest possible, and seminars were almost always conjunct. In the room were Pablo Navarro, Cristina Redondo, Ernesto Garzón Valdés (who would often come down from Mainz), Eduardo Rivera López, Ricardo Caracciolo, Roberto Gargarella or Silvina Ramírez (to name some of the Argentinians), as well as Marisa Iglesias, Jordi Ferrer, Josep Maria Vilajosana, José Juan Moreso (coming from Girona at the time), Neus Torbisco, Josep Lluis Martí or Héctor López Bofill (to name some of the locals, to which I add Susanna Pozzolo from Genoa, where she had studied with Riccardo Guastini and Paolo Comanducci). The group was soon joined by a young constitutional scholar that was returning from Yale: Víctor Ferreres Comella. Setting aside the welcoming support of Marc Carrillo at those initial moments, and Owen Fiss later on, Víctor is the person I owe indisputably the most in terms of professional orientation and education in constitutional law. The clarity and insight

[15] *Doxa* https://doxa.ua.es/; *Isonomía*, https://isonomia.itam.mx/index.php/revista-cientifica; *Analisi e Diritto*, www.journal.edizioniets.eu/index.php/aed.

of his scholarship (which combines constitutional and normative theory with overdoses of analytic clarity) was a model for my generation.[16] He was also determinant for my deciding to go to the United States to continue my graduate studies – an option that was, at the time, far less common for constitutional lawyers in Spain than going to Germany or Italy.

With the passage of time, several currents featuring different emphasis and areas of interest developed out of this lively intellectual breeding ground. Some people continued doing highly abstract analytic work in legal theory. Others came to use their analytic background to develop scholarship in different specific areas (constitutional law and interpretation, supranational and international legal integration, evidence theory, criminal law, political theory, bioethics, multiculturalism, etc), and the group working in Alicante developed the 'law as argumentation' approach. Juan Ruiz Manero and Manuel Atienza developed this approach in the context of what they call a 'postpositivist' theory of law.[17] This label intends to underline that a plausible understanding of the law must of course be positivist (in the sense of vindicating the social sources of law and rejecting natural law) but also understand law as a human creation that cannot be reduced to a system of norms and their modes of identification. Any meaningful conception of the law must go 'beyond' (ie 'post') positivism, and understand it as a social practice oriented by goals and values.[18] Legal theorists must therefore not only describe legal phenomena but engage with social realities and provide orientation and evaluation criteria to those that participate in legal practice – among them criteria on how to make good legal arguments.[19] This understanding has obvious connections to the views of American legal theorist Ronald Dworkin, who considers law part of practical reason and postulates the ultimate unity of the latter, with those of Robert Alexy on principles, discourse theory and proportionality, and those of Owen Fiss and other scholars I will mention later on.[20]

The mapping of this period must make space to mention the towering work of Carlos Nino, who greatly contributed to all 'renovated' areas of scholarship.

[16] See Víctor Ferreres Comella, *Justicia constitucional y democracia* (Madrid, Centro de Estudios Políticos y Constitucionales, 1998); *El principio de taxatividad en materia penal y el valor normativo de la jurisprudencia: una perspectiva constitucional* (Madrid, Civitas, 2002); *Constitutional Courts and Democratic Values* (New Haven, Yale University Press, 2009); *The Constitution of Arbitration* (Cambridge, Cambridge University Press, 2021).

[17] Manuel Atienza and Juan Ruiz Manero, *Para una teoría postpositivsta del derecho* (Lima, Palestra, 2003); Manuel Atienza and Juan Ruiz Manero, 'Dejemos atrás el positivismo jurídico' (2007) 27 *Isonomía* 7–28; Manuel Atienza, 'Ni positivismo jurídico ni neoconstitucionalismo: una defensa del constitucionalismo postpositivsta' (2017) 2(3) *CAP Jurídica* 59–101.

[18] Manuel Atienza, 'Dejemos atrás …' (n 17). For an excellent global reconstruction of his thought, see Isabel Lifante Vidal, 'Diez ideas sobre el pensamiento iusfilosófico de Manuel Atienza' (2023) 46 *Doxa* 243–57.

[19] Manuel Atienza, *Curso de argumentación jurídica* (n 14).

[20] Ronald Dworkin, *Law's Empire* (Cambridge MA, Harvard University Press, 1986); *Freedom's Law: The Moral Reading of the American Constitution* (Cambridge MA, Harvard University Press, 1996); *Justice for Hedgehogs* (Cambridge MA, Harvard University Press, 2011).

Despite his premature death at 49 years old in 1993 in Bolivia, where he had gone to support the works of the Constituent Assembly, his imprint and legacy have been enormous.[21] He renovated legal theory, constitutional law and criminal theory;[22] he made important contributions in moral and political philosophy, especially on the notions of personal and collective autonomy;[23] and he was a theorist of deliberative democracy and one of the first Latin American scholars to publish in English and teach at an American University – Yale Law School.[24] He also had a central role in the Argentinian transition to democracy as an advisor to President Raúl Alfonsín. Nino nurtured from his post the political dynamics that made possible the trial of the military Juntas in 1985, and he developed individual and collective academic work that made possible the 1994 constitutional reform approved shortly after his death.[25] He wrote on the perils of hyper-presidentialism and laid important theoretical ground to the trials of the Juntas in *Radical Evil on Trial*.[26] His disciples and friends have continued, expanded and transformed many of the seeds he planted. They are an academic generation with which I have shared most of my professional life.

II. A JOURNEY INTO AMERICA: NORMATIVE CONSTITUTIONALISM AND THE BUILDING OF NEW PRACTICES OF CONSTITUTIONAL ADJUDICATION

After being awarded a graduate scholarship sponsored by La Caixa Foundation in the style of the Fulbright grants, and having endured the habitual anxieties of the application processes, I arrived in New Haven (Connecticut, USA) in 1998 to complete a Master of Law (LLM) at Yale. The idea was later to apply, if possible, to the Juris Science Doctor (JSD) Program and write my doctoral thesis under the supervision of the professor that Víctor Ferreres had so strongly recommended: Owen Fiss.

Studying at the Yale Law School opened immense horizons, whose approximate contours I would apprehend only years later. For starters, it was an amazing

[21] For a comprehensive overview of his work, see Victoria Roca Pérez, *Derecho y razonamiento práctico en Carlos S. Nino* (Madrid, Centro de Estudios Políticos y Constitucionales, 2005).

[22] Carlos Santiago Nino, *Fundamentos de derecho constitucional: análisis filosófico, jurídico y politológico de la práctica constitucional* (Buenos Aires, Astrea, 1992); *Ética y derechos humanos* (Barcelona, Ariel, 1989); *Introducción al análisis del derecho* (Buenos Aires, Astrea, rev. 1996); *Fundamentos de derecho penal* (ed. G. Maurino; Barcelona, Gedisa, 2008).

[23] See Eduardo Rivera López (n 12) 161–64.

[24] Carlos Santiago Nino, *The Constitution of Deliberative Democracy* 2nd edn (New Haven, Yale University Press, 1998).

[25] Owen Fiss, 'Carlos Nino: The Death of a Public Intellectual' in *Pillars of Justice: Lawyers and the Liberal Tradition* (Cambridge MA, Harvard University Press, 2017) 139–51.

[26] Carlos Santiago Nino, *Radical Evil on Trial* (New Haven, Yale University Press, 1998); 'El híper presidencialismo argentino y las concepciones de la democracia' in Carlos Santiago Nino, Roberto Gargarella et al, *El presidencialismo puesto a prueba* (Madrid, Centro de Estudios Políticos y Constitucionales, 1992).

incursion into an entirely new way of teaching and learning law. The way of being in class, what was expected from students, the assignments we were given or the facture of the examinations – they were all a great novelty for me. I took classes under different formats, from professors with highly different styles, but the teaching 'technology' was amazing all along – the approach to legal learning is no doubt the feature that I admire the most in American legal education.[27] At Yale, I also discovered inter-disciplinarity. My best window into it was Carol Rose's Property course, where she would combine philosophy, history, law and economics, feminism, jurisprudence and classic common law, as if it were the easiest and most natural thing to be done.[28] Another great learning outlet was the Capitalism or Democracy? seminar offered by Owen Fiss and George Priest. We would discuss readings in small groups, spurred by the interchange between two professors that argued with passion and unconditional mutual respect despite their deep disagreements.

(My days as graduate student in the United States were also marked, I should add, by uninterrupted suffering with the poverty of my oral English. My classmates from Latin America and other countries where English is not a public language felt similarly. Yet in my mind, my situation was always worse. I remember working all the time, living on hummus rolls, feeling miserable in view of the distance between what I intended to say or write and what I was actually saying or writing, and asking myself if I could really do it.)

Second, my graduate education at Yale exposed me to an extraordinarily varied and rich range of conceptions of the law, much wider than my former legal education in Spain. As Owen Fiss has explained so well, in the decade of the 1970s, Yale Law School became the preserve of the liberal tradition (ie the liberal-equalitarian tradition, as we would put it in Europe and Latin America) against the two other currents that have dominated United States universities for quite long: critical legal studies (which, to say it with Fiss's remarkable economy of words, defends the proposition that law is politics), and the law and economics movement (which, again in Fiss's words, defends the proposition that law is efficiency).[29]

When I arrived at the school in the late 1990s, however, the course catalogue did certainly include all three currents. While I ignored the law and economics option I actually took a course on critical race theory, another one with Roberto Mangabeira Unger – which I enjoyed enormously – and another one with the un-classifiable Jack Balkin, acquiring some familiarity with variations of critical

[27] Owen Fiss, 'The Law According to Yale' in Myres S McDougal and W Michael Reisman (eds), *Power and Policy in Quest of Law* (The Hague, Martinus Nijhoff, 1985). For an expanded version, 'Eugene Rostow: The Law According to Yale' in *Pillars ...* (n 25) 91–105.

[28] For an illustration, Carol M Rose, 'Property as Storytelling: Perspectives from Game Theory, Narrative Theory, Feminist Theory' (1990) 2 *Yale Journal of Law and the Humanities* 37–57. With less methodological mix but quintessentially Carol Rose, 'Crystals and Mud in Property Law' (1988) 40(3) *Stanford Law Review* 577–610.

[29] Fiss, *Pillars ...* (n 25) 12–13, 113, 125.

theory. A number of courses adopted the habitual historic, self-centred perspective that makes United States constitutional law so boring for outsiders – despite the great learning that comes from theorisations of its centuries-long historical practice and interpretation. Other scholars, however – starting with Owen Fiss, Reva Siegel and Robert Post, to name only professors who work in the area of constitutional law – would evaluate legal practice in light of broadly appealing normative theories, developing the sort of enlightening scholarship that makes the Yale law faculty a reference for academia worldwide. While Yale's emphasis as a law school is largely normative and theoretical, not empirical, I was exposed to a style of doing scholarship that prizes clarity, that is openly argumentative, and that is explicitly and permanently in dialogue both with the level of normative values and with the evaluation of social consequences. Iconic articles such as 'Why Equal Protection No Longer Protects', 'Equality Talk' or 'She the People' by Siegel, to raise a few examples among infinite others, attest to the illumination and generative power of this kind of scholarship.[30]

Third, at Yale I encountered a community that would be become central for me to this day: the Latin American graduate students of my generation. Some of them were classmates at the LLM, others arrived later on. I have subsequently collaborated with them continuously, as much in Yale-related spaces as in the context of the academic communities already mentioned or to be soon mentioned in this chapter. At the end of my LLM, I was awarded a summer scholarship to go to Argentina under the sponsorship of the Linkage programme that Owen Fiss and Robert Burt had set up in memory of their close friend Carlos Nino. The project was a continuation of the cooperation the three of them had started in the context of Argentina's and Chile's transitions to democracy.[31] During our summer stay in Buenos Aires as Linkage fellows in 1998, we travelled to La Serena in Chile, and I attended SELA (the *Seminario en América Latina de Teoría Constitucional y Política*, Latin American Seminar on Constitutional Law and Theory) for the first time. Some of the UPF people were there, the disciples of Nino from Argentina were there, professors from Diego Portales University and the University of Chile were there, and many young and middle-aged professors from Colombia, Paraguay, Puerto Rico, Brazil and Perú were there (professors from Mexico, Ecuador, Cuba, Venezuela and other universities in the United States would join the seminar in future years).

The SELA has now taken place for almost 30 years and has fulfilled many crucial functions in Latin America. With time, the seminar has grown, become more diverse, and its thematic and methodological focus has expanded, moving away from philosophy and getting closer to socio-legal studies. It has at the same

[30] Reva B Siegel, 'Why Equal Protection No Longer Protects: The Evolving Forms of Status-Enforcing State Action' (1997) 49 *Stanford Law Review* 1111–48; 'She the People: The Nineteenth Amendment, Sex Equality, Federalism, and the Family' (2002) 115 *Harvard Law Review* 947–1046; 'Equality Talk: Antisubordination and Anticlassification Values in Constitutional Struggles Over Brown' (2004) 117 *Harvard Law Review* 1470–547.

[31] Fiss, *Pillars* … (n 25) 192.

time nurtured and witnessed the transformation of the Latin American public law academy (including a new approach to legal education and the production of legal scholarship), providing a background space where hundreds of other individual and collective projects have found ways to develop.

During my doctoral dissertation under the supervision of Owen Fiss, from 1999 to 2005, I affirmed an approach that I will generically call, for abbreviation, 'standard substantive constitutionalism'. It is an approach based on the critical construction/reconstruction of constitutional practices in light of the normative commitments expressed in the high positive norms of the system – which in contemporary democracies invariably affirm equality, autonomy and social justice. This approach sits at the intersection of the visions of the law and the constitution we might derive – to name only individuals who have already appeared in our narration – from Atienza, Alexy, Fiss, Dworkin or Nino. It uses the tools they offer to develop 'engaged' or internal views about the meaning and the implications of constitutional principles. Owen, who in the 1970s produced theorisations of anti-subordination and substantive equality that are still massively used today, was the best teacher I could ever have had.[32]

The tools and goals that underlie standard substantive constitutionalism provided me the resources to traverse the next stage of my professional life: clerking at the Mexican Supreme Court. After moving to Mexico for personal reasons, I got into contact with Rodolfo Vázquez at Instituto Tecnológico Autónomo de México (ITAM) – another absolutely central person without whose work and initiatives many of the developments and communities we have surveyed would not exist. Rodolfo had close bonds with the universities I had been associated with in Spain (and their partners in Italy) and with the academic community articulated around the figure and legacy of Carlos Nino. José Ramón Cossío Díaz, a renowned Mexican constitutional lawyer, was the Dean of ITAM at the time. He was appointed Justice to the Supreme Court of Mexico in 2004, and he invited me to join his clerking team.

My stay at the Supreme Court (2004–11) was as influential and formative as my former experiences – or more. The entrance of Cossío to the court was an authentic revolution in an institution that had been integrated for many years only with career judges, not academics, practitioners or (only sporadically) people with experience in public office.[33] The work we developed under Cossío's direction and encouragement was crucial to bolster the legal transition that Mexico started with some delay with respect to its political transition.[34] The paradigm we were fighting against was traditional Latin American formalism – which was not very different from traditional European formalism,

[32] See Owen Fiss, 'Groups and the Equal Protection Clause' (1976) 5(2) *Philosophy and Public Affairs* 107–77.

[33] See Pablo Mijangos y González, *Historia mínima de la Suprema Corte* (Mexico City, El Colegio de México, 2019) 222–23.

[34] See Héctor Fix-Fierro, *El poder del poder judicial y la modernización jurídica en el México contemporáneo* (Mexico City, IIJ UNAM, 2020) 1–19.

as it grew and became common in the civil law tradition before the advent of post-war constitutionalism.

The characterisation of formalism in theoretical terms is a complex endeavour. At the level of judicial practice, it can be easily related to a well-known package of attitudes and ways of doing which include, among others: the privileging of literal (textual) interpretation, complemented only if necessary with systematic interpretation or consultation of legislative intention; the treatment of legal provisions as categorical rules, not as open-ended principles, wherever possible; and the presentation of legal meaning as something unproblematic and evident, and not as something intrinsically associated to a practice of asking and giving reasons.[35]

At the time we arrived at the Supreme Court, this formalistic attitude meant also almost automatic deference to the legislative and the executive branches. Both historic case law, developed in times of PRI single-party hegemony, and the conceptual and procedural resorts of *amparo* litigation (the Mexican rights protecting complaint), definitely worked in defence of public authority, not in defence of the people. This situation was, at that moment, already in stark contrast with the Mexican constitution, which had been amended to include a large collection of new rights, and with the international treaties massively signed by Mexico. As the literature has often observed, while over the decades of the 1980s and 1990s the Supreme Court had fulfilled its function well of adjudicating conflicts between the different power branches and territorial levels of government – something Mexican hyper-powerful presidents had done in the past – its role in terms of rights protection was poor.[36] Seen from the perspective of what constitutional courts were doing in countries like Colombia, Argentina, Brazil or Costa Rica, legal developments in the Mexican judiciary were out of step both with constitutional provisions and the ethos of the time. Our collective task was therefore to do as much as possible in terms of promoting a new way of reading the constitution and deciding cases, in view of its normative force, especially (but not exclusively) in the domain of rights. Justice Cossío pushed forward countless debates within the court and, slowly but steadily, prepared the jurisprudential setting ready for the more ambitious achievements that would come after the human rights' constitutional reform of 2011.[37]

[35] For an illustration of the sort of moves that singularise a formalistic approach to constitutional interpretation see, for instance, Roberto Lara Chagoyán, 'Diez patologías formalistas en la cultura jurídica mexicana. Tras los pasos de M. Atienza' (2023) 47 *Doxa* 225–42.

[36] See Karina Ansolabehere, 'More Power, More Rights? The Supreme Court and Society in Mexico', in Javier Couso, Alexandra Hunneus and Rachel Sieder (eds), *Cultures of Legality: Judicialization and Political Activism in Latin America* (Cambridge, Cambridge University Press, 2010); Ana Laura Magaloni, '¿Por qué la Suprema Corte no ha sido un instrumento de defensa de los derechos fundamentales?' in Eduardo Ferrer Mac-Gregor and Arturo Zaldívar Lelo de Larrea (eds), *La ciencia del derecho procesal constitucional. Estudios en homenaje a Héctor Fix Zamudio en sus cincuenta años como investigador del derecho* (Mexico City, IIJ UNAM, IMDPC, Marcial Pons, 2010).

[37] About the main contents and goals of the June 2011 constitutional reform, see Miguel Carbonell and Pedro Salazar (eds), *La reforma constitucional de derechos humanos: un nuevo paradigma*

It was during my time at the Supreme Court that I started to expand my knowledge about judicial review in other Latin American countries. Knowing that comparative developments were among our main sources of inspiration – the court's historic doctrines were useless and international human rights sources played a very modest role in the country before the 2011 constitutional reform afforded them the same hierarchical status as the constitution. Justice Cossío used an existing internal clerk-supporting programme to send us for brief but intensive stays to other national or international courts, to read rulings, and get to know their decision-making styles and protocols. In my visit to the Constitutional Court of Colombia – the first of others to come – I discovered the *tutela*, the public action of unconstitutionality, the procedural doctrines produced by the court to amplify access and strengthen the remedial reach of its rulings, as well as an impressive amount of pathbreaking doctrines that influenced rights protection in all Latin America.

Colombia was the first step along a path that, over the course of the years and pretty 'organically', has led to my gaining more knowledge about constitutional dynamics and adjudication in Latin American countries. Mutual awareness of judicial developments, a shared conversation around common problems, common constitutional features or inter-American developments among regional legal elites, including networks of public interest litigation and activism – surely aided by the common use of Spanish and swift linguistic bridges with Brazil – are definitely features of legal dynamics in Latin America.

III. MAPPING OUT AND EXPLAINING THE WORLD: COMPARATIVE CONSTITUTIONAL STUDIES AND THE SOCIO-LEGAL TURN IN PUBLIC LAW

In 2011, after almost eight years at the Supreme Court, I went into full-time academic dedication in Mexico. It was the first time I had a full-time position at the university – even though I had been teaching in Barcelona in my pre-doctoral period and briefly in Mexico before entering the Supreme Court. Because I had poured every last drop of knowledge inside me into the court's drafting and advisory tasks, it really felt like a return to books, study and preparation. I had not lost contact with academic life, but I had to catch up. There was a lot of new stuff out there to be apprehended.

Developments around constitutionalism have seen an extraordinary expansion over the last decades, after the third wave of democratisation reached Central and Eastern Europe and Latin America. In these countries, prevailing understandings have invariably conceptualised the constitution as a true norm

(Mexico City, IIJ UNAM, 2011). For an assessment of the many developments triggered by the reform after ten years, see José Luis Caballero and Eduardo Ferrer MacGregor (eds), *La reforma constitucional sobre derechos humanos. Una evaluación con perspectiva de futuro* (Mexico, Tirant lo Blanch, 2022).

that binds both individuals and state authorities, that is enforceable by courts, and that sets down a substantive horizon of goals, rights and values that must effectively preside over the organisation of social life. Over this period, constitutionalism has indeed been a thing, and has generated an unprecedented degree of analysis at different levels, with different methodologies, from different fields, in different spaces. More generally, we may say that law, and specifically constitutions, have been over the last decades more important than ever before and have become an important object of study for disciplines where it had not been prominent in the past (such as comparative politics, anthropology, political science, sociology or history).

During the 10 years I spent at ITAM Law School and currently at the UNAM Institute for Legal Research (which I joined in 2022), I have developed professionally amidst this crisscrossing of perspectives and fields. The epistemic communities I mentioned in the former sections have not disappeared. They have evolved, but they remain there. In the Alicante postpositivist hub, the European and Latin American scholars that nurtured themselves in the group of Manuel Atienza, Juan Ruiz Manero and Josep Aguiló are in their forties and fifties and already have their own projects and bodies of scholarship, followed by many other younger academics. The Alicante Master of Legal Argumentation has been taken by several generations of jurists from all Latin countries, and the resulting transnational community has now a new space called *i-latina* (*filosofía del derecho para el mundo latino*, philosophy of law for the Latin world).[38]

The analytic philosophers are also still there, even if work on legal language, norms or meta-ethics is far less central and most people have moved to 'applied theory'. Prominent among them is the Girona-based evidence theory group, founded by Jordi Ferrer – who started his career at UPF – which has attracted philosophers in the analytic tradition working on other fields and is now a power-house of applied legal theory influencing legal theory, legal practice and education in Spain and Latin America. Incidentally, women legal theorists have discovered that they are far less in number in their field than in other fields of philosophy (let alone public law). They have launched interesting visibility-enhancing initiatives such as the seminar 'In Theory There are Women (in Theory)', which celebrated its fourth edition in September 2024.[39]

The SELA value-engaged community continues to meet every year around Owen Fiss's indispensable leadership. The SELA members of my generation (also around our fifties, and half of them women) are now mature scholars. Many have been or are currently deans, justices in supreme, constitutional or special courts, prosecutors, Constituent Assembly members, governmental advisors, members of cabinet or directors of civil society organisations and academic networks. As is habitual in presidential systems, but with special

[38] Asociación de Filosofía del Derecho para el mundo latino: www.i-latina.org/.

[39] Conferencia internacional 'En teoría hay mujeres (en teoría)': https://istitutotarello.org/2023/01/23/iii-conferencia-internacional-en-teoria-hay-mujeres-en-teoria-7-y-8-de-julio-de-2023-milano-italia/.

smoothness in Latin America, where administrative structures and systems of professional career are weaker than in Europe, people move often between state structures and the university – even if the degree of professionalisation of the legal academia in the region is higher than ever before.[40]

Despite these signs of continuity, the methodologies around the study and use of public law have diversified. New approaches have appeared, all grown out of or bolstered by the extraordinary expansion of constitutionalism. I would classify the tasks engaged by current scholarship on constitutionalism under several entries, covering at least: categorisation, explanation, evaluation and participation in constitutional developments and practice.

I will close this chapter by briefly suggesting how these tasks are deployed in two areas where I have been working recently: the study of Latin American constitutionalism, and the comparative study of constitutionalism worldwide, as an identifiable recently emerged academic field. A feature that emerges as we analyse the contours and methods of the work done in these areas is, in my view, the prominence of the *explanation-evaluation* combination. This combination has turned these fields into spaces that bring together lawyers, political scientists, socio-legal scholars and legal anthropologists. What should be underlined in the context of this project, in other words, is that a good part of what contemporary 'globalised' constitutionalists do at the moment implies continuous interaction with 'law and society' approaches. They combine theory with a variety of empirical measurements and evaluations which render the socio-legal extraordinarily preeminent within the legal.

In the context of the study of Latin American constitutionalism, for instance, one thing scholars have been doing over the last two decades is, first, developing theories and *categorisations* that intend to characterise regional constitutionalism in view of some explicit or implicit setup (historic models, North-Atlantic democracies, political theory, western or non-western epistemologies, etc). These are instrumental at deepening our comprehension of the phenomenon. The adjectivisation of regional constitutionalism as forward-looking,[41] aspirational,[42] transformative,[43] liberal or radical,[44] hybrid,[45] structurally

[40] See Javier Wilenmann, Diego Gil and Samuel Tschorne, 'It Now Exists: The Birth of the Chilean Professional Legal Academia in the Wake of Neoliberalism' (2023) 48(3) *Law & Social Inquiry* 971–98.

[41] Ruti Teitel, 'Transitional Jurisprudence: The Role of Law in Political Transformation' (1997) 106(7) *Yale Law Journal* 2009–80.

[42] Mauricio García Villegas, 'Constitucionalismo aspiracional: derecho, democracia y cambio social en américa latina' (2012) 25(75) *Análisis Político* 89–110.

[43] Armin von Bogdandy et al (eds), *Transformative Constitutionalism in Latin America: The Emergence of a New Ius Commune* (Oxford, Oxford University Press, 2017).

[44] James Crawford and Daniel Bonilla (eds), *Constitutionalism in the Americas* (New York, Routledge, 2018).

[45] Francisca Pou Giménez, 'Hybridity and Constitutional Taxonomy in Latin America' (2022) 16(2) *Law and Ethics of Human Rights* 245–72.

inegalitarian,[46] pluralist,[47] pluri-national, communitarian and intercultural,[48] environmental or eco-centric[49] then emerges. In their (socio-legal) maps of intellectual thinking about regional constitutionalism, Javier Couso and Alberto Coddou focus on a subset of categorisations that seem to additionally defend a certain normative understanding of regional constitutions, with the goal of impacting legal and political practice. It is at this level that Couso compares Latin American (progressive) neo-constitutionalism – a category where he includes *ius constitutionale commune en América Latina* (ICCAL) as developed by the scholars that converge around the Max Planck Public Law Institute in Heidelberg[50] – and New Latin American (radical) constitutionalism – which places in their best light the distinctive features of the innovative constitutions of Ecuador and Bolivia.[51] Coddou, on his part, adds to those two currents one that he calls 'egalitarian-dialogic constitutionalism' – similar to the one Natalia Ángel Cabo and Domingo Lovera-Parmo call 'Latin American social constitutionalism'.[52]

Aside from these important taxonomic exercises, an important part of more specific inquiries in the domain of constitutional law in Latin America is today inextricably associated to efforts at *explanation* and *evaluation* that imply work at the level of the socio-legal. The study of judicialisation in Latin America,[53]

[46] Roberto Gargarella, *The Legal Foundations of Inequality: Constitutionalism in the Americas: 1776–1860* (Cambridge, Cambridge University Press, 2010); *Latin American Constitutionalism, 1810–2010: The Engine Room of the Constitution* (Oxford, Oxford University Press, 2013).

[47] Raquel Z Yrigoyen Fajardo, 'The Horizon of Pluralist Constitutionalism: From Multiculturalism to Decolonization', in César Rodríguez Garavito (ed), *Law and Society in Latin America: A New Map* (New York, Routledge, 2014); Daniel Bonilla Maldonado, *La constitución multicultural* (Bogotá, Siglo del Hombre Ed.-Instituto Pensar, 2006).

[48] María Elena Attard Bellido. 'El constitucionalismo boliviano en clave de género e interseccionalidad', in Francisca Pou Giménez, Ruth Rubio Marín and Verónica Undurraga Valdés (eds), *Gender, Women and Constitutionalism in Latin America* (New York, Routledge, 2024).

[49] Germana de Oliveira Moraes, 'O Constitucionalismo Ecocêntrico na América Latina, o Bem Viver e a Nova Visão das Águas' (2013) 34 (1) Revista da Faculdade de Direito 123–55; Daniel Bonilla Maldonado, 'El constitucionalismo radical ambiental y la diversidad cultural en América Latina: los derechos de la naturaleza y el buen vivir en Ecuador y Bolivia' (2019) 24 *Revista Derecho del Estado* 3–23.

[50] Bogdandy et al (n 43).

[51] Javier Couso, 'Latin American New Constitutionalism: A Tale of Two Cities' in Conrado Hubner Mendes, Roberto Gargarella and Sebastián Guidi (eds), *Handbook of Constitutional Law in Latin America* (Oxford, Oxford University Press, 2022) 354–65.

[52] Alberto Coddou McManus, 'A Critical Account of Ius Constitutionale Commune in Latin America: A Map of Contemporary Latin American Constitutionalism' (2022) 11(1) *Global Constitutionalism* 110–38.

[53] See, for instance, Diana Kapiszewski, Gordon Silverstein and Robert A Kagan (eds), *Consequential Courts: Judicial Roles in Global Perspective* (Cambridge, Cambridge University Press, 2013); Gretchen Helmke and Julio Rios-Figueroa (eds), *Courts in Latin America* (Cambridge, Cambridge University Press, 2010); Couso, Hunneus and Sieder (n 36); Diego Werneck Arguelhes and Evandro Proença Süssekind, 'Building Judicial Power in Latin America: Opposition Strategies and the Lessons of the Brazilian Case' (2018) 27(1) *Revista Uruguaya de Ciencia Política* 175–96; Sandra Botero, Daniel Brinks and Ezequiel González-Ocantos (eds.), *The Limits of Judicialization: From Progress to Backlash in Latin America* (Cambridge, Cambridge University Press, 2022).

for instance, or the study of constitutional change in the region,[54] have been spaces where political scientists, lawyers and even legal anthropologists have worked hand in hand over the last decades. The abundant work on sexual and reproductive rights and gender and constitutionalism, to raise another example, generally adopts the same integrative approach. It is rare to find scholarship in the area that confines itself to tasks of doctrinal reconstruction; relevant works rather pause to explore what is behind the legal developments under analysis, evaluate the outcomes of legalisation processes and generally adopt an anti-necessitarian stance.[55] We could go on with more and more examples, since much of the work on fundamental or human rights in the region inhabits this amplified methodologic space.

Some of this work is actually adjacent already to instances of *participation*, that is, to instances of direct academic engagement with constitutional practices, which include impact-oriented critical comment on reforms or judicial rulings, writing and signing of amicus curie, op-eds and blogposts, support for social activism, and a long etcetera. In Latin America, in a context where, as we observed, constitutional law is bonded with a transformative normative program, an important part of constitutional scholarship, especially in the domain of rights, inhabits the terrains of 'constitucionalismo vivo' (living constitutionalism), 'investigación-acción' (action research), or more simply, critical analysis of constitutional practice, which is pretty dynamic. Incidentally, this analysis of practice is sometimes damaging of the professional status of younger academics, many of them women, who are not awarded the prestige that accrues to practitioners of 'high theory'.

The same socio-legal turn is perceptible, more generally, at the level of 'comparative constitutional studies' at a broader scale – an approach that develops in an identifiable space enclosing certain academic seminars, reference journals, informal networks, and so on.[56] In a book that was enormously successful in

[54] See, for instance, Gabriel Negretto, *Making Constitutions: Presidents, Parties and Institutional Choice in Latin America* (Cambridge, Cambridge University Press, 2013); Richard Albert, Carlos Bernal and Juliano Zaiden Benvindo (eds), *Constitutional Change and Transformation in Latin America* (Oxford, Hart, 2019).

[55] See, for instance, Paola Bergallo, Isabel Cristina Jaramillo Sierra and Juan Marco Vaggione, *El aborto en América Latina: Estrategias jurídicas para luchar por su legalización y enfrentar las resistencias conservadoras* (Buenos Aires, Siglo XXI Editores, 2019); Francisca Pou Giménez, Ruth Rubio Marín and Verónica Undurraga Valdés, *Women, Gender and Constitutionalism in Latin America* (Abingdon Routledge, 2024).

[56] The spaces associated to the International Society of Public Law ('I-con') are central: the *International Journal of Constitutional Law*, the Annual Icon Meetings and the activities of Icon national chapters, the I-connect blog and associated blogs at the national level. Other spaces are Global Constitutionalism, Comparative Constitutional Studies, Law and Ethics of Human Rights, the *American Journal of Comparative Law, Law and Society Review* or *Law and Social Inquiry* (academic journals), the annual meetings of the Law and Society Association (for many years a space for discussion of law-related work well beyond the original 'law and society' approach), in permanent conjunction with all kinds of smaller seminars and initiatives at national level but with a loosely articulated transnational web of participants and audiences.

changing the prevailing nomenclature, Ran Hirschl included a chapter entitled 'From Comparative Constitutional Law to Comparative Constitutional Studies' where he identified a shift in the study of constitutionalism towards a methodological approach that openly brings in the social sciences.[57] The emergence of 'large-n' constitutional analysis has changed the framing of many discussions, as paradigmatically illustrated by the work of Zachary Elkins, Tom Ginsburg or James Melton on the basis of the 'comparative constitutions' database (now open to all),[58] the work by Mila Versteeg and collaborators,[59] or the work by David Law.[60] Non-quantitative, theoretically oriented comparative constitutional scholarship, still majoritarian, equally deploys context-informed and socially situated analysis.[61] These past years, for instance, debates on constitutional design, theory and doctrine have made an effort to come to terms with the implications of radical change in the political conditions that had operated for decades as background assumptions in the study of contemporary constitutionalism. Much work in comparative constitutional studies at the moment examines new developments associated with phenomena like democratic retrogression, the crisis of political parties or environmental collapse, or reexamines previous debates in view of these new developments in the political and social scene.[62]

[57] Ran Hirschl, *Comparative Matters: The Renaissance of Comparative Constitutional Law* (Oxford, Oxford University Press, 2014) 151–91; Mila Versteeg, Tom Ginsburg and David Landau, *Comparative Constitutional Law: A Global and Interdisciplinary Approach* (Oxford, Oxford University Press, 2022); Mila Versteeg and Adam Chilton, 'Introduction: A Second Wave of Comparative Constitutional Studies' (2022) 51 *Journal of Legal Studies* 321–28.

[58] For an illustration, see Zachary Elkins, Tom Ginsburg and James Melton, *The Endurance of National Constitutions* (Cambridge, Cambridge University Press, 2009); Tom Ginsburg and James Melton, 'Does the Constitutional Amendment Rule Matter At All? Amendment Cultures and the Challenges of Measuring Amendment Difficulty' (2015) 13(3) *International Journal of Constitutional Law* 686–713; Zachary Elkins and Tom Ginsburg, 'Ideation and Innovation in Constitutional Rights' (2022) 16(2) *Law and Ethics of Human Rights* 217–44. See the databases: https://comparativeconstitutionsproject.org/ and www.constituteproject.org/.

[59] For an illustration, see Mila Versteeg and Alan Chilton, *How Constitutional Rights Matter* (Oxford, Oxford University Press, 2020); 'Small-c Constitutional Rights' (2022) 20 *International Journal of Constitutional Law* 141–76; 'The Effect of Constitutional Gender Equality Clauses' (2022) 51 *Journal of Legal Studies* 329–70; 'Rights without Resources: The Impact of Constitutional Social Rights on Social Spending' (2017) 60 *Journal of Law & Economics* 713–48.

[60] See, for instance, David Law, Aharon Barak and Yeong-Chin Su, 'Constitutional Adjudication in Comparative Perspective', in *Constitutional Interpretation: Theory and Practice*, vol 10 (Nangang, Academia Sinica, 2020); 'Constitutional Dialects: The Language of Transnational Legal Orders', in Gregory Shaffer, Tom Ginsburg and Terence Halliday (eds), *Constitution-Making and Transnational Legal Order* (Cambridge, Cambridge University Press, 2019) 110–55; 'Generic Constitutional Law' (2005) 89 *Minnesota Law Review* 652–69.

[61] David Law, *Constitutionalism in Context* (Cambridge, Cambridge University Press, 2021); Rebecca Cook, *Frontiers of Gender Equality* (Philadelphia, University of Pennsylvania Press, 2023).

[62] Jeff King, 'Social Rights as Capstone', in Katharine Young (ed), *The Future of Economic and Social Rights* (Cambridge, Cambridge University Press, 2019) 289–323; Tom Ginsburg and Aziz Huq, *How to Save a Constitutional Democracy* (Cambridge, Cambridge University Press, 2018); Yaniv Roznai and Tamar Ostowsky Brandes, 'Democratic Erosion, Populist Constitutionalism, and the Unconstitutional Constitutional Amendments Doctrine' (2020) 14(1) *Law and Ethics of Human Rights* 19–48.

The turn towards methodologies that embrace socio-legal sensitivities is even more important in the epistemic communities committed to developing comparative constitutional analysis from a critical stance, cognisant of the power asymmetries that still pervade the production of legal knowledge even among a community that self-perceives itself as progressive.[63] The Eurocentric and colonial assumptions of traditional comparative law are transparent,[64] but even within the apparently 'neutral' and more inclusive frames of comparative constitutional studies, there remain abundant unconscious gender, class and geo-political biases – narratives of Latin American constitutional 'failure' provide an example.[65] Different levels of economic, institutional, cultural and personal resources exert a notable impact on what is written, discussed or celebrated, and what remains ignored in the English-speaking constitutional comparative conversation. The slowly increasing presence of authors from more diversified backgrounds and the expansion of topics and writing styles is an important step forward even if it diminishes only marginally the in-built biases of existing intellectual debates.[66] Designing and developing with a socio-legal sensitivity comparative constitutional research projects should be actually seen in this case not as a way of integrating 'context', but as a way of deconstructing the traditional dichotomies about what is central and what is contextual while remaking (in a pluralist spirit) what we have learned to perceive as abstract or conceptual – and the other way around.

IV. CONCLUDING THOUGHTS

At one level, this chapter has outlined how a little girl from Felanitx in the venerable island of Mallorca went to Barcelona, then to Yale Law School, then to Mexico, and ended up making a life as an academic up and down the American continent and beyond.

As a surely far more interesting one, the journey has been instrumental to the identification of epistemic communities, events and fields of academic knowledge that are not always identified as such, and even more rarely placed in connection with one another – especially in English-speaking academic spaces. For sure, the unification we accomplish by following the accidents of

[63] See Daniel Bonilla, 'The Political Economy of Legal Knowledge' in Crawford and Bonilla (n 44). I thank Esteban Restrepo Saldarriaga and Héctor López Bofill for insightful remarks about the nature of contemporary constitutional comparativism as a field and epistemic community.

[64] See Daniel Bonilla, *Legal Barbarians: Identity, Modern Comparative Law and the Global South* (Cambridge, Cambridge University Press, 2021).

[65] Jorge Esquirol, 'The Geopolitics of Constitutionalism in Latin America' in Crawford and Bonilla (n 44); 'The Latin American Tradition of Legal Failure' (2011) 2 *Comparative Law Review* 2–19.

[66] See, for example Cook (n 61); Helena Alviar, Karl Klare and Lucy A Williams, *Social and Economic Rights in Theory and Practice. Critical Inquiries* (Abingdon, Routledge, 2015); Francisca Pou Giménez, Laura Clérico and Esteban Restrepo Saldarriaga, *Proportionality and Transformation: Theory and Practice from Latin America* (Cambridge, Cambridge University Press, 2022).

my trajectory as a public lawyer is precarious. The resulting map of disciplines, strands of scholarship and epistemic communities is quick and radically incomplete. For each field that I identify, the absence of others flashes out. For each of the individuals I mention, hundreds of others go unnoticed – among them, regrettably, the dozens of academics and close friends of my generation on two sides of the Atlantic, and the younger generation that follows our footsteps. From each of the sites I mention departs a bundle of arrows towards others, and from each of the latter depart others towards still others, forming a network of incredible density that we have here merely started to visualise. The survey, however, is pertinent to the reconstruction of socio-legal trajectories in Europe for at least three reasons that I will briefly bring up, in hope of enjoying opportunities for further development in the future.

First, and despite this chapter not having really engaged the exercise, a socio-legal perspective is indispensable to reconstruct the political economy that is behind the academic landscape that we usually take for granted. At a specific level, for instance, a deepening into my life trajectory from the sociological perspective would ground an important vindication of welfare states, public education, scholarship programmes, institutional creation (journals, seminars, universities, programmes) and collective networks and platforms. And the thing about my life is, of course, not its being remarkable in any sense, but its not being atypical. It portrays an evolution that is representative of certain things at certain times and places. The socio-legal perspective may help us also evaluate what does it mean to work in the English-speaking global sphere of comparative constitutional studies – what it implies for different people in different places and circumstances, and what it suggests about the possibilities, problems, challenges or relevance of the field. In my view, a broader socio-legal examination may be more illuminating than a mere reading of life trajectories under the lenses of intersectionality and structural advantage/disadvantage – associated to narratives and identity cleavages that do not exhaust the texture of existing power dynamics.

Second, and more importantly, this chapter documents how socio-legal methodologies have entered the mainstream of contemporary constitutionalism – even if I have described only one important and identifiable strand among what is done in the domain of constitutional law, and not all of them. Again, I don't think this chapter recounts something that has happened specifically to me, but something that has occurred out there in the world and can be documented for the case of important academic groups. It is interesting to ponder, in any case, whether I would have entered so smoothly the sociologically informed world of constitutional studies if I had not migrated to Latin America, or had remained far from the influence of the United States' legal education styles. After all, sociology and attention to empirical analysis were esoteric at the time of my legal education in Spain. The approach to the study of constitutionalism that I have described might be less influential in European constitutional law and scholarship – but this is something that must be in any case established by careful independent research. If it were the case, that would not automatically imply, of course, that there are fewer academic spaces for sociologically oriented constitutional analysis in Europe, only that they might be developed within the boundaries of other disciplines – such as sociology or political science, for instance.

In other words, the lines of interaction between different methodologies in the domain of public law are surely drawn differently in different places, and the formal disciplines and institutions where they find shelter vary. Viewed historically, from the perspective of the southern European countries that regained democracy in the 1980s and the Latin America countries that followed suit in the 1990s, there seems to be logic in a journey where relative emphasis moves, over time, from analytic legal theory to standard normative constitutionalism and, later, to socio-legally informed public law – along the lines we have described. While analytic philosophy and legal theory provide important tools to understand what normativity is about (something that looks sensible if one is to replace a political conception of the constitution with a legal one), standard normative constitutionalism and related approaches seem to be appropriate once the normativity of the constitution is undisputed and the task of the day is fleshing out the scope of constitutional commitments and their consequences in specific cases. Similarly, once the modus operandi of the normative constitution has been reasonably mainstreamed and stabilized, it makes sense to turn to detailed explanation and evaluation, especially in the context of constitutions that conceive themselves as transformative, as occurs in Latin America, and aspire to contribute to progressively transform a reality still largely defined by violence, arbitrariness, inequality and poverty. An expanded methodological palette that includes the socio-legal is necessary for that.

This leads us to the third and final invitation this chapter puts forth, associated to the need to continue and enlarge investigation about what sociology of law or socio-legal approaches should count for in our time and age. What is the relation between the sociology done in the classic tradition of Max Weber and Emile Durkheim, the legal sociology of Renato Treves or Adam Podgórecki, and contemporary constitutional studies after the socio-legal turn? Is this question viewed and answered differently in different countries, traditions or legal cultures? The collective project this chapter lays an important preliminary ground to know more about these questions. It shows how the substance and the disciplinary boundaries at the intersection between the sociological and the legal have radically varied from one country to another, sometimes for unexpected reasons. I hope this piece contributes to identify new domains to be charted.

10

Socio-Legal Studies in the United Kingdom: A Personal Reflection

SALLY WHEELER

THERE ARE NUMEROUS accounts of how socio-legal studies has developed to become a central part of the intellectual life of the academy in the last 40 years or so. Indeed, I have provided, in different guises, several of these accounts. This chapter offers the opportunity to integrate something of an autobiographic turn on how this transformation on, or, perhaps more contentiously within, legal studies in the United Kingdom has occurred – because unlike other parts of the world it is primarily legal studies where socio-legal studies has had traction and not other social science or related disciplines. I draw on my previous accounts and reflect on those of others, recognising that an autobiographic narrative is likely to take us to a place where recollections and interpretations of events, practices and motives will likely differ at times. I tell a story that focuses on evolving scholarly and professional identities and the shape and contents of disciplines. Both identities and disciplines are dynamic and fluid and are influenced and sculpted by large scale external environmental factors such as the Research Assessment Exercise (RAE) and the Research Excellence Framework (REF), student demand and the desirability and availability of grant funding. For the discipline of law, we can also add the requirements (and the varying interpretation of them) of the legal profession of legal education. There are less obvious but more pervasive evolutionary ideas such as higher education study not for specific employment paths in a vocational sense but as a general liberal education[1] with a multitude of different possible outcomes. There is also an internal dimension to account for an individual's own interests in research terms, their ambitions for that research in terms of policy impact, contribution to theoretical development and the provision of new knowledge and their understanding of their position within the academy. This chapter is

[1] A Bradney, *Conversations, Choices and Chances: The Liberal Law School in the Twenty-First Century* (Oxford, Hart, 2003) and SJ Clark, 'Law School as Liberal Education' (2013) 63 *Journal of Legal Education* 235.

arranged in a roughly chronological sequence. The first section is demonstrably autobiographical covering my discovery of socio-legal studies. The second section considers how and why socio-legal studies has become the intellectual force it is and the final section offers some thoughts on how I hope socio-legal studies will evolve in the future, followed by a conclusion.

I. THE BEGINNINGS OF SOCIO-LEGAL STUDIES AND MY BEGINNING WITHIN IT

Socio-legal studies began for me with a studentship from the Economic and Social Research Council (ESRC) to the Oxford Centre for Socio-Legal Studies in 1985 for a D Phil (PhD in anyone else's terms). My undergraduate law degree had been at Oxford, and despite the centre being founded in 1972, I was blissfully unaware of it and of socio-legal studies. From other academics' accounts of their undergraduate education, I was not alone in my ignorance of a world of ideas outside the doctrinal study of law.[2] As Cownie explains,[3] legal research and consequently legal education at that time was largely a search for order, coherence and general principles, often reasoning through analogy within legal instruments: cases, statutes, delegated legislation, parliamentary reports, and so on. The case and problem method dominated legal education,[4] and legal research was disseminated through the publication of case notes, short articles and textbooks aimed at the student market.[5] Despite the sometimes trenchant critiques of technocentrism,[6] positivism[7] and repetition and replication[8] levelled at doctrinalism, this does not mean that high level doctrinal study with its intense internal perspective[9] was uninteresting – far from it. Shortly before my finals in June 1985, I became aware of the first edition of Paul Craig's book *Administrative Law*[10] and my summer holiday reading in 1984 had been

[2] The two people I think of here are Andy Boon and Nikki Lacey, but I am sure that many others would agree with this observation. See A Boon, 'Integrating Socio-Legal Studies into the Law Curriculum' (2012) 39 *Journal of Law and Society* 616, 620 and N Lacey, 'William Twinning and the Law in Context Series: A Personal Reflection' (2020) 16 *International Journal of Law in Context* 464.

[3] F Cownie, 'Law, Research and the Academy' in P Trowler, M Saunders and V Bamber (eds), *Tribes and Territories in the 21st Century: Rethinking the Significance of Disciplines in Higher Education* (Abingdon, Routledge, 2012) 57.

[4] D Capper, 'Contract Law Teaching: Teaching from the Case Law' in W Swain and D Campbell (eds), *Reimagining Contract Law Pedagogy* (London, Routledge, 2019) 167.

[5] G Wilson, 'English Legal Scholarship' (1987) 50 *Modern Law Review* 818.

[6] M Thornton, 'Technocentrism in the Law School: Why the Gender and Colour of Law Remain the Same' (1998) 36 *Osgoode Hall Law Journal*, 369.

[7] R Collier, 'Masculinism, Law and Law Teaching' (1991) 19 *International Journal of the Sociology of Law* 427.

[8] P Goodrich, 'Of Blackstone's Tower: Metaphors of Distance and Histories of the English Law School' in P Birks (ed), *Pressing Problems in the Law, volume 2. What are Law Schools for?* (Oxford, Oxford University Press, 1996) 59.

[9] For a discussion of this introspection and its intellectual mission, see C McCrudden, 'Legal Research and the Social Sciences' (2006) 122 *Law Quarterly Review* 632.

[10] P Craig, *Administrative Law* (London, Sweet & Maxwell, 1983).

Carol Harlow and Rick Rawlings' *Law and Administration*[11] and David Yates' *Exclusion Clauses in Contracts.*[12] All three of these texts, none of which had appeared on my reading lists, radically changed my understanding of the relevant norms and concepts in their respective fields. Nevertheless, as the daughter of a small-town provincial solicitor with a criminal and civil legal aid practice, I was always aware that law as practised and law as experienced in the world outside Oxford (and nearly all other universities, with the exception perhaps of Warwick) was rather different. The beginning point for socio-legal studies is much harder to discern. There were small fractures and fissures emerging in the model of legal education and research that I set out above from the 1960s onwards. Two of the larger fractures were created by Critical Legal Studies and the Sociology of Law. Both emerged during this period but did not grow to maturity in the form of a large movement of scholars identifying as being part of them. They were both always, in my view, more vibrant fields in the United States and Canada than they were in the United Kingdom, despite being populated by some leading scholars of the time: Maureen Cain and Colin Campbell, for example. A determining factor for them might have been that in both the United States and Canada legal studies existed outside the organising edifice of the law school, in departments of rhetoric, sociology and social policy, for example. Legal education in those jurisdictions was confined to the postgraduate sphere leaving space for the discussion of ideas around law as a concept in other disciplines studied by undergraduates.[13] In the United Kingdom, legal studies did not exist outside the law school, which focused on undergraduate education. Neither Critical Legal Studies nor Sociology of Law could make substantial or sustained[14] inroads into a curriculum heavily influenced by what academic lawyers thought the legal profession wanted students to be taught; both were too oppositional for this.[15] Both had also largely run their course by

[11] C Harlow and R Rawlings, *Law and Administration* (London, Weidenfeld and Nicolson, 1984).

[12] D Yates, *Exclusion Clauses in Contracts* 2nd edn (London, Sweet & Maxwell, 1982).

[13] I wonder if this, in part, explains the emergence of interdisciplinary interactions around law such as Critical Race Theory and Law and Literature in the United States some years before they became part of the scholarship to be found within United Kingdom law schools. See eg R Delgado and J Stefancic, 'Critical Race Theory: An Annotated Bibliography' (1993) 79 *Virginia Law Review* 461 and E Gemmette, 'Law and Literature: An Unnecessarily Suspect Class in the Liberal Arts Component of Law School Curriculu' (1989) 23 *Valparaiso Law Review* 267.

[14] Critical Legal Studies deserves more discussion and credit than the very truncated reference it receives here for reasons of space and focus. It flourished for some years as a noisy, if not dominant, discourse in a range of law schools (Birkbeck, Middlesex Kent, Warwick, Lancaster) but more recently has become the province of individual scholars. Most accounts of the CLS movement and its tenets are United States focused but for the United Kingdom, see C Douzinas and A Gearey, *Critical Jurisprudence. The Political Philosophy of Justice* (Oxford, Hart, 2005) and A Gearey, 'Anxiety and Affirmation: Critical Legal Studies and the "Critical Tradition(s)"' (2006) 31 *NYU Review of Law and Social Change* 585.

[15] Critical Legal Studies scholars at least felt at home in the law school in a way which Sociology of Law scholars did not seem to. See G Teubner, 'The King's Many Bodies: The Self-Deconstruction of Law's Hierarchy' (1997) 31 *Law and Society Review* 763.

the time the huge expansion of law student numbers in the United Kingdom occurred in the 1980s, a period identified by Twinning as marking the birth of the 'modern British Law School',[16] and so missed the opportunities afforded by the law degree being thought of as something other than a route into legal professional work.

The Law School at the University of Warwick, founded in 1967 some two or so years after the university itself, became home to the Law in Context approach to legal research and education.[17] William Twinning arrived there in 1972 via the Law School at the University of Khartoum in the Sudan, then playing a key role in founding of a law school at the fledgling University College in Dar es Salaam and a chair at Queen's Belfast, all locations that would have presented challenges for the delivery of conventional legal education, albeit for different reasons. Together with figures such as Patrick McAuslan[18] (Twinning's colleague at Dar es Salaam), Patrick Atiyah and Martin Partington, he put together a law school curriculum[19] that focused on 'broadening the study of law from within' by taking as the 'starting point … phenomena and problems which have been identified and classified in social rather than legal categories'.[20] It is through this approach that *new* optional subjects such as Housing and Planning emerged to become part of the law school diet.[21] At around the same time, Twinning and Robert Stevens became the founding editors of the *Law in Context* book series, the first volume of which appeared in 1970 and was published originally by Weidenfeld and Nicholson and now by Cambridge University Press. I suspect that many of the volumes produced in the first 20 years or so were at best on 'secondary' reading lists for undergraduates, if they were encouraged at all.[22]

The Law in Context approach is the most obvious forerunner of socio-legal studies. However, Law in Context makes small claims for itself;[23] it does not offer a theory or theories about law or legal concepts.[24] Rather, 'it merely

[16] W Twinning, 'Remembering 1972: The Oxford Centre in the Context of Developments in Higher Education and the Discipline of Law' (1995) 22 *Journal of Law and Society* 35.

[17] R Folsum and N Roberts, 'The Warwick Story: Being Led Down the Contextual Path of the Law' (1979) 30 *Journal of Legal Education* 166 and G Wilson (ed), *Frontiers of Legal Scholarship* (London, Wiley, 1995) in particular the opening chapter by R Cranston, 'A Wayward, Vagrant Spirit: Law in Context Finds its Rich and Kindly Earth'.

[18] W Twinning, 'McAuslan in Context: Early Days in Dar and Warwick' in T Zartaloudis (ed), *Land Law and Urban Policy in Context* (London, Birkbeck Law Press 2017) 35.

[19] W Twinning, 'Geoffrey Wilson Obituary' *The Guardian*, 8 November 2015.

[20] W Twinning, 'Some Jobs for Jurisprudence' (1974) 2 *British Journal of Law & Society* 149, 166.

[21] D Cowan and S Wheeler, 'The Sociology of Housing Law' in J Priban (ed), *Research Handbook for the Sociology of Law* (Cheltenham, Edward Elgar, 2021) 332.

[22] S Wheeler, 'Gone and Almost Entirely Forgotten: The Watkinson Report' (2009) 60 *Northern Ireland Legal Quarterly* 263.

[23] J Webb, 'When "Law and Sociology" is not Enough: Transdisciplinarity and the Problem of Complexity' in M Freeman (ed), *Law and Sociology* (Oxford, Oxford University Press, 2006) 90.

[24] Z Bankowski and G Mungham, 'Warwick University, Ltd (Continued)' (1974) 1 *British Journal of Law and Society* 179.

provides a flexible framework for diverse ways of breaking out from a narrow tradition'[25] from within the discipline of law. Socio-legal studies purports to offer a much broader intellectual horizon although as my section 'Going Forward' below explains, there is a critique that suggests that it still has some way to go in really delivering on this promise. That broad intellectual horizon was the cornerstone of the Oxford Centre. It had two distinctive features. One was that although there were other clusterings of socio-legal scholars, notably ones in Warwick, Sheffield and Cardiff, the Oxford Centre received block funding from the then Social Science Research Council (later to become the ESRC) for its core posts, from 1972 to 1992.[26] This gave the Oxford Centre a feeling of permanence and socio-legal studies in the United Kingdom a clear anchor point.[27] United Kingdom-based scholars were welcomed there for study periods and consultant contracts. The centre had a very active visitor programme for overseas scholars which offered an international connection for United Kingdom socio-legal studies scholars long before the internet facilitated those connections to become the norm in academic life. The second was that core research council funding allowed the centre to operate free from the constraints that would have come from being located within the funding model of a conventional university department. This allowed the appointment of academics from other disciplines: inter alia economists, sociologists, psychologists. They worked alongside legal academics on several broad themes such as regulation and dispute resolution[28] in a series of ever evolving projects. This depth of collaboration across disciplines has never been replicated within the one academic unit.[29] It occurs in individually funded research projects and research programmes[30] based around particular questions, but that is very different from the free form ongoing space for thinking and development that the centre allowed.

[25] W Twinning, *Jurist in Context: A Memoir* (Cambridge, Cambridge University Press, 2019) 169. David Sugarman provides typically insightful discussions of Twinning's contribution to legal academia in D Sugarman, 'William Twinning: The Man Who Radicalized the Middle Ground' (2020) 16 *International Journal of Law in Context* 475 and 'Twining's Tower and the Challenges of Making Law a Humanistic Discipline' (2020) series 2, 2 *Amicus Curiae* 334.

[26] K Hawkins, 'Prologue: Donald Harris and the Early Years of the Oxford Centre' in K Hawkins (ed), *The Human Face of Law: Essays in Honour of Donald Harris* (Oxford, Oxford University Press, 1997).

[27] The scale of the focus on the Oxford Centre is clear from the ESRC *Review of Socio-Legal Research* (1994) at p 31 which points out that between 1985 and 1991 it received over a third of the ESRC's total support for socio-legal research.

[28] For an overview of research themes in that period see D Galligan, 'Introduction' (1995) 22 *Journal of Law and Society* 1.

[29] Interdisciplinary inquiry is always talked about by universities, governments, industry and research funders as being hugely desirable. However, implementing it within university structures has always been very difficult. See J Klein, *Crossing Boundaries: Knowledge, Disciplinarities and Interdisciplinarities* (Charlottesville, University Press of Virginia, 1996) and B Hansson, 'Interdisciplinarity: For What Purpose?' (1999) 32 *Policy Sciences* 339.

[30] The 1990s saw the ESRC promote a shift towards team-based research but not to the extent that it was going to continue core funding of the Oxford Centre. See M Henkel, *Academic Identities and Policy Change in Higher Education* (London, Jessica Kingsley Publishers, 2000).

It was a hugely exciting place to begin an academic career. I acknowledge that my recollection of it as a welcoming home to scholars from anywhere and everywhere engaged in socio-legal work is not the recollection of all.[31] Some of the work done there, which I touch upon later on, both pre- and post- this core funding, has fundamentally changed the way in which academics, policy makers and regulators think about legal concepts, legal structures and the professional groups which are encompassed therein.

II. THE RISE OF SOCIO-LEGAL STUDIES: INTERNAL AND EXTERNAL FACTORS

In 1990, the Socio-Legal Studies Association (SLSA) was formed at a conference in Bristol by a core group of scholars with a constitution, a membership function and a founding chair, Professor Hazel Genn, then a researcher at the Oxford Centre. It replaced what had been a much more informal grouping – the Socio-Legal Group set up in 1974. The fledgling SLSA was supported financially by the Oxford Centre until its core funding ended and then by other funders including the *Journal of Law and Society* and the publisher Butterworths. The SLSA quickly added to its governance structures an annual conference, a postgraduate conference, a code of ethics for socio-legal research and a high-quality regular newsletter funded by Cardiff Law School and subsequently a consortium of other law schools.[32] Programmes to make small grants available to members to support a variety of research activities followed. It became a member society of the Academy of Social Science. In 1992, the annual SLSA conference boasted 161 participants and 97 papers.[33] In 2004 at the annual conference held in Glasgow, there were some 300 participants including 25 from universities outside the United Kingdom and Ireland.[34] In 2023, there were 930 papers listed in the conference brochure for the annual conference held in Derry/Londonderry.[35]

The exponential growth in the functions and popularity of the SLSA mirrors the success of socio-legal studies at colonising *law schools* (a point returned

[31] See eg Alan Hunt's appraisal of it from a distance in A Hunt, 'Governing the Socio-Legal Project: Or What Do Research Councils Do' (1994) 21 *Journal of Law and Society* 520.

[32] Much of the early history of the SLSA is covered in P Thomas, 'Socio-Legal Studies: The Case of Disappearing Fleas and Bustards' in P Thomas (ed), *Socio-Legal Studies* (Aldershot, Dartmouth, 1997) 3, 10–12. Thomas' recollections of the Socio-Legal Group are somewhat at odds with those expressed by Hunt, see n 31.

[33] Information taken from material supplied to the author by Fiona Cownie.

[34] This information was obtained from the SLSA Archive which is held at the Institute of Advanced Legal Studies, accessible by appointment (information accurate at 9 June 2024), see https://ials.sas.ac.uk/ials-library/archives with the class mark, SLSA/5/10.

[35] The brochure is available at www.slsa.ac.uk/images/conferences/SLSA_2024_Ulster_Brochure.pdf.

to later). This success is seen in terms of academics and research outputs, less so legal education, although socio-legal influence in this area has undoubtedly developed since I began my teaching career in 1985.[36] Cownie's research in 2004[37] on what she describes as the 'private life' of law schools and academic lawyers as opposed to the 'public life' of academic law[38] revealed that half her interview sample considered themselves to be socio-legal scholars. Others who did not identify as such asserted that their approach to law included the consideration of contextual issues such as social, political and economic context. Socio-legal studies has moved from being located in a distinctive hub at Oxford and a largely below-the-radar alternative to traditional approaches to academic legal studies in a very small number of law schools to occupying, and some might claim becoming, the mainstream of legal academia.[39] This journey to the mainstream has been accompanied by more than several accounts or reflections on what socio-legal studies is and what it can be defined as[40] – a paradigm,[41] a movement,[42] as something that can only be described by reference to something that it is not[43] and so on with nomenclature selected to appeal to different stakeholders within and outside the university. The emphasis has been on establishing a broad church of scholarship aligned to that endorsed by the SLSA, creating a self-reinforcing yet porous circle around socio-legal studies within the edifice of the law school. These discussions of definition have replaced earlier ruminations on the position of law as an academic subject within the university[44] and its relationship to the legal profession.[45] At the same time, those working in

[36] The divide between the research that occurs in law schools and the dimensions of what is taught to law students remains an issue particularly in relation to the subjects which are considered foundational, C Hunter (ed), *Integrating Socio-Legal Studies into the Law Curriculum* (London, Palgrave Macmillan, 2012).

[37] F Cownie, *Legal Academics: Cultures and Identities* (Oxford, Hart, 2004).

[38] Cownie, above n 3, 64.

[39] A Ogus, 'Reflections on the Development in Britain of Interdisciplinary Approaches to Law: Utility and Disability' (1999) 50 *Northern Ireland Legal Quarterly* 421.

[40] For a non-exhaustive list see P Hillyard, 'Invoking Indignation: Reflection on Future Directions of Socio-Legal Studies' (2002) 29 *Journal of Law and Society* 645; R Cotterrell, 'Subverting Orthodoxy, Making Law Central: A View of Socio-Legal Studies' (2002) 29 *Journal of Law and Society* 632; Bradney, see n 1; S Wheeler and P Thomas, 'Socio-Legal Studies' in D Hayton (ed), *Laws Future(s)* (Oxford, Hart, 2000) 267.

[41] P Thomas (ed), *Socio-Legal Studies* (Aldershot, Dartmouth, 1997) 3, 19. See also P Thomas, 'Socio-Legal Studies in the UK' in F Bruinsma (ed), *Precaire Waarden, Liber Amicorum Voor Por. Mr A A G Peters* (Netherlands, Gouda Quint, 1994). The term 'paradigm' was used to signal a call to academic lawyers to review the values and standards of traditional legal education with the idea that such a review would facilitate change and development.

[42] S Wheeler, 'Company Law' in P Thomas (ed), *Socio-Legal Studies* (Aldershot, Dartmouth, 1997) 285, 302. The term 'movement' was used to address the position of marginality for socio-legal studies within law schools.

[43] H Sommerlad, 'Developments in Socio-Legal Studies: Subjects and Methodologies – The Anglo-Saxon Model' (2015) 36 *Recht de Werkelijkheid* 55.

[44] An account of this can be found in N Duxbury, *Jurists and Judges* (Oxford, Hart, 2001).

[45] L Gower, 'English Legal Training: A Critical Survey' (1950) 13 *Modern Law Review* 137.

university law schools have embraced qualifications that bring them into line with colleagues in other disciplines. They are far more likely to hold a doctorate in law than they are to hold a professional legal qualification.[46]

One might wonder why there is this attention paid to the purpose of trying to define socio-legal studies when it appears to be in the ascendency and well established. It was, and continues to be, hugely successful in law schools. Why was this not just seen as a natural evolution of legal studies without further discussion and explanation? Disciplines evolve and change organically all the time,[47] even if their container labels (ie academic departments and their names) don't, often because of the pressure of external factors: student demand for example. Equally, internal factors such as changes in ideology or innovation in methodology leading to disciplinary fragmentation and eventual reassembly might play a role.[48] The answer in relation to socio-legal studies lies, I think, within the academy around the issue of recognition. Early proponents and advocates of socio-legal studies wanted, particularly after the removal of core funding from the Oxford Centre and the loss of that as a focal point, to establish and secure both a place and an identity within the university. Creating a professional association and selecting as the first chair someone whose first degree was in Anthropology but who had produced a groundbreaking account of the way insurance for personal injury actually worked[49] was a way of both asserting distinctiveness around the work of individuals engaged in the field and establishing a territorial claim to the ground occupied by professionally orientated doctrinal research.

The stories that are then told about what socio-legal studies is and what it does are a way of creating a hinterland of intellectual rigour. There is a considered genealogy and broadly shared research practices that propel it into the academy, as, in Beecher's terms,[50] a soft discipline. It is distinct from law's previous position as an applied discipline for the acquisition of knowledge and skills thought to be relevant to a professional career in law. Indeed, it was as recently as 1987 that research in law (meaning doctrinal legal research) was compared to a 'disposable plastic cup' because 'each adjective strengthens the message that

[46] In 1966, 78 per cent of legal academics held professional legal qualifications. See J Wilson, 'A First Survey of University Legal Education in the United Kingdom' (1966) 9 *Journal of the Society of Public Teachers of Law* 5. The information provided by P Leighton, T Mortimer and N Whatley, *Today's Law Teachers: Lawyers or Academics?* (London, Cavendish, 1995) and any subsequent examination of the public profiles of law school staff web pages would suggest that this figure is vastly reduced now.

[47] Klein, above n 29.

[48] M Dogan and R Pahre, *Creative Marginality: Innovation at the Intersections of Social Sciences* (Boulder Colorado, Westview Press, 1990) 58, 84–85.

[49] H Genn, *Hard Bargaining: Out of Court Settlements in Personal Injury Actions* (Oxford, Oxford University Press, 1987).

[50] T Beecher, *Academic Tribes and Territories: Intellectual Enquiry and the Culture of Disciplines* (Buckingham, Open University Press, 1989).

one cannot expect much in terms of quality … from it'.[51] Once socio-legal studies is grounded within the academy, it becomes less important for individuals to deconstruct why and how that identity is embraced by them. Across the university sector, it is not unusual for some labels to be appropriate to describe what one teaches and others to describe what one researches. Academics frequently talk about themselves as being 'from X School' when in a representative capacity but describe their research interests thematically 'as being about Y' and feel more comfortable doing that.[52] This is certainly true for me on a personal level. And perhaps it is one explanation for why socio-legal studies academics have colonised law schools but have not interspersed so readily themselves into other academic units.[53]

Changes to the external environment of universities have also contributed to the rise and entrenchment of socio-legal studies. Some of those changes have already been highlighted as the expansion of student numbers throughout the 1990s and, specifically in relation to legal education, the reframing of the law degree as a liberal education. This positioned a legal education encapsulating socio-legal studies as of broad interest rather than simply the academic stage of training for a professional career in law. Turner offers the view that disciplines are always market-based in that they are 'a kind of protectionist device that responds to the alteration of the markets by the action of others'.[54] The late twentieth and current twenty-first century law school is a clear example of this. The connection to the legal profession through the teaching of foundational subjects allied to the much broader material provided by socio-legal studies results in student demand and job market demand, and so teaching income flows from either or both of those pillars. Law schools have expanded and remained a source of academic employment whereas other social science and humanities disciplines have contracted. It is perhaps unsurprising given the existence of opportunity in the law school and not elsewhere that socio-legal studies has flourished here and augmented legal study rather than the study of the other social sciences.

Universities in the United Kingdom have transitioned into a market driven system of mass high education over the last 40 years where the user, that is, the student, pays. This has been accompanied by inter alia the imposition of an audit and measurement culture of every facet of university activity: broadly education, student outcomes and research quality. This is not the place to

[51] G Wilson, 'English Legal Scholarship' (1987) 50 *Modern Law Review* 818.

[52] A Brew, 'Disciplinary and Interdisciplinary Affiliations of Experienced Researchers' (2008) 56 *Higher Education* 423.

[53] The Nuffield Report on empirical socio-legal studies found that socio-legal studies scholars were primarily located in law schools. See H Genn et al, *Law in the Real World: Improving Our Understanding of How Law Works* (London, The Nuffield Foundation, 2006). There is nothing to suggest that this situation has changed.

[54] S Turner, 'What are Disciplines? And How is Interdisciplinarity Different?' in P Weingart and N Stehr (eds), *Practising Interdisciplinarity* (Toronto, University of Toronto Press, 2000) 47, 50.

explore these developments in any detail or pronounce on their desirability, not least because numerous accounts exist elsewhere.[55] They have transformed the workplace that I joined in 1987 and are no longer limited to the United Kingdom. Internationally, most university systems have been subsumed to one degree or another by a neoliberalist ideology and have quality metrics imposed upon their activities.[56] The most important development for socio-legal studies has been the measurement of research performance through what is now called the Research Excellence Framework as opposed to its earlier guises of Research Selectivity and Research Assessment.[57] Successive processes have valued the fruits of socio-legal work, both empirical and theoretical, more highly than the production of the doctrinal textbook and materials[58] that focus on keeping the legal profession informed of recent developments.[59] In the United Kingdom, unlike many other jurisdictions with a similar policy towards assessing research quality, the results of these research evaluation exercises are turned into a funding formula to distribute money to universities. Socio-legal research and researchers are attractive to law schools, and socio-legal studies has thrived in these conditions.

Socio-legal research is more likely to attract funding from one of the British research funding councils, international funders or a charitable funder than traditional doctrinal legal studies. Whilst the percentage of overhead cost recovery varies from funder to funder, there is no cost recovery in the absence of external funding. The amount of external funding obtained by each academic unit submitted to the research evaluation exercise influences the view that is taken of its research environment. Moreover, in an era when public funding for universities is declining, producing research without obtaining additional external funding becomes increasingly difficult. All funders are interested in the impact of the research they fund. For many of them, the potential for impact and ideas about impact are a key part of the application process. Assessing the societal impact of research became part of the Research Excellence Framework

[55] See eg two accounts from opposite ends of the time period, P Scott, *The Meanings Of Mass Higher Education* (Buckingham, Open University Press, 1995) and P Mandler, *The Crisis of the Meritocracy: Britain's Transition to Mass Education since the Second World War* (Oxford, Oxford University Press, 2020).

[56] In the specific context of education quality, see J Brennan and T Shah, 'Quality Assessment and Institutional Change: Experiences from 14 Countries' (2000) 40 *Higher Education* 331.

[57] I McNeely, 'Research Excellence and the Origins of the Managerial University in Thatcher's Britain' (2023) 37 *Contemporary British History* 1.

[58] The 1996 and 2001 Research Assessment Exercises both included in their assessment criteria for law the phrase 'student textbooks and books written for the legal or other professions will be regarded as research output provided that they exhibit significant scholarly material'. This delivered a clear message that legal research in the law school was likely to occur outside these formats, see Research Assessment Exercise 1996 www.rae.ac.uk/1996/36.html and RAE 2001 www.rae.ac.uk/2001/Pubs/5_99/ByUoA/crit36.htm.

[59] R Collier, '"We're All Socio-Legal Now?" Legal Education, Scholarship and the "Global Knowledge Economy" – Reflections on the UK Experience' (2004) 26 *Sydney Law Review* 503.

in 2014,[60] was refined in 2021 and looks set to remain as part of the next exercise proposed for 2029. This focus on impact can only support the growth of socio-legal studies still further. It also deflects a challenge that has been made against socio-legal studies from its earliest days: it is too focused on policy goals and too reactive to the agendas of policy-makers.[61] The danger of this was said to be that its research would replicate the authority of the state through law and so limit the degree of political engagement that researchers could have beyond an assessment of existing legal structures and established societal relations.[62] The reality is that, in the current iteration of higher education policy and the wider funding environment, user involvement has become the norm for researchers in many disciplines including socio-legal studies. This includes their involvement in research design, ideas of co-creation between researcher and researched and the seeking out of policy makers as an audience for research. Funding is so competitive and time so tight that socio-legal scholars are unlikely to be producing work that does not think through the 'relationship between empirical research and critical scholarship'.[63]

III. GOING FORWARD

My career as a salaried academic within the academy is much closer to its end than its beginning. As I reflect on all that has changed over the last 37 years or so, the success of socio-legal studies is a highpoint. That success was founded on the hard work of some key individuals. It is perhaps invidious to call them out in print, but they worked at creating and growing the SLSA, founding and editing socio-legal journals and book series and lobbying the ESRC for a continued place at the table. This meant that socio-legal studies was supported in funded doctoral training centres. This has raised the level of methodological sophistication of work undertaken at the PhD level considerably.[64] The *Journal of Law*

[60] See G Samuel and G Derrick, 'Societal Impact Evaluation: Exploring Evaluator Perceptions of the Characterization of Impact under the REF2014' (2015) 24 *Research Evaluation* 229 for a discussion of how impact was constructed, albeit for Panel A rather than Panel C where law is situated.

[61] Socio-legal studies research, in common with other interdisciplinary inquiries, is often problem-focused rather than question-focused, and this instrumentality is seen as being vulnerable to corporate interests as there is insufficient examination of the assumptions that give rise to the problem. See J Hearn, 'Interdisciplinarity/Extradisciplinarity: On the University and the Active Pursuit of Community' (2003) 3 *History of Intellectual Culture* 1.

[62] A Sarat and S Silbey, 'The Pull of the Policy Audience' (1988) 10 *Law and Policy* 97. For an assessment of these arguments see F Bell, 'Empirical Research in Law' (2016) 25 *Griffith Law Review* 262.

[63] R Hunter, 'Would You Like Theory with That? Bridging the Divide Between Policy-Oriented Empirical Legal Research, Critical Theory and Politics' (2008) 41 *Studies in Law, Politics and Society* 121, 122.

[64] See D Vick, 'Interdisciplinarity and the Discipline of Law' (2004) 31 *Journal of Law and Society* 163, 188–90 for a discussion of the challenges faced by those adopting research methodologies and methods drawn from fields in which they have no formal training.

and Society and *Social and Legal Studies* both attract a global authorship and readership. But there is more to be done.

Early socio-legal work was contemporaneously labelled as being 'anti-theoretical',[65] and a little later chastised for being 'value free' and indulging in policy studies that were characterised by technocratic instrumentalism.[66] Looking back now, this seems unfair. It does not recognise as groundbreaking the research that I found challenged my world view and that I have returned to time and time again over the years for inspiration. I think here, inter alia, of McBarnet's *Conviction*,[67] Adler and Asquith's *Discretion*,[68] Hawkins' *Environment and Enforcement*,[69] the 'Compensation Study'[70] and the work that flowed from it. Inspirations and influences for individuals will differ, but the point being made here is that there certainly was a considerable amount of early socio-legal work that laid out the modern administrative state in a way that had not been a concern for lawyers previously. It gave accounts of the relationship between agency, organisational capacities and institutional cultures that social scientists had no empirical knowledge of. Far too often, socio-legal work is seen as being concerned with the 'gap'[71] where this gap is presented as the law in action (as described by socio-legal work) versus the law described in law textbooks. Socio-legal work considers how law is experienced by users, activists and professional groups as opposed to doctrinal accounts of its contents. Macaulay's *Non-Contractual Relationships in Business: A Preliminary Study*[72] is a good example of this. It is not assisted by its rather prosaic title, but even that makes clear that the piece is not about how doctrinal contract law does not work or how it might be improved. It is instead about how businessmen construct and maintain their relationships with each and plan their transactions.[73] These are

[65] N Lacey, 'Normative Reconstruction in Socio-Legal Theory' (1996) 5 *Social and Legal Studies* 131, 132.

[66] The quote continues 'concerned with social engineering through existing social order and not with explaining that order or transcending it by critique', making clear that from its standpoint socio-legal studies is a failed political project, C Campbell and P Wiles, 'The Study of Law in Society in Britain' (1976) 10 *Law and Society Review* 547.

[67] D McBarnet, *Conviction: Law, State and the Construction of Justice* (Abingdon, Palgrave Macmillan, 1981).

[68] M Adler and S Asquith, *Discretion and Welfare* (London, Heinemann Educational, 1981).

[69] K Hawkins, *Environment and Enforcement* (Oxford, Oxford University Press, 1984).

[70] The work of the Oxford Centre on legal process particularly in tort law and medical negligence, see as exemplars of this D Harris et al, *Compensation and Support for Illness and Injury* (Oxford, Oxford University Press, 1984), Genn (n 49) and L Mulcahy and S Lloyd-Bostock, 'Managers as Third-Party Dispute Handlers in Complaints about Hospitals' (1994) 16 *Law and Policy* 185, was recognised 'as one of the greatest achievements in the study of law over the last fifty years', *SSRC/ESRC – The First Forty Years*, 12, https://esrc.ukri.org/files/news-events-and-publications/publications/ssrc-and-esrc-the-first-forty-years/.

[71] J Gould and S Barclay, 'Mind the Gap: The Place of Gap Studies in Sociolegal Scholarship' (2012) 8 *Annual Review of Law and Social Science* 323.

[72] S Macaulay, 'Non-Contractual Relations in Business' (1963) 28 *American Sociological Review* 55.

[73] S Wheeler, 'Visions of Contract' (2017) 44 (SI) *Journal of Law and Society* 74.

rather different things. It is a hugely significant piece of work for those interested in how private transactions are structured and concluded but is often portrayed as a small number of manufacturers in Wisconsin not using contract law.

The challenge for socio-legal inquiry now is to move away from being thought of as providing focused impact for discrete groups of users through empirically and theoretically informed small scale research studies. The inquiry needs to be clear that what it provides is a narrative about who is and who is not being regulated by law, how that regulation occurs, and about how and when laws are enforced and in relation to whom. Critics are right when they suggest that the 'socio' part of socio-legal studies is underdeveloped and under-utilised.[74] There is an absence of both a clear ethical and political underpinning to socio-legal studies[75] and a lack of a consistent conceptual framework. It needs to create these things to make clear that its offer, if you like, to the world is that law is a both a social practice and a social construct. The nature of intellectual endeavour within the study of law is about inquiry rather than the search for authority.[76] Rather than explaining that it is 'where law meets social sciences and the humanities',[77] it might want to suggest overtly, and this is a personal view, that its themes are power, accountability, governance and social inequality. Its perspectives are, individually and intersectionally, feminism, gender and colonialism. And, it is interested in the relationship between institutions, the state and individuals.

IV. A BRIEF CONCLUSION

Socio-legal studies has moved a long way from its beginnings in the late 1960s. It has overcome challenges from within the academy and withstood, if not drawn strength, from external environmental factors. My academic career has moved with it, and I have undoubtedly benefitted from the rising profile that it has had within the academy. Nothing is more refreshing than to go to an SLSA or American Law and Society conference where one knows very few people in a large list of attendees. It demonstrates that socio-legal studies is secure and flourishing.

[74] Lacey, n 65.

[75] S Silbey, 'What Makes a Social Science of Law: Doubling the Social in Socio-Legal Studies' in D Feenan (ed), *Exploring the 'Socio' of Socio-Legal Studies* (Abingdon, Palgrave Macmillan, 2013) 20.

[76] M Feeley, 'Three Voices of Socio-Legal Studies' (2001) 35 *Israel Law Review* 175.

[77] This is the rider to the header on the website of the SLSA, see www.slsa.ac.uk.

Index

Abel, R 101
Abel, R and Lewis, PSC
Lawyers in Society 90, 91, 97
Abel, RA et al
Lawyers in 21st Century Societies 84
academic habitus
academic recruitment in France 106
comparative 3–7
epistemic communities 10–13, 14, 16–17
Germany 122–123
globalisation 61, 63, 85, 153
Hungary 43–47
institutional and political economies 14, 16, 171
Adler, M and Asquith, S
Discretion and Welfare 184
Agersnap, T 92
Aguiló, J 156, 165
Albania *See* **Western Balkans**
Alchourrón, C 156
Alexy, R 158, 162
Alfonsín, R 159
Althusser, L 107
analytic tradition in legal theory 152, 153, 156, 165, 172
Andenæs, K 99–100
Ángel Cabo, N 167
anthropology, legal 21, 140, 168
Denmark 99
explanation-evaluation combination 166
Hungary 40, 48
Anzola, S 99
Argentina 155–157, 159, 161, 163
Arnaud, A-J 105
Atienza, M 155–156, 158, 162, 165
Atiyah, P 176
Aubert, V 88, 90, 91, 97
Austro-Hungarian Monarchy 20, 21, 45, 64
autonomous law 74

Balibar, E 146
Balkin, J 160–161
Banakar, R 84, 91–92, 93, 103
Bancaud, A 109, 110
Barzilai, G 146, 147–148
Becker, H
Outsiders 108
Beecher, T 180
Berdica, J
Law and Society 80
Bertilsson, M 90–91
Bičanić, R 69
black letter law 17, 115, 116
Boatcă, M 21
Bobbio, N 76, 155, 172
Bogišić, B 68–69, 71
Current Legal Customs of South Slavs 68, 85
Boigeol, A 109, 110, 111, 112
Bolivia 167
Bologna reforms 67, 79
Bonet, J 154
Borch, C 92
Borucka-Arctowa, M 24–25
Bosnia and Herzegovina *See* **Western Balkans**
Bourdieu, P 7, 13, 94–95, 102, 106, 109
'The Biographic Illusion' 89
Outline of a Theory of Practice 94
The Rules of Art 94
Sketch for a Self-Analysis 87, 88–89
The Social Structure of the Economy 94
The State Nobility 91, 94
The Weight of the World 94
'Who Created the Creator' 89
'Why the Social Sciences Must Take Themselves as Their Object' 88
Bovan, S 80
Božič, TS 79
Brazil 163, 164
Broady, D 95
Brzozowski, S 22
Bucholc, M 2, 6–7, 15
Bulygin, E 156
Burt, R 161
Butter, T 99

Cain, M 175
Calavitta, K 112
Calsamilgia Blancafort, A 155
Campbell, C 175

Canada 175
Caracciolo, R 155, 157
Carbonnier, J 76, 78, 106, 110
Carnap, R 156
Carrillo, M 157
Carrió, G 156
cause lawyering 112, 113, 114, 118
Cayla, O 116
Certeau, M de 146
Chamboredon, J-C
  La délinquance juvenile 108
Chicago school of sociology 108
Chile 161
Coddou, A 167
Cohen, A 94
Colombia 163, 164
  tutela 164
colonialism 15, 185
Colson, R 106
Comanducci, P 157
Commaille, J 106, 109–110
Communism *See also* **Marxism; socialist era**
  bourgeois ideology 74
comparative law
  constitutional studies 168–170
  generally 3, 151
  Germany 128
  Hungary 45
  Scandinavia 91, 97
  transnational latin network 164, 165, 166, 168–170
  Western Balkans 62, 68
comparative social science 3, 4
comparative socio-legal histories *See also* **academic habitus**
  agency and 7–10
  comparative heuristics 4, 7–16
  epistemic communities 10–13, 14, 16–17
  generally 3–7
  individual biographies 5–7, 16
  institutional and political economies 14, 16, 171
  nature of research 5
  positionality 5, 9–10
constitutional law
  analytic approach 152, 153, 165
  comparative 168–170
  constitucionalismo vivo 168
  egalitarian-dialogic constitutionalism 167
  globalised constitutionalism 166
  ius constitutionale commune en América Latina 167
  New Latin American constitutionalism 167
  socio-legal studies 151–155, 166–170, 171–172
  standard substantive constitutionalism 162
  transnational latin network 163–172
Cossio, C 156
Cossío J 162–164
Costa Rica 163
Cotterell, R 3
Couso, J 167
Cowan, D 59, 102, 179
Cownie, F 174
Craig, P
  Administrative Law 174–175
criminology, sociology of law and 63, 90, 92
critical theory
  critical race theory 132
  German critical legal studies 9, 10–11, 119–122, 129, 131–132
  Israel 146–147
  UK critical legal studies 175–176
Croatia *See* **Western Balkans**
Cummings, S 99, 101
Cywiński, Z 19
Czarnowski, S 22

Dahrendorf, R 28
Dalberg-Larsen, J 88, 90, 96
Danish Council for Independent Research 99
Däubler, W 127
Dębska, H 24–25
Deleuze, G and Guattari, F 146
Denmark *See* **Scandinavia**
Derrida, J and Nancy, J-L 146
Dezalay, S 98
Dezalay, Y 13, 91, 94, 98, 112
Díaz, E 155, 156
Didry, C 109
discourse theory 158
Dokić, M 80
Đorđević, J 69, 70
Dorlin, E 149
Duguit, L 70, 73
  Les transformations du droit public 70
Durkheim, E 21, 70, 73, 74, 76, 105, 172
  The Division of Labor in Society 107
  The Suicide 107
Dworkin, R 96, 158, 162

Ecuador 167
Edelman, L 112
Ehrlich 19, 21, 22, 65, 70, 79
Ehrlich, S 19, 26, 36
Elkins, Z 169
England, KVL 5
English language 11–12, 17, 93, 184
Germany 134
Hungary 11, 45, 58–59
Israel 141
journals 183–184
Scandinavia 11, 92, 103
transnational latin network 11, 159
Western Balkans 11, 61
environmental law, Poland 33
ethnography 5, 115
autoethnography 5–7
ethnomethodology 108
European Court of Human Rights
Poland 34, 35
European Research Council 115
European Union
Eastern Europe 94
legal education and judicial training 95
Life Long Learning Programme 95
Polish membership 30, 33, 35, 36
socio-legal studies, effect upon 30
Europeanisation
legal scholarship and 63
Western Balkans 61, 65
explanation-evaluation combination 166–167

Falke, J 129
Fekete, B 7, 11, 12, 13, 15
feminism *See also* **gender; women**
Polish anti-feminist backlash 31
socio-legal studies 132, 185
Ferrer, J 157, 165
Ferreres Comella, V 157–158, 159
Field, S 106
Fiss, O 157, 158, 159, 160–161, 162, 165
Foblets, M-C 59
Forić, S 11, 12, 13, 15
formalism 162–163
Foucault, M 146
framework law 102
France 69, 70
academic recruitment 106
access to courts 116–117
Année sociologique 69
black letter law 116
Constitutional Court 117
Droit et société 109, 113
empirical legal studies 115–116
ethnography 115
French apex court lawyers 116–117
Institut d'Histoire du Temps Présent 111
international scholarship 115
law and economics perspective 116
legal education 114–115
Marxist ideology 107
policy-oriented approach to law 116
sociology 106–108, 114
sociology of law 105–109, 114–118
structuralists 132
US influence 11, 105
World War II 110–112
Freeman, MDA
Lloyd's Introduction to Jurisprudence 96
Freirechtsschule 21
Fuszara, M 31

Galanter, M
'Why the Haves Come Out Ahead?' 113
Gargarella, R 157
Garth, BG 91, 94, 98, 111–112
Garzón Valdés, E 156, 157
Geiger, T 87, 90
gender
feminist legal studies 132, 185
gender studies in legal scholarship 63, 132, 134
inequality 31, 34
intersectionality 132
knowledge of law 52
Polish anti-feminist backlash 31
positionality of researcher 9
role 17, 153
socio-legal studies 185
Genn, H 178
Paths to Justice 101
Gény, F 70
Germany
academic habitus 122–123
collective bargaining 124–125
critical legal studies 9, 10–11, 119–122, 129, 131–132
empirical jurisprudence 133
English language publications 134
Federal Labour Court 124–125, 126, 127, 128
Federal Republic 16, 125–129

Hamburger Universität für Wirtschaft und Politik 122
interdisciplinary legal studies 119–134
Kritische Justiz 122, 127, 129
labour law, interdisciplinary study 119–134
legal education 120–121, 132
Rechtswissenschaft als Sozialwissenschaft 129
research funding 122, 128
right to strike 125
sociology of law trajectory 11, 12, 119–124
Sozialwissenschaftliche Forschungsgruppe 128
systems theory 131
Vereinigung für Recht und Gesellschaft 131
Weimar tradition 16, 120, 124–125
Wirtschafts- und Sozialwissenschaftliches Institut 130
Works Constitution Act 123
Zeitschrift für Rechtssoziologie 119–120, 121, 127–128, 129, 132
Zentrum für Europäische Rechtspolitik 129
Giddens, A 90
Ginsburg, T 169
Goffmann, E 108, 109
Goldschmidt, V et al 87
Goričar, J 74, 79, 85
Graber, D 135–136, 144
Graff, A 31
Grebo, Z
Marx and Kelsen 75
Greenland 87
Groupe d'information et de Soutien des Immigrés 114
Guastini, R 157
Gurvitch, G 70, 73, 74, 76, 78, 79, 105

Habermas, J 65, 77, 79, 88, 90, 123, 129
Habsburg Empire 41, 45
Halevy J 139
Hammerslev, O 7, 11, 12
Harlow, C and Rawlings, R
Law and Administration 175
Hart, HLA 155
Hauriou, M 70, 73
Hawkins, K
Environment and Enforcement 184
Heller, T 132
Hertogh, M 41, 59, 102
Hirschl, R 169
Höland, A 129, 131
Horváth, B
Rechtssoziologie 49–50
human rights law 31, 33–35
Hungary
1959 Civil Code 51
academic culture 43–47
contemporary period 55–59
democratic backlash 59
English language publications 11, 45, 58–59
ethnological/anthropological approach 47
German influence 41–42, 45, 46
Habsburg Empire 41, 45
Horváth's *Rechtssoziologie* 49–50
interwar period 42
Kulcsár's national surveys 50–53, 54, 58
legal anthropology 40
legal consciousness 50–51, 54, 55–56
legal culture 56–58
legal education 46
legal sociological tradition 41–59
normative/doctrinal approach 41, 45
post-socialist era 42
punitiveness in 57–58
qualitative research tools 58
quantitative research methods 58
regional cooperation 39, 59, 61
research funding 14, 55–59
Sajó's *Látszat és valóság a jogban* 43, 53–55
social stratification 51–52
socialist era 15–16, 42, 50–55
socio-legal scholarly community 12, 43, 44–47
socio-legal studies tradition 39–43
Szilágyi 43
teaching methods 46
women researchers 45–46
Hutchinson, A and Cohen, D 143
Hydén, H 84, 103

Iglesias, M 157
Igličar, A 79, 80
images of law 24, 29
interdisciplinary legal studies
conceptual 140
Germany 119–134
instrumental 140

Israel 135–150
research funding 140
socio-legal 2, 7, 144, 152
transnational latin network 151–153, 154
United States 160
International Institute for the Sociology of Law workshop 1, 7, 14, 93
International Journal of Law in Context 4
International Political Science Association 26
International Working Group on the Legal Professions 97
internationalisation
academic interchanges 61, 63, 85, 153
electronic communications 98
geopolitical order, transformation 97–98
methodological nationalism, limitations 98
sociology of law 88, 92, 102
Western ethnocentrism 98
intersectionality 132, 185
Israel
critical theory 146–147
cultural affiliations with Europe 141
interdisciplinary legal studies 135–150
language 141
Law and Society Association 146
legal education 141, 148
Mizrahis 138, 142
occupied territories 136, 141, 142, 146, 147–149
Palestinian citizens 139, 142, 147–148
repudiated violence, trials of 136, 138–139, 142–145, 149
rules of engagement 139
settler-colonial nature 137, 138, 141, 142, 145, 146, 147–150
socio-legal studies 135, 137, 145–150
Theory and Critique 146
US influence 141, 147
Israël, L 2, 7, 8–9, 11, 13, 149

Jabareen, H 148
Janković, I 77
Johnsen, JT 100
Joseph, I 108, 109
Journal of Law and Society 4, 6, 184
Jovanović, S 69, 70
judiciary
Poland 33
Scandinavia 87, 92
JussBuss 100–101

Kaczyński, J 26
Kahn-Freund, O 124–125, 127
Karpik, L
French Lawyers: A Study in Collective Action 112
Kaupen, W 121
Kelsen, H 75, 156
Kittner, M 126
Klausa, E 120
Kocher, E 9, 11, 12, 13, 16
Kohte, W 129, 131
Komornik, M 32
Korolczuk, E 31
Kosić, M 70
Kosovo *See* **Western Balkans**
Kregar, J 80
Introduction to Sociology 79
Krzywicki, L 22
Kulcsár, K 50–53, 54, 56, 58
Kurczewski, J 22, 24

La Caixa Foundation 159
labelling theories 109
labour law
collective bargaining 124–125
Federal Republic of Germany 125–129, 130
interdisciplinary study 119–134
Labour Law Research Network 134
power imbalance 125
right to strike 125
socio-legal tradition and 124–134
Weimar Republic 120, 124–125
Lande, J 23–24
language
English *See* English language
Israel 141
Lascoumes, P 109, 110, 111
latin network, transnational 12, 151–153
analytic tradition 152, 153, 156, 165, 172
applied theory 165
comparative law 164, 165, 166, 168–170
constitucionalismo vivo 168
constitutionalism 163–172
English language publications 159
evidence theory group 165
explanation-evaluation combination 166–167
formalism 162–163
human rights 163–164, 168
i-latina 165
investigación-acción 168

ius constitutionale commune en América Latina 167
judicialisation in Latin America 164, 167–168
SELA 161–162, 165–166
socio-legal trajectory 152–155, 166–170, 171–172
women legal theorists 165, 168
law
brutal expressions of 143
motivational aspects 24
postpositivist theory 158, 165
and socio-legal studies, split 29–30
as a threat 142, 144
Law, D 169
Law and Society Association 9, 93, 94, 98, 112, 114, 121
counter-movement to 120
interdisciplinary events 105
Lawyers in Twenty-First Century Society 98
lebendes Recht 21
legal aid schemes 100, 101
legal argumentation approach 156, 158
legal consciousness 118
emotional-volitional dimension 54
evaluative dimension 54
Horváth 50
Hungarian research into 55–58
Kulcsár 51, 54, 56
legal knowledge distinguished 51
Polish research into 19, 24, 27–28, 29, 35
Sajó 53–55
social stratification, influence 51–52
legal dogmatics 154
legal duality paradigm 70
legal education
European Union 95
France 114–115
Germany 120–121, 132
Hungary 46
Israel 141, 148
neoliberalist ideology 182
United Kingdom 173, 174–179, 181–182
United States 159–161, 171, 175
Western Balkans 61, 81
legal-empirical research under Communism 25–26
legal ethics
sociology of 99
university curricula 30
legal pluralism 21
legal pragmatism 90
legal scholarship
doctrinal model 63
socio-legal studies 63
sociology of law 20, 45, 63
Western ethnocentrism 98
legal socialisation 24, 29, 35
Legradić, R 72
liberalism 28, 160–161
Lochak, D 114
Lomell, HM 99
López Bofill, H 157
Loveman, M 113
Lovera-Parmo, D 167
Lucas Gioja, A 156
Luhmann, N 11, 65, 77, 79, 88, 123
Lukić, RD 69, 73, 75, 76
On the Concept of Sociology of Law 70–71
Lundberg, A 103

Macaulay, S
Non-Contractual Relationships in Business 184
McAuslan, P 176
McBarnet, D
Conviction 184
McCann, M 112
Rights at Work 112
Madar, R 7, 9, 12
Madsen, MR 13
Maine, HS 68
Malem, J 155
Mandić, O 73–74, 86
Mangabeira Unger, R 160
Marí, E 156
Marković, BS 70
Marković, SS 69
Martí, JL 157
Marx, K 88
Marxist-Leninism
France 107
Hungary 50–53
legal-empirical research 25–26, 27
Poland 22–27
sociology 27, 67
Western Balkans 67, 72, 75
Mathiesen, T 91, 97, 99, 100–101
Mautner, M 146
media, impact on public opinion 50
Melton, J 169
memory studies
Poland 32, 33
Western Balkans 61–62

Mertz, E 114
Mexico 157, 162–165
amparo litigation 163
constitutional law 163–165
judicial review 164
Supreme Court 162–164
migration and asylum law 33–35
Mitrović, DM 78, 80
Montenegro *See* **Western Balkans**
Moreso, JJ 157

Nafstad, I 84
Navarro, P 157
Nelken, D 59
neo-Kantianism 49
Nielsen, Stine Piilgaard Porner 99, 101, 102
Nikičević, T 68
Nino, C 155, 156, 157, 158–159, 161, 162
Radical Evil on Trial 159
Nipperdey, H-C 126
Nordmann, J 110–112
Noreau, P 105
North Macedonia *See* **Western Balkans**
Norway *See* **Scandinavia**

Olesen, A 99, 101
Ottoman Empire 64

Padjen, I 75–76
Palmer Olsen, H 96
Papendorf, K 99
Partington, M 176
Perić, B
Structure of Law 73
Petersen, H 92
Petrażycki, L 19, 22–23, 28, 36, 78
equal rights for women 31
Poland under Communism 23–25, 26, 27
Petrović, Prince Nikola 68
Pfarr, H 122, 130
Philippopoulos-Mihalopoulos, A 136
Płatek, M 31
Pleasence, P et al 101
pluralism 90
Podgórecki, A 24–25, 29, 65, 172
Poland
abuse of binding law 32–33
anti-Communist opposition 26, 28
anti-feminist backlash 31
constitutional debate 32–33
environmental law 33
European integration 30, 33, 35, 36
human rights law 31, 33–35
inequality 31, 33, 34, 35
institutional sociology 22
judiciary 33
law/socio-legal studies split 29–30
legal consciousness, research into 19, 24, 27–28, 29, 35
legal pluralism 21, 22–23, 28
legal socialisation, research into 24, 29, 35
legal-empirical research under Communism 25–26
LGBTIQ rights 33, 35
marginalised fields 30–31
Marxist influence 22–23, 24, 25–27
memory studies 32, 33
migration and asylum law 33–35
ML v Poland 34
national-conservative political turn 32–36
neo-institutional paradigm 29
partitions 20–21, 28
Petrażycki 19, 22–25, 26, 36
post-socialist era 19–20, 27–32
Prawo i Sprawiedliwość 32–34
pre-1945 20–23
professional ethics 30
reproductive rights 31, 33–34
restoration of Polish statehood 21, 22
rule of law crisis 20, 34
socialist era 15–16, 23–27
socio-legal research traditions 19–20, 23–32
sociology of law 2, 20, 22, 30–31
state of emergency, regulation 33
women's rights 31, 33–34, 35
policy recommendations as epistemic obstacle 135–136, 142
Pollock, F 68
positionality and subjectivity 5, 9–10
positivism
Hungary 41, 42, 48
postpositivist theory 158, 165
Scandinavia 89
United Kingdom 174
Western Balkans 75
Post, R 161
post-modernism 90
postcolonial legal criticism 132
postpositivist theory 158, 165
Pou Giménez, F 7, 9, 11, 12
Pozzolo, S 157
pre-state law 24

Priest, G 160
proportionality 158
public opinion
formation 50
pooling 50
Pusić, E 77

queer legal theory 132

Rabossi, E 156
race
critical race theory 132
intersectionality 132
positionality 9
Ramírez, S 157
Ramm, T 127
Rask Madsen, M 94, 96–97
Redondo, C 157
regional cooperation
conferences and workshops 61–62
Hungary 39, 59, 61
Poland 36
Scandinavia 87–103
Western Balkans 61–62, 63, 84
Rehder, B 126, 127
research *See also* **academic habitus**
epistemic communities 10–13, 14, 16–17
funding *See* research funding
positionality and subjectivity 5, 9–10
qualitative tools 58
quantitative methods 58
Research Committee on Sociology of Law 25, 73, 98
International Working Group on the Legal Professions 97
research funding 11, 14
European Research Council 115
Germany 122, 128
Hungary 14, 55–59
interdisciplinary research 140
Scandinavia 14, 88, 93–95
United Kingdom 14, 177, 182–183
Rivera López, E 157
Robert, P 110
Rogowski, R 120
Röhl, KF 120
Rønning, OH 99–100
Rose, C 160
Ross, A 87–88, 90, 96
Rottleuthner, H 120, 128
Rousso, H 110–111
Ruiz Manero, J 156, 158, 165
rule of law
brutal expressions of 143
cultural preconditions 55–56
Hungarian research 55–56
Hungary, erosion in 59
Polish crisis 20, 34
Russell, B 156

Sajó, A
Látszat és valóság a jogban 43, 53–55
Salvador Coderch, P 154
Sarat, A 112
Sarat, A and Scheingold, S (eds)
Cause Lawyering 112, 115
Scandinavia
comparative Lawyers in Society project 91, 97
critique of positivism 89
English language 11, 92, 93, 103
framework law 102
homelessness, research into 102
Independent Research Council Denmark 91
international socio-legal methodology 92
judges, focus on 87, 92
JussBuss 100–101
legal aid schemes 100, 101
legal clinics 96
Menu for Justice project 95
Nordic Bourdieusian association 94
publications 88, 90, 96–97
realism 156
regional cooperation 87–103
research funding 14, 88, 93–95, 102
Retfærd 92, 95
Scandinavian legal realism 87
socio-legal studies trajectory 88–103
sociology of law, marginalization 89, 92
sociology of law as scientific field 92
'stepchild debate' 91–93
university law departments 93–94, 95–97
welfare state law 101, 102, 103
Scheingold, S 112
Schultz, U 59, 97
Sebba, L 146, 147
Seminario en América Latina Seminario en América Latina 161–162, 165–166
Serbia *See* **Western Balkans**
Serverin, E 109, 111
Shamir, R 146

Shenhav, Y 146–147, 148
Siebeck, M 123
Siegel, R 161
Silbey, S and Ewick, P
  The Common Place of Law 113
Sinzheimer, H 124, 126, 127
Sitnić, A 80
Skąpska, G 20, 25–26, 28, 32–33
Slovenia *See* **Western Balkans**
social media campaigns 132
socialist era
  Hungary 15–16, 42, 50–55
  Poland 15–16, 22, 23–27, 28
  Western Balkans 15–16, 65, 67, 71–77
socio-legal identifications
  Israel 142–145
  law and, generally 135–137
  limits 138–141
socio-legal studies
  anti-theoretical 184
  Bologna reforms 67, 79
  challenge for 185
  constitutional studies 151–152
  delineation from other study areas 48, 62–63
  discovery of law in social facts 70–71
  explanation-evaluation combination 166–167
  historical context and trajectories 14–16
  law in context approach 176–177
  legal scholarship and 63
  limitation 144–145
  national/regional disparities 15–16
  normative or non-normative 70
  sociology of law and 2, 20, 63–64
  theoretical/empirical distinction 140, 143–150
  use of term 2
Socio-Legal Studies Association 178–179, 183
sociology of law
  criminology and 63, 90, 92
  critical legal studies and 9, 10–11, 119–122, 129, 131–132, 146
  decolonising 21, 103
  discovery of law in social facts 70–71
  empirical 2, 8, 19, 20, 22, 24–27, 50, 63, 70, 71, 74, 88, 115–116
  goal 45, 63
  instrumentality condition 64, 67, 71, 73, 77, 81, 82–83, 85
  international methodology 92
  intersectionality 132
  Kelsenian turn 75
  labour law, interdisciplinary study 119–134
  legal duality paradigm 70
  legal realism 117
  liminality dilemma 64, 67, 71, 73, 77, 83, 85
  opposition to 119–121
  postcolonial legal criticism 132
  scientific field, recognition as 92
  socio-legal studies and 2, 20, 63–64
  state-made law 21, 23, 70
  systems theory 131
  theoretical 19, 22–23, 26, 29, 30, 49, 54, 63, 71–73, 74, 88
  translation, issue raised by 113
  United Kingdom 2, 175–176
  Weberian 76, 111
  Weimar tradition 120, 124–125
sociotechnique 24
Sommerlad, H 97
Soubiran-Paillet, F 109
Spain
  1978 Constitution 153
  constitutional law 157–158
  legal argumentation approach 156, 158
  post-dictatorship era 153–154, 156
Stalin, J 25
Stanković, J
  Basics of General Sociology of Law 78–79
Stanziani, A 110
Stevens, R 176
structuralists 132
Sweden *See* **Scandinavia**
Swedish Research Council 99
Swiss Network for Law and Society 139–140, 144
symbolic interactionism 108
synoptical approach 49–50
systems theory 131
Szilágyi, IH 43

Tasić, Đ 69–71, 80, 85
technocentrism 174
technocratic instrumentalism 184
Thénault, S 149
Todorović, D 69, 70
Tomašić, D 69
Tomić, IM 83
Torbisco, N 157

transitional social actions 74
translation, issue raised by 113
Travers, M 93
Treves, R 65, 76, 155, 172
Turner, S 181
Twinning, W 176

Ukraine
Russian invasion 35
United Kingdom
'Compensation Study' 184
critical legal studies 175–176
Journal of Law and Society 4, 6, 183–184
law in context approach 176–177
legal education 173, 174–179, 181–182
legal research 174
Research Assessment Exercise 173
Research Excellence Framework 173, 182–183
research funding 14, 177, 182–183
Social and Legal Studies 184
Socio-Legal Group 178
socio-legal studies 2, 63, 120, 173–185
Socio-Legal Studies Association 178–179, 183, 185
sociology of law 2, 175–176
United Nations global goals 99
United States
critical legal studies 41, 175
empirical legal studies movement 115–116
European socio-legal approach compared 11, 41
influence 11, 105
law and society tradition 106
legal education 159–161, 171, 175
realism 156
socio-legal studies 117–118, 185
sociology of law 175

value-neutral scholarly orientation 48
Vanneuville, R 115
Vauchez, A 94
Vázquez, R 162
Vernengo, R 156
Versteeg, M 169
Vienna Circle 156
Vilajosana, JM 157
Vinogradoff, P 68
Visković, N 76, 85
Concept of Law 76
Von Wright, GH 156
Vrban, D 68
Sociology of Law 79–80
Vukosavljević, S 69
Vuković, D 80
Legal State and Shadowed Order 80
Society and Law 80

Wandall, R 92
Weber, M 21, 48, 76, 77, 79, 88, 90, 106, 172
Weis Bentzon, A 92
Weiss, M 127
welfare state law 101, 102, 103
Welti, F 131
Wesołowski, W 26–27
Western Balkans
Albania 64, 65, 67
Belgrade 61, 62, 65–66, 69, 72, 73, 77–78, 80
conferences and workshops 61–62
disparities within 64–67
Eastern legal traditions bordering 64
educational publishing 66
English language publications 11, 61
Europeanisation 61, 65
historical background 64–67
independent states 64–65
instrumentality condition 64, 67, 71, 73, 77, 81, 82–83, 85
interwar period 69–71
Kelsenian turn 75
'Law and Society' Working Group 72, 75–76, 77
'Law and Society – Fundamental Research' 72
legal duality paradigm 70
liminality dilemma 64, 67, 71, 73, 77, 83, 85
Ljubljana 65, 66, 74, 79
memory studies 61–62
North-South divide 65–67, 79
Novi Sad 65
post-socialist transition 65, 77–82
postgraduate legal education 81
private law codification 68
publications 68, 78–81, 85, 86
regional cooperation 61–62, 63, 84
Slovenia 61
socialist era 15–16, 65, 67, 71–77
socio-legal studies trajectory 12, 61–86
Sociological Review 69–70
sociology, institutionalisation 68–69, 71

Yugoslav Society for Theory, Philosophy and Sociology of Law 78
Yugoslav state 65, 66, 67, 69–70, 72–77
Zagreb 62, 65–66, 69, 73, 77, 79, 80
Wheeler, S 13, 14
Wiatr, J 26–27
Wittgenstein, L 151, 156
women
feminism 31, 132, 185
reproductive rights 31, 33–34
sexual violence against 138
women researchers in Hungary 45–46
women's rights 31, 33–34, 35
Worms, R 68

Yates, D
Exclusion Clauses in Contracts 175
Yiftachel, O and Kedar, AS 146
Ystehede, PJ 99
Yugoslavia *See* Western Balkans

Zanaj, Fatmit 66–67
Ždralović, A 80
Ziv, N 146
Znaniecki, F 22
Žun, A 74, 79
Zvekić, U 77
Zweigert, K 129

www.ingramcontent.com/pod-product-compliance
Ingram Content Group UK Ltd.
Pitfield, Milton Keynes, MK11 3LW, UK
UKHW020816290926
15470UKWH00003B/1201

9 781509 982622